ENTREPRENEUR MAGAZINE

The *Entrepreneur* Magazine Small Business Series

Published:

The Entrepreneur Magazine Small Business Advisor
Starting an Import/Export Business
Making Money with Your Personal Computer

Forthcoming:

Home-Based Business Guide
Small Business Legal Guide
Guide to Mixed-Media Marketing
Organizing and Promoting Seminars

ENTREPRENEUR MAGAZINE
Making Money with Your Personal Computer

John Wiley & Sons, Inc.

New York • Chichester • Brisbane • Toronto • Singapore

Copyright © 1995 by Entrepreneur Media, Inc.
Published by John Wiley & Sons, Inc.

Library of Congress Cataloging-in-Publication Data:

Entrepreneur magazine : making money with your personal computer.
     p.   cm. — (The Entrepreneur magazine small business series)
   Includes index.
   ISBN 0-471-10982-7 (cloth : alk. paper). — ISBN 0-471-10981-9
(paper : alk. paper)
   1. Home-based businesses—Data processing. 2. New business
enterprises. 3. Small business—Management. I. Entrepreneur
(Santa Monica, Calif.) II. Series.
HD62.38.E57   1995
658′.041—dc20   95-17898

Printed in the United States of America

10 9 8 7 6 5 4 3 2 1

ACKNOWLEDGMENTS

ENTREPRENEUR MAGAZINE GROUP

Editor	Charles Fuller
Assistant Editor	Ken Ohlson
Copy Editors	Heather Page
	David Pomije
	Imran Husain
Contributing Editors	Gina Farrell Gladwell
	Terry O'Rourke
	Anne Callot
	Maura Hudson Pomije
	Lauren Fischbein
	Meredith Kaplan
Editorial Assistants	Kimberly Hoelscher
	Glen Webber

CONTENTS

INTRODUCTION

When *Entrepreneur* magazine reported on the world's first and only hobby-computer store in 1977, even we didn't anticipate the high-tech explosion that was to follow. Within a few years, the microcomputer industry had become a multibillion-dollar business, creating dozens of ancillary industries for computer manufacture, sale, and service, plus an aftermarket.

The advent of the moderately priced microcomputer made it possible for individual entrepreneurs to operate full-fledged businesses. More importantly, they were able to conduct business from their home, saving on start-up costs and overhead during the initial stage. Many entrepreneurs have continued in business at home indefinitely. Today, more than 30% of U.S. households have computers, and some researchers expect the number to reach nearly 50% by 1996. For the more than 40 million people who are home-based entrepreneurs, the figures aren't surprising. With start-up investments as low as $1,000, these entrepreneurs have turned their home computers into highly profitable instruments for making a living.

If you don't know much about computers, don't despair. You don't have to be a computer programmer or software publisher to make money with your computer, though both these skills can lead to lucrative home-based businesses. Instead, if you're able to use a computer confidently (or can learn to do so), are willing to keep on top of the latest technological advancements that pertain to your business, and know how to market yourself and your product or service, you can start and run your own computer-based business within your home.

This book will give you an idea of the range of small business opportunities available to an entrepreneur equipped with a computer. The choices are many, varied, and continuously changing, which is why you should think of this book as a "survey" of opportunities available to you. Essentially, any product or service that can be generated from computer know-how and is useful to the business sector is likely to find a market. As *Fortune* magazine reported in April 1994, "American business is . . . outsourcing like crazy." Companies are continuing to downsize and the work needed to fill in the gaps is highly specialized. The key is to find a niche within your selected business offering and then get out there and get yourself known.

Products and services for busy American families are also in demand: referral services, home inventory cataloging services, and computer setup and tutoring services. Personalized children's books and local specialty newsletters and newspapers are also popular. Retail computer-based businesses, which require extensive facility preparation and inventory buying, are outside the scope of this book. (However, a few of these businesses have been analyzed in depth in other *Entrepreneur* business start-up guides.)

It's important to determine whether you're ready to make a commitment to being self-employed. Buying this book was a step in the right direction. Now ask yourself: Can I do without company-paid health insurance and retirement plans? Will I miss office socializing and the comfort of a steady paycheck? Can I get by without access to the equipment and support staff that I once took for granted? Will I manage my time and be willing to knock myself out getting new clients?

If the answer is yes, you could become one of the hottest entrepreneurs in the country, making more money from your home-based venture than you ever thought was possible. According to Dun & Bradstreet (D & B), new business incorporations in 1993 reached their highest annual level since the mid-1940s. Even more impressive: of the businesses studied by D & B that had started in 1985, 70% were still active in 1994 (*Business Week,* May 23, 1994). What does this mean for you? The time has never been better for taking the plunge into entrepreneurship and making your new business last for the long haul.

1

THE COMPUTER REVOLUTION

Computers have come a long way since the magnetic core systems that were prevalent in government and big business before the advent of the microchip. Today's systems, based on microchip technology (millions of circuits stamped on a silicon chip), are smaller (compare a desktop to an entire room devoted to a floor standing system), more powerful (a Pentium or Power PC computer can process data much faster than those behemoth magnetic core computers), portable (try taking a floor standing magnetic core computer, or even one of today's mainframe systems, on the road), and far less expensive (a full-featured multimedia personal computer costs about $2,000). Personal computers have freed the masses from manual system bondage. Even the smallest businesses, referred to on Madison Avenue as the SOHO (small office home office) market, have the ability to enter into the information age.

No longer is the question *whether* a business should computerize; the question is *when*. That maxim is even more significant in relation to the SOHO market. Small commercial office operators and home-based businesses (both full- and part-time) can benefit and have realized great rewards from personal computer technology through the creation of the "virtual office." Using their personal computers, they have not only created opportunity, but have also projected an image of their

3

small commercial or home-based office that is worthy of a much larger enterprise, and communicated a professionalism that permeates their business relationships.

More importantly, these entrepreneurs are maximizing their investment in computer technology. They are producing savings in operating expenses through greater efficiency, and they are generating revenue. Perhaps the greatest empowerment personal computers have given these entrepreneurs is the opportunity to pursue a dream of owning their own business. They are liberated from the shackles of a 9-to-5 job that makes someone else rich.

THE GROWING PERSONAL COMPUTER MARKET

As this book will illustrate, millions of entrepreneurs have started and are currently operating a lot of good business opportunities based on computer technology. In fact, Link Resources, in New York, estimates that, in 1994, *more than 43 million people generated their income from work done at home,* and *nearly 60% of them used computers.* Figure 1–1 shows the number of home-based income earners during 1990–1994. Figure 1–2 tracks the steady growth of the use of computers in home-based work in the same years.

Of the total number of individuals earning income from their home, at least 24.9 million are home-based business owners operating

Figure 1–1   Home-Based Income Earners in the United States, 1990–1994

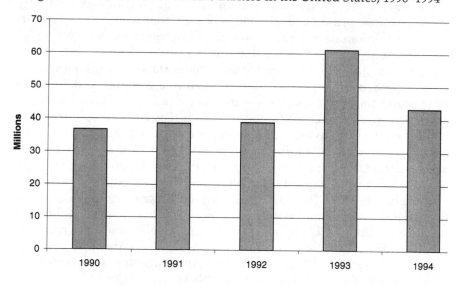

Source: Link Resources Corp.

Figure 1–2 United States Households Using a
Computer in their Home-Based Work, 1990–1994

Source: Link Resources Corp.

either full- or part-time, according to Link Resources. Of that total,
Link estimates that 12.7 million are self-employed individuals whose
home-based business is their primary occupation. The remaining 12.2
million are part-time home-based business owners. Although industry
growth estimates vary, those who make charting industries their business agree unanimously that the number of home-based businesses
will increase dramatically in the coming years.

More importantly, current sales of desktop PCs, portables, and
software to this market ($33.2 billion) are expected to grow to $44.6 bil-
lion by 1998. That 6.1% growth rate is faster than overall industry
sales, according to BIS Strategic Decisions of Norwell, Massachusetts.
Sales to the SOHO market are currently $6.2 billion or 18.6% of the
total desktop market. By 1998, BIS Strategic Decisions expects that figure to grow 11%, to $10.4 billion.

Those numbers reflect both the predicted move toward telecom-
muting by large companies and the enormous impact that computer-
oriented home-based entrepreneurs will have on the market. Most of
these opportunities are outgrowths of expertise that entrepreneurs
acquired when they were doing the same type of work for a previous
employer(s). As relentless corporate downsizing continues, talented
individuals with key computer skills are being laid off, and companies
that have a need to get the work done are losing those skills on-
premises. Enter the phenomenon known as *outsourcing:* companies
contract with former employees to provide the same type of support
they previously had provided while under their employ. The former
employee, now turned entrepreneur, has a ready source of income,

and the company saves money by not having to foot the bill for payroll taxes and benefits. A win–win situation exists for both parties.

In addition to skills that can be outsourced, many entrepreneurs starting computer-oriented businesses have specific expertise that many companies—and consumers—don't have. Uniqueness is especially characteristic of new and emerging technologies like multimedia services, which include a whole array of opportunities from simple marketing presentations to interactive kiosks.

Exactly what types of businesses are these small, home-based business owners running? The list depends on whom one asks and where one looks. A 1993 readership survey by *Home Office Computing* indicated these top 10 businesses for home-based computer entrepreneurs:

1. Business support services.
2. Consulting.
3. Programming/Computer services.
4. Communications.
5. Secretarial/Word processing.
6. Financial support services.
7. Graphic/Visual/Fine arts.
8. Marketing/Advertising.
9. Medical services.
10. Real estate.

The business you start does not have to be sophisticated to be a moneymaker. For example, *Parents* magazine highlighted one reader who was anxious to stay home with her children and asked subscribers/readers to send in business ideas that she could implement from home. Among the suggestions that poured into the magazine were: calligraphy services, invitation and flyer designer, catering and baking, and becoming owner/editor of her own local newspaper, to name a few.

Business opportunities are nearly limitless. Computer technology has changed the way the world conducts business today, and has opened new doors for entrepreneurs. Telecommunications giant AT&T reportedly works with more than 130 subcontractors, some of which are home-based companies. Like many other large companies, Ernst & Young, a nationwide consulting firm, has used computers to cut down office space and save millions of dollars per year. Consultants from the firm are equipped with portable computers, modems, and all the software they need. They "set up shop" within the offices of their clients during the time they are servicing them. In between, they use whatever space is available at their Ernst & Young home-base, and they bring their computer, files, and modems with them.

CHOOSING YOUR BUSINESS

The first step toward targeting your market and getting your business going is selecting what that business will be. Home-based business owners should specialize—at least during start-up and the first several months of operation—before branching out into add-on services. This approach is important for several reasons:

1. It keeps start-up and operating costs to a minimum. For example, a word processing and computer maintenance/repair service might seem compatible, but the two businesses require significantly different software and supplies, and the up-front outlay of cash to provide two services will not likely accelerate your break-even point.
2. There is only one of you, and unless you plan to start with a staff—and their wages and taxes—you cannot easily produce quality work in one field while you're putting out fires in another.
3. Potential clients gain confidence in home-based ventures when the home-based entrepreneur is an expert. Cement yourself as an exceptional graphic artist or business consultant or specialty producer. You can add other business offerings later.

You must ask yourself some key questions when making your business choice:

What Expertise and Experience Can I Offer?

When you start a business, your proven skills and existing know-how offer many advantages—you know what supplies and equipment you will need, and you have already established vendor and client contacts in the industry. Your home-based business does not need to recreate your previous position with another company (though it can), but you might expand on areas that you saw were deficient while working for someone else, or specialize in a product or service that was only a small part of your former employer's portfolio.

What Do I Love Doing?

This may be the most important consideration of all. As an entrepreneur, you will spend thousands of hours each year on your business. If you are a home-based entrepreneur, you will never leave your "office." You must not only believe that your business is the greatest thing since indoor plumbing, you must also convince potential clients, bankers, investors, suppliers, and others to share that belief. To be truly successful over the long haul, doing something you love is a must. If you hated the work you once did as an employee, then you are probably better off starting a business where you may have less experience, but more passion and eagerness to learn.

What Can My Living/Office Arrangements Support?

It is important to assess, up front, what you can afford in living/office space. For example, you may love the mail-order business and have 10 years' experience as a mail-order company supervisor, but if you currently can afford only a one-bedroom apartment or condominium and have no garage space, the inventory space required for this business will be difficult to accommodate. There are ways around most of these logistical hurdles (i.e., renting storage space nearby), but you must take a good look at your situation and decide what you can live with. We will offer advice on choosing your location later in this chapter.

What Does My Service/Product Offer to the World?

Having a product or service does not mean having a market. If your passion and experience are in an area that does not lend itself to meeting a current market demand, rethink your business. Many successful entrepreneurs started businesses offering a product or service that they knew would fulfill a particular market demand before they started. A good example is Charles Fletcher, publisher of *Lower Columbia Business* magazine. Already a writer and home-based desktop publisher, Fletcher created his magazine when clients in his county complained about the quality of business news available to them. His magazine met a need for the community and helped him ward off growing competition in desktop publishing in his area.

IDEAS FOR COMPUTER-BASED BUSINESSES

The possibilities for entrepreneurs are seemingly endless, and it is impossible to outline here every computer-related business that exists today. Throughout the discussion dealing with choice of a business, a diverse group of 24 businesses that currently are in most demand in the marketplace is examined in detail. If the exact business niche that captures your interest or relates closely to your acquired skills and expertise is not specifically named, the in-depth descriptions of the 24 businesses will be relevant for parallel information and decisions. The potential market segments of each of the 24 businesses are summarized in Figure 1–3. Each type of business is analyzed in the following sections.

1. Architect/Computer-Aided Design

Your market as an architect or computer-aided design service will likely include upper-bracket, two-income families who are buying or renovating a home—especially first-time homeowners. Today, to get their foot in the door of homeownership, many families opt to buy condominiums or other association-based homes that limit their ability to customize but are regarded as investments. These people are ready to customize when they move to a more permanent residence. If they can make the jump to buying their "dream home," the fun begins for them—as does the expense. Though many house purchasers will spend good money to make their new house into their idea of a perfect home, they often want to see what the finished product will look like—before they invest.

Today's high-tech computer-aided design software can test alternate ideas and bring a custom-designed home to life on a computer screen, before clients' eyes. Architectural skills serve as a solid foundation for building clients' confidence and getting the job done right. These skills will also appeal to landlords who own small commercial buildings in select neighborhoods. Many award-winning architects began with a small project in the outskirts of a city and caught the attention of larger businesses. Their clientele doubled or tripled within a relatively small geographic area.

2. Bulletin Board Service

Capitalizing on the ever-growing on-line service boom, bulletin board services (BBSs) are an exciting and popular enterprise. According to *Boardwatch* magazine, the more than 53,000 public dial-up BBSs operating in North America have over 13 million subscribers. These services include both general information boards and highly specialized offerings (birds, history, cooking, legislation, and the Middle East, to name only a few). Bulletin boards that let people chat on-line are among the most popular, simply because people love to talk to each other.

Your market will be as varied as the type of BBS line you choose. The key to success in the BBS business is originality. To attract to your service users who will be willing to be paying members (many hobby bulletin boards are free) on top of paying for connection time, you

Figure 1–3   The 24 Computer-Based Businesses Most in Demand

Business	Potential Market Segments
1. Architect/ Computer-Aided Design	Upper-bracket, two-income families who are buying or renovating a home; landlords who own small commercial buildings in select neighborhoods.
2. Bulletin Board Service	Market varies with type of BBS; however, key to success is originality: offering a "value-added" program that users could not otherwise access for free.
3. Business Consulting	Companies of all sizes, including banks, insurance operations, health care service enterprises, manufacturers, and large retailers, as well as any businesses experiencing unexpected and rapid growth, a sudden loss of revenues, or other indication of a need for change.
4. Business Plan Writing	New entrepreneurs or small business owners looking to expand.
5. Computer Consulting/Training	Businesses of all sizes; home computer owners, students, job-hunters, children.
6. Computer Repair/ Maintenance and Programming	Any business that uses a computer but cannot afford to keep management information systems (MIS) staff on salary, including law offices, doctors' offices, publishing firms, CPAs, and home-based businesses; also, home computer owners.
7. Data Detective	Companies of all sizes that have proprietary operating systems and product or service information they need to protect; also, law firms.
8. Database Management/ Mail List Service	Small to medium-size businesses, political campaigns, coupon and publishing houses, entrepreneurs.
9. Electronic Clipping Service	Company marketing departments, publications, freelance writers, politicians, academia, and entertainment and public relations (PR) firms.
10. Freelance Writing	Market varies with type of freelancing to be done and publications or companies targeted; however, specializing increases market potential.
11. Graphic Design	Ad agencies, PR firms, new entrepreneurs, mail-order companies, salespeople.
12. Home Inventory Cataloging/ Organizing	Busy, two-income families with more disposable income than time.

Figure 1–3   *(Continued)*

Business	Potential Market Segments
13. Information Broker/Research Service	Companies of all sizes; market varies; specializing can increase market potential.
14. Inventory Control Service	Small to medium-size businesses, especially new entrepreneurs.
15. Mail Order	Market varies with products; however, most catalog shoppers are female, married, college-educated howeowners in a two-income family earning above $30,000 annually.
16. Multimedia	Businesses (all sizes) that need training, educational, or sales presentations; malls, museums, libraries in need of interactive video kiosks.
17. Newsletter Publishing	*Service-based business:* small to medium-size businesses; associations; other organizations that desire a quality publication but lack staff. *Subscriber-based business:* market varies with topic; includes communities of all sizes.
18. Personalized Children's Books	Parents, grandparents, all relatives with children; gift stores, bookstores, hospitals, mall kiosks.
19. Referral Service	Market varies with companies selected for referral; market research should target both those in need of referrals and companies that would want to be listed on your service.
20. Sales/Marketing Service	Small business owners looking to expand, and independent salespeople representing various companies or products.
21. Sign Making	Local retailers, libraries, schools, community organizations, restaurants, caterers, party-planning services.
22. Software Design/Custom Software	Vertical market that has a specialty niche with unmet needs (wide general-audience product will compete with large publishers). Market varies with type of software developed.
23. Utility Bill Auditing	Medium-size and large businesses with high-energy usage operations and multiline telephone systems; nonprofit organizations with special tax exemptions.
24. Word Processing	Small businesses, professionals (lawyers, doctors, dentists), job-hunters, students.

need an original, worthwhile product that you must constantly maintain. If your BBS offers a product (shareware, graphics, word games, and so on), you must keep the offering fresh. If you offer information, it must be up-to-date and thorough. If you offer a chat line, you will need to facilitate on-line conversations as needed and to prompt discussions by providing information on the subject being discussed. (Remember, if your BBS is not a "value-added" program that users could otherwise access for free, it will be difficult to make money.)

You must find out everything you can about the people who may be attracted to your offering. If you offer a recipe-swapping BBS, for example, read everything available and gather as much data as possible about Americans who are interested in cooking and also fit the market for purchasing on-line services. Kevin Behrens, owner of Aquilla BBS Inc., in Illinois, says: "We build a personal relationship between the users and ourselves. Users have to be people we can understand and relate to. . . . You need to tailor your marketing content to the specific group or population you're addressing. For example, if you're advertising to a school population, you need to specifically address the educational aids you offer on your service."

3. Business Consulting

If you're making a move from the corporate world to entrepreneurialism, business consulting can be a great opportunity. Many large companies' managers, faced with hiring freezes and reengineering, are able to sidestep caps on hiring by looking to temporary help in the form of consultants. It is surprising how many companies will not allow managers to hire full-time staff but will fork over significant hourly wages to consultants whom they know they can let go when their budget allotment is exhausted.

Some companies hire business consultants to help them reorganize and refocus their efforts; they gain knowledgeable business problem solvers, motivators, and cheerleaders. Others are hired to complete specific tasks: put a proposal system on-line; create a new marketing approach for 1996; help train management/employees; evaluate line operations to see where fat can be trimmed and efficiency improved. In general, the tasks completed by business consultants could be done by existing company personnel. The problem is that staff cutbacks or shifting business priorities leave a gap between projects that company executives want completed and the number of people who can dedicate time to completing them.

The types of companies that will be attracted to consulting services include banks, insurance operations (especially those involved in health care), health care service enterprises, manufacturers, large re-tailers, and any businesses experiencing unexpected and rapid growth, a sudden loss of revenues, or any other condition that indicates a need for change—and an expert outsider's point of view.

4. Business Plan Writing

In this role, you can consider yourself an entrepreneur for entrepreneurs. Though every new business owner knows about the probable benefit from a business plan, and those seeking funding *have* to pull one together, many otherwise skilled businesspeople cringe at the idea of having to develop their own business plans.

This is exactly why there will always be a market for a home-based business plan service. The service is tailor-made for individuals who find financial projections, profit-and-loss statements, and marketing plans a pleasant challenge. Potential clients include both hopeful entrepreneurs and existing business owners looking to expand. Clients tend to be charismatic go-getters with a dream who have trouble getting their business idea translated into a professional and marketable overview that will attract investors and can serve as a guidepost for all phases of business operations.

5. Computer Consulting/Training

Computer consulting and training covers a broad spectrum of opportunities, from having individuals learn basic computer programs in your home to helping select the right hardware/software/accessory packages for growing businesses.

Consulting and training are paired because they complement one another in experience, equipment, and operational needs. Often, a computer consultant who helps a company select and install a new computer setup for its employees will be asked to return to provide training and instruction. Some entrepreneurs package their services to include a single price for both. Likewise, when you are offering computer training to individuals, they will look to you to provide them with recommendations on putting together the best possible system for their computing needs.

The market you select will depend on the type of business you want to run. Ask yourself the following questions:

- Do I want to work from home, or simply have a home office?
- Am I an effective speaker and presenter? Can I remain calm and focused in front of a group, or do I do better one-on-one?

- What fascinates me: learning more about emerging computer technologies or finding new and simpler ways to make computer products work?
- Do I prefer scheduling many projects in a week, or focusing on fewer, longer-term projects?

If you want to work from home, can communicate well with people one-on-one, and enjoy finding and teaching new and simpler ways to use computer programs, then you should market computer training services to job-hunters, students, and home computer users in your local area. To do so, advertise in the Yellow Pages, in local newspaper classifieds, on school information and job boards, and in school papers. Emphasize that you can train clients in "the need-to-know computer programs that employers are demanding." Leave your business cards and brochures with retail computer stores that can refer you when someone buys a new home computer setup, and do some networking communitywide. Once you are established, you may begin to get referrals from previous students.

If you can identify a need for assistance in computer operations in your area, you could become a computer instructor serving both the business and large-scale consumer markets, providing instruction in classrooms rented out on a per-day or per-evening basis.

Facilities can be found in schools, civic organization halls, or local computer stores. You'll have to negotiate a fair rent with your land-lord—either a flat rate or a rate based on the amount of business you do. In no case should the rent exceed 25% of gross income, and you should do everything possible to bring that percentage down.

One technique for keeping your rent down in a government organization space would be to stress the public service angle of your business. If you rent from a private-sector organization, consider offering a 25% discount to organization members who enroll in your classes, as a means of keeping your rent down and stabilizing your revenues.

If you don't mind working on the road and are an effective communicator who can stay calm in front of groups of professionals, you may prefer company training. If you also enjoy staying abreast of new computer technology, you can market your computer consulting skills. Marketing by direct mail can be effective, though your business will thrive if you can build referrals. "When I am talking to a client, I'll say, 'Well, do you know anyone else in this industry that I can talk to?" says entrepreneur Eric Bott, a telecommunications and computer consultant. "If I am doing a good job, most of them are open to suggestions." Bott also points out that, when doing consulting projects, which can last two weeks, a month, or more, you need only five calls or so from a direct-mail campaign to keep you busy. Add referrals and contacts through networking, and you can stay busy for the next 6 to 12 months.

6. Computer Repair/Maintenance and Programming

The market for computer repair/maintenance and programming includes just about any business that uses a computer but cannot afford to keep management information systems (MIS) staff on salary. Law offices, doctors' offices, publishing firms, CPAs, and, of course, home-based businesses, all need their computers to be reliable and efficient, but will not likely hire a full- or even part-time staffer to repair, maintain, and program them.

If you're interested in long-term projects, you may want to market your programming skills to major manufacturers and R&D firms that need custom programming for specific projects. If you prefer a flexible schedule and variety, you should market your talents to local businesses and to home computer users (via Yellow Pages, local newspaper classifieds, coupons, and direct mail). One business owner we spoke with started off by offering computer preventive maintenance services and basic repairs, but soon expanded into other areas when he realized how many of his clients needed help with things like loading software, configuring systems, adding accessories like modems and fax connections, and so on.

7. Data Detective

As the entire world grows more and more dependent on computers—not only for easier production and efficiency, but also as communication tools and convenient store, houses of information—an alarm suddenly sounds. If I can retrieve hundreds of megabytes of information from my system, so can others (including those I would rather not allow access).

As increasing numbers of people swing into the information superhighway, the vulnerability of all this private information becomes evident. Information theft through computers is such a growing problem that the U.S. Department of Defense created the Computer Emergency Response Team (CERT) center in Pittsburgh, at Carnegie Mellon University. The team's job is to find hackers on the Internet and other on-line services.

Companies of all sizes face the same security problems. Nationwide, increasing emphasis is placed on the need to protect data and programs that hold the key to ma ¬y companies' success. The result is a need for data detectives: high-tech programmers who can not only make their way through the most complex of systems, but can also think like a potential hacker.

As a data detective, your market will include small, medium and large companies with proprietary operating systems and/or product or service information.

8. Database Management/Mail List Service

Numerous businesses and other ventures require up-to-date mailing lists, yet lack the staff and equipment needed to maintain them. Armed with a database management setup, your services will be attractive to small and midsize businesses, publishing houses, coupon houses, political campaigns, and many new entrepreneurs.

Some mail list service businesses specialize—for example, they market their services to local political campaigns on an ongoing basis. (Even though political races generally are decided only once every two years, or annually in the case of special elections, the preparations start one to two years in advance.) Specializing provides benefits because the lists you work with have a common thread. You can utilize lists from various clients to build databases and lists that you can then sell to others.

When marketing, count in large part on referrals from local sources: the chamber of commerce, city clerk, local newspapers, word processing services and sales/marketing consultants, as well as any business or business plan consultants in your area. Referrals are important because they are free. You should also use the Yellow Pages, local newspaper advertising (especially offering your own coupons, to gather more names and addresses for your local database), and ads in various civic and business publications, including newsletters.

9. Electronic Clipping Service

People need various types of information, often of such a broad and immediate nature that they are too busy to collect it themselves. Electronic clipping services handle such topics on both a project basis and an ongoing basis. For example, a client involved in research for a masters' thesis might ask you to provide him or her with the latest published information on standardized testing in elementary schools. A small film company may need copies of all reviews of their newly released documentary from the entertainment sections of hundreds of newspapers and magazines nationwide. Elected officials or public figures may need to keep abreast of how recent health care cutbacks are being dealt with not only in their own small communities, but in communities across the country. Your clipping service puts such information at their fingertips—in some cases, providing regular updates and thus a regular income for you.

Potential markets for an electronic clipping service include:

- Company marketing departments, which are often too busy to gather all the research material they need for a new campaign or a record of when and where their companies are being mentioned in the media.
- Publications, including magazines, newspapers, and corporate newsletters, which are always wanting to remain on top of the latest information.
- Freelance writers on assignment, or looking for story ideas.
- Politicians and campaign consultants.
- Academia, including university departments (for grant proposals, etc.), students, and organizations.
- Public relations firms.

10. Freelance Writing

If writing is both your talent and your passion, then freelance writing could be for you.

The market for freelance writers is huge. Look at the latest version of *Writer's Market* for evidence on how many publications are looking for new and established writers who can write interestingly about a variety of topics and contribute articles and ideas. You can also offer your talents to small businesses or larger corporations that have cut back on their communications staffing. Especially if you specialize, you can market your services to both publications and business.

For example, on the topic of health care alone, you will find more than 50 related magazines, hundreds of newspaper reports on medical topics, and literally thousands of hospitals, physicians' groups, and other health care service companies that produce publications—often open to a good freelance writer. Once your contacts are established and growing in the health care field, you may find subjects for articles that are appealing to mainstream magazines or to newspapers looking for "special to" exclusives.

The key to marketing as a freelance writer is selling your idea and selling yourself. The standard means of doing both is the "query" letter, describing your story ideas and your background. If you are approaching businesses, you will want something standardized and professional, always including your business and/or rolodex card(s). With publications, your queries should be customized to illustrate your understanding of *their* market, as well as your article ideas and your background. After you become published, include one or two writing samples with each query letter. As with all marketing endeavors, *know all you can about the potential client you are approaching*—do your research.

11. Graphic Design

Graphic designers are often used on a freelance basis by ad agencies and public relations (PR) firms. Other potential clients include new entrepreneurs needing logos for their businesses, mail-order houses that need someone to design their catalogs, and salespeople desiring customized visual aids for use in sales presentations or training sessions. A good niche for graphic designers, in fact, is to design standard presentation packages that can be sold to salespersons and easily adapted to their on-the-road presentation needs.

Actually, clients exist all around you. By bringing samples of your work to show local business owners, you can illustrate how your skills can enhance their current marketing pieces—signs, business cards, Yellow Pages ads, brochures, and more. You can even market pieces to publications, on-line services, and newsletter publishers, who are often looking for design elements to plug into pieces as needed.

When marketing your skills, stress the quality of your work as well as your ability to handle several projects at once and to complete them before or by concurrent deadlines. Your talents and creativity will be evident in your samples, but your professionalism will clinch the sale.

12. Home Inventory Cataloging/Organizing

If you have a knack—better yet, an obsession—for organization, this can be a highly satisfying home-based business. Your target market will be today's busy, two-income families that have more disposable income than time. With your help, they can be ready for insurance claims should disaster strike (fire, flood, earthquake, theft), have their records for the past seven years organized, filed, and catalogued on computer, and/or finally have an organized book/CD/video/photo library in their home.

Early marketing may be difficult: most people are uncomfortable having a stranger in their home, and their discomfort is heightened when that stranger will be looking at their personal records, possessions, and "clutter." Networking will be vital to gaining early contacts and references. Try affiliating yourself with general contractors, real estate agents, insurance agents, and others who have contact with families and are entrusted with their homes and possessions. You might also become bonded and state that fact in your brochure. Once you have some client references behind you, and some experience organizing and inventorying various sizes of homes and types of possessions, try offering local seminars or a free newsletter on organization, to attract new clients. Yellow Pages listings are also worthwhile.

13. Information Broker/Research Service

Janet Gotkin, a partner in New York-based InfoLink, advises: "Your biggest challenge in starting this business will be being committed to constant, ongoing marketing. You're a service that's difficult to define. People need it, but they don't know how to reach what you offer—how to reach you."

In fact, the market for an information broker/research service is nearly unlimited and will take defining by you, based on your areas of interest and your skills—much like a BBS line operator or freelance writer. You can receive information from databases nationwide and even worldwide, by modem, and can disseminate that information to clients who live thousands of miles from you. Similarly, many local entities, such as medical and legal offices and nonprofit organizations, need masses of numerical data but either are too busy or lack the resources to gather it themselves.

It is essential to define specifically the type of information and research you will offer, and then find out everything you can about the people who may be attracted to your offering. If, for example, you offer a nationwide travel information service, you need to find out all you can about the people who travel within the United States—their average age, earnings, preferred types of trips (resort, camping, cruises), information most sought before traveling, and so on. Because this type of research will become your lifeblood, you should be able to do a thorough job of your own market research before turning around and offering your services to clients.

As with many businesses that have a ready consumer need but lack easy definition, referrals and networking are important to marketing strategy. So is simply getting your name out there via exposure. Targeted direct mail, attendance at trade shows, circulation of press releases, and reprints of published articles will serve you well by simply letting people know that your service exists. In addition, depending on your information specialty, you may employ direct sales techniques, including cold calls to businesses that need your services. Entrepreneur Josh Blackmun, an attorney, offers his legal research services to lawyers and business executives, and employs salespeople to generate new client leads.

At first, advertise in the business section of your local newspaper, or in local journals. This should bring in enough business to get you started. Mail a brochure to every business, organization, or association that might require the type of research you perform. Stress that your expertise as an information broker has given you experience in finding valuable information from sources that they have never considered or with which they may be unfamiliar. The speed with which you are able to give clients the information they need will greatly determine your success, so be sure that your advertising emphasizes both promptness and thoroughness—and that you deliver as promised.

14. Inventory Control Service

Inventory normally represents merchants' greatest cost. Helping small business owners get a better handle on inventory control is what this business is all about.

Your marketing goal is to target new and small business owners who lack the time or know-how to set up initial inventory tracking systems, and, in the first several months of business, may not want to hire personnel or spend money on sophisticated systems to track their inventory properly. Through direct mail (targeting mailing lists of small businesses), telemarketing, personal contact, and the Yellow Pages, you play up the fact that inventory mismanagement spells disaster for small business owners by taking away from planned returns on investment and leaving them with unsatisfied clients.

Play up the figures. A merchandise consultant interviewed for this book indicated that it costs the average retailer anywhere from 20% to 30% of the original investment in inventory just to maintain it. If a potential client turns over its inventory four times during the fiscal year, the cost will be 5% to 7.5% of sales just to maintain that inventory. If inventory is maintained improperly, costs will rise while sales and profits fall.

You can also sell the very real fact that business owners, even more than homeowners, must know what stock they have on hand in case of disaster (fire, flood, earthquake, theft). Your service provides the business owner with peace of mind—for daily operations, record-keeping and taxes, and insurance preparedness.

15. Mail Order

If trends continue in their current patterns, catalog sales will reach $66.4 billion by 1996, according to statistics produced by the WEFA Group, an economic research and forecasting firm. You can grab a piece of the action by starting your own mail-order business.

As with many of the businesses we've discussed, your market will be as varied as the type of product line you choose to offer. However, according to research by Deloitte & Touche, most catalog shoppers are female, married, college-educated homeowners in a two-income family earning $30,000 to $99,000 in annual household income.

You can offer general catalog merchandise, but keep in mind that you will have to compete with larger, more established companies. Specializing can be beneficial for newcomers, as long as the items offered have proven appeal. Increasingly, consumers are turning to catalogs to purchase gifts for the winter holidays, because catalog shopping takes care of the thought, the wrapping, and the shipping. Holiday catalogs also have a market with businesses that choose to remember clients and associates at the holidays.

Whatever market you choose, an advantage to this business is that you are automatically marketing your service each time you mail a catalog. In the beginning, you will likely need to purchase lists through list brokers. Eventually, catalog orders and call-ins will produce generous and more productive lists.

16. Multimedia

Taking optimum advantage of the advances in technology, multimedia services combine sound, music, graphics, and video into incredible, and often interactive, presentations. Successful multimedia companies such as Statmedia in California have produced award-winning training simulators that can test and license state smog technicians. Less complex presentations serve as stunning sales presentations or employee orientation pieces. Some companies specialize in multimedia presentations for law firms, health care entities, and libraries.

Essentially, the following multimedia products will find ready markets:

- Training products—for organizations, companies, and non-profit groups.
- Business presentations—especially for companies that rely on impressive sales presentations to beat out their competition.

- Interactive kiosks—automated directories featuring particular products and services or their locations—which can be attractive to shopping malls and museums.
- Entertainment or educational products—targeted to consumers and organizations that hope to educate, as well as to advertising firms, trade show organizers, and similar communications sources.

According to Market Intelligence, a market research firm, there are more than 130,000 multimedia developers in the United States—a relatively small number, reflecting the newness of the medium. If you can build a reputation for your skills in combining various media to produce an integrated and impressive on-screen product, you can soon find your efforts rewarded with sales in the six figures.

17. Newsletter Publishing

Newsletters are the publication medium of the decade. As costs for trade journals and other communication vehicles increase, simple but professional newsletters allow people who have ideas, stories, and information to share to do so without spending a fortune.

Often, however, they need an expert who can pull their newsletter together. Thus, opportunities for newsletter publishing are plentiful. Market prospects include:

- Small to medium-size businesses that wish to communicate with their clients and prospects.
- Associations and other organizations that do not have a communications staff or would hire an outside business to produce the final newsletter in conjunction with their staff.
- Communities of all sizes, and even subcommunities within a community. For example, entrepreneur Charles Fletcher publishes the *Lower Columbia Business* magazine, targeting the business community in southern Oregon.
- Solo practitioner offices, such as lawyers, doctors, dentists, word processors, and others.

You can also go with an original idea and market to subscribers nationwide. The secret to success in newsletter publishing is to *limit your market* by narrowing the newsletter's focus. Books, magazines, and newspapers deal with subjects in a general way. Subscribers look to a newsletter for specifics. Choose a topic on which you are an expert or in which you have great interest. The *Oxbridge Directory of News-letters* estimates that there are roughly 4,000 subscription newsletters in the United States and Canada; of these, 3,500 are business-oriented and only 500 cater to consumer interests. This industry is ripe for expansion.

For your newsletter, look for a subject that hasn't already been exploited to its maximum by magazines or other newsletters. Many entrepreneurs have discovered their niche in the market quite accidentally: in looking for a product or service for which they themselves had a need, they discovered that no such product or service exists. For example, an avid bottle-top collector may be interested in receiving a newsletter written expressly for collectors of bottle caps, only to find that there is no newsletter of this type. This seems to be a perfect opportunity to take advantage of a gap in the market, but how can this entrepreneur be sure that others would be interested in this newsletter?

Testing the market is an important step in the direction of success in the newsletter industry. Using the example given above, this entrepreneur could test his or her idea by placing "test ads" in publications targeted at collectors. The ad should not mention anything about buying the newsletter, but should advise interested parties to write in for more information. In this way, you can get an idea of what the response to your newsletter will be. If this response is significant enough (perhaps 1% of the total number of subscribers to the publications in which you advertised), then you are on your way to being a newsletter publisher.

18. Personalized Children's Books

Approximately 4 million babies are predicted to be born each year in the United States through at least the end of the 1990s. This means millions of parents, grandparents, aunts, and uncles will want to shower them with the perfect educational and self-esteem enhancing gift: personalized children's books.

You do not need to be a writer or artist to succeed in this truly self-contained business. What you need is a good computer system, custom software packages designed to produce the books, and a good marketing strategy. Many entrepreneurs take their business on the road—county fairs, holiday boutiques, special community functions, and other gatherings where parents and children will be found. Others rely on local advertising—leaving brochures with family service businesses and hospitals, or building accounts with community bookstores and gift boutiques. Direct mail can also be effective, as can catalogs and Yellow Pages ads.

19. Referral Service

When a businessman recently arrived from India wanted to reserve space at a recording studio, he was frustrated. Of the three recording studios listed in the Yellow Pages, two didn't answer and the third was extremely rude. They said they didn't do voice recordings and suggested he "try the Yellow Pages" because they didn't have time to deal with him.

Rather than sit and fume, he got an idea for a business, because he had a hunch that other consumers might feel the same frustration. What was needed, he felt, was a new type of generic Yellow Pages, a service that a consumer with a need could call to get specific referrals. Say, for instance, you're stumped by the task of finding a sculptured brass candle holder, or you want to find out where to grab takeout Chinese food at 3:00 A.M. You could simply call a single toll-free number, talk to an operator, and get the needed information.

That was the idea. Soon, with nearly 8,000 companies listed on his service (each of which paid $50 per month, for a total of $400,000 in income), his idea had more than paid off. The beauty of this type of business is that it could work in practically any community.

All businesses know they have to advertise, and because traditional Yellow Pages place businesses head-to-head in a competitive marketplace, they'll jump at the chance to get a personal referral. That's where a professional referral service comes in. By using personal computers and a bank of operators, business information can be passed on quickly to consumers 24 hours a day.

Select a market that appeals to consumers who prefer a referral to a simple ad (i.e., professional services such as law firms, dentists, physicians, and general contractors), or select a product, service, or other entity that is generally difficult to locate. You could start a referral service that listed all restaurants, community centers, and other organizations that allow private parties to be held on their premises, and give your callers a basic rundown of costs, available seating, type of surroundings, additional services (catering, bar tending, music).

20. Sales/Marketing Service

Most salespeople don't have the time to sit down and compose letters to individual clients. They'd rather finalize a deal on the phone or in person, but letter writing is often an unavoidable part of their job. A letter tells the client that its business is important—and that your salesperson is professional and courteous.

Other small companies that make the leap into the big leagues find they must produce, for prospective clients, high-quality proposals that will rival those of larger firms. Without a professionally written and designed proposal, they will not be considered "players." That's where sales/marketing services come in.

If you are a strong writer with a background in—or, at a minimum, a strong understanding of—the sales process, then your own sales/marketing service can be lucrative. It is important to define yourself as an expert with excellent written communication skills. Potential clients include small business owners looking to expand, and independent salespeople representing various companies or products. An example is a mortgage broker who also has a real estate license, works for a couple of firms as an independent contractor, and essentially operates as a single-person business with no support staff.

Reciprocal advertising referrals with office supply warehouses, computer hardware/software stores, printers, copier services, and courier/messenger companies work well for a sales/marketing venture. Offer to hand out their business cards and literature to your clients in return for letting you leave your cards and brochures for pickup at their businesses. Networking is also crucial. You should become well known among the chamber of commerce, real estate and insurance associations, salesperson groups, toastmasters, and wherever else referrals—and clients—are likely to be found.

21. Sign Making

Today, it is possible to make a vinyl sign for a client in as little as 10 to 15 minutes—allowing plenty of opportunity for making high profits with your company. The business has automatic appeal because it is fast and efficient, a must for today's consumers. The biggest challenge as a business is simply to get the message out that you exist and are ready to serve.

A sign-making business generally opens its doors to a multitude of potential clients:

- Local retailers.
- Libraries, schools, and community organizations.
- Restaurants, caterers, and party-planning services.
- Consumers wanting to announce births or celebrate birthdays, anniversaries, or other momentous occasions.

To be sure that your service is thought of first in your community, take advantage of all marketing media: networking, brochures, direct mail, catalogs, reciprocal advertising, donating signs to special causes (in return for placing your company name on the banner or having your business cards or brochures on hand), Yellow Pages, and community newspaper ads.

22. Software Design/Custom Software

Will the market for small software designers and custom programmers continue? Perhaps columnist Peter Coffee in *PC Week* said it best when explaining his reaction to the statement that "programmers are on their way out because end users will soon be creating their own applications from off-the-shelf objects." His response: "No way, hipsters, it's not going to happen." Why? Because even as companies such as Novell develop software that allows computer users to custom design, "programming, no matter how visual the tools may be, is inherently abstract," says Coffee. The majority of users want a ready-to-use product.

However, you should be aware that, as the software industry matures, it's increasingly difficult to make money. The best approach seems to be to focus on a narrow, or vertical, market. For example, there is a firm that offers cemetery-management software. In addition to helping cemetery owners with their financial planning, this software contains data about the permissible number of plots per acre, which varies from state to state. This makes it possible for cemetery owners to "model" various cemetery layouts.

Whatever vertical market you decide to attack, you'll need to understand the needs of that market in great detail. It may be helpful to hire employees who have already worked in the vertical market you plan to take on. Direct-mail and direct telephone sales, as well as well-placed trade journal or consumer magazine ads, will help make the right people aware of your new product.

Software publishers can help get your product to market. Most make custom arrangements with programmers based on a number of considerations. Usually (but not always), publishers purchase the rights to your software, duplicate the disks, create the manuals, and market the finished product. In return, you get cash—either up front or in the form of royalties. Some deals include both a cash advance *and* royalties. Publishers may distribute the product to dealers themselves or use outside distributors. Some publishers also sell software through their own mail-order operations. A number of hardware manufacturers have software-publishing arms: IBM, Tandy (Radio Shack), and Apple are examples. They may or may not require exclusive rights to your software. Unless the price they offer is substantial, stay away from exclusive deals. A lawyer who is familiar with this field can advise you.

23. Utility Bill Auditing

The more than 23 million businesses in the United States have at least one thing in common: a desire to save money. Utility bill auditing services do just that, saving anywhere from 50% to 75% of utility charges for numerous clients across the country.

Auditors working from their home examine gas, sewage, electric, water, and telephone bills for inaccuracies in rate classification, billing, meter usage, and taxes. Most charge a fee based on savings, so their potential clients have nothing to lose by letting them dive in and take a money-saving look at their bills.

Getting the first couple of clients is the biggest challenge. A dynamic personality and a competent grasp of tariffs (legal documents filed by utility and telephone companies with appropriate government agencies) can give you a chance at your first successes. From there, successful auditors say, other clients will climb on board eagerly to see whether they can save money, too.

24. Word Processing

If you're a competent typist, you may have already thought about setting up a word processing business in your home. Thousands are doing so and finding small businesses and professional people—doctors, lawyers, dentists, and so forth—eager to use their services, either on a contract or piecework basis.

The demand for such services isn't confined to large cities. Smaller communities, where technology is slow to arrive, sometimes offer the best ground-floor opportunities for starting word processing services. Competition in smaller communities may be minimal, and potential clients may respond more favorably to higher fees because their experience with technology is more limited. A word-processing service that charges more than a local typist, however, must be ready to justify the cost. In most cases, this means providing the highest quality and fastest turnaround in town, or supplementing your word processing services with other expertise. For example, you can help job-hunters write a successful resume, word process a professional finished resume for them, and store the resume on disk for updates and subsequent needed revisions.

At this point, straight and simple word processing is still the most popular service being offered out of private homes and small offices. It may be the one way to open other doors of opportunity for you, particularly if you're a competent typist, your word processing package is fairly sophisticated, and you're well-versed in its use.

FINDING YOUR MARKET

The market for many home-based computer business is comprised of both business and consumer segments. A computer-based business originally designed to appeal to one segment or the other may expand to include both. Start by finding out who your most likely customers will be. You can expand your marketing efforts later. The amount of specialization offered by your business products or services can greatly alter your expected target market.

To find out what kind of market exists for your intended home-based business, begin by learning as much as you can about your business and community.

Read Everything

This is the cheapest and quickest way to learn the basics about your future venture, avoid "reinventing the wheel," and prepare properly for start-up. As Amar Bhide stated in his *Harvard Business Review* article, "How Entrepreneurs Craft Strategies that Work" (March/April 1994): "Entrepreneurs typically lack the time and money to interview a representative cross section of potential customers, let alone analyze substitutes, reconstruct competitors' costs, or project alternative technology scenarios. . . . Yet all ventures merit some analysis and planning." If you do nothing else to prepare for your new business, invest some time in reading everything you can find on related subjects and existing entrepreneurs.

Look at the Competition

Analysis of the competition in your local area is especially important, both to see whom you are up against and to gauge how they are doing. The mere existence of competition does not preclude you from moving forward; in fact, it can help you to a better focus for your business strategy. By making a list of all your competitors and noting their locations, specialties, and business practices (hours of operation, inventory, and so on), you can better weigh the advantages and disadvantages of your own business.

Network with Local Businesses

Some established businesses will have clients similar to those you hope to target. Other home-based entrepreneurs can be especially helpful in anticipating community reaction to your business. You may be able to barter with these local business owners, before your business is up and running, by offering them your products and/or services in exchange for information. Word of mouth goes a long way for new entrepreneurs.

Show a Prototype of Your Work to Potential Buyers

Early purchasers could not picture substituting a photocopier for the carbon paper used in their offices. So, too, most people find it hard to picture the benefits of various products and services before they see them in a working context. Even businesses that do not seem to lend themselves to visual aids—like business consulting, bulletin board, or referral services—need to have visuals for marketing.

Create a Chart or Brochure that States Known Benefits

Businesses/consumers have benefited from products/services like yours in the past. Specific (and brief) write-ups that explain specifically how they benefited will encourage your new prospects. Show a sample of the reports, findings, or sources that will be given through your business. Offer free services/products to a handful of local individuals (like the business owners mentioned above) and take pictures, get them to serve as references, and present your service as a viable investment.

When all is said and done, however, nothing beats conducting thorough market research before you drill your home-based business full bore. Don't spend time unnecessarily on "nice to know" projects; instead, invest time on specific research that will help you launch your business successfully.

MARKET RESEARCH

The purpose of market research is to provide relevant data that will help solve the marketing problems a business will encounter. This research is absolutely necessary in the start-up phase. Conducting thorough market surveys is the foundation of any successful business. In fact, strategies such as market segmentation (identifying specific segments within a market) and product differentiation (creating an identity for your service that separates it from your competitors') would be impossible to develop without market research. According to William A. Cohen, author of *The Entrepreneur and Small Business Problem Solver* (John Wiley & Sons, 1990), the marketing research process can be broken down into specific stages:

1. Determine the problems that must be solved.
2. Determine whether those problems require research in order to solve them.
3. List the goals and objectives that will be defined through market research.

4. Identify the type of data that should be gathered to meet those goals.
5. Plan the method that will be used to acquire the desired information.
6. Define the sample audience that will best provide the data required.
7. Conduct market research and gather the information.
8. Analyze the data.
9. Develop conclusions based on the information gathered, and determine a course of action.

There are four primary research methods you'll have to choose from:

1. The historical method uses past data to define current market conditions.
2. The observational method studies current market data in order to predict future conditions.
3. The experimental method, using appropriately controlled tests, seeks to discover whether specific marketing activities will be effective.
4. The survey method, the most prevalent method, uses research on existing markets.

How to Do a Market Survey

A thorough market survey will help determine a reasonable sales forecast for your business. According to Dan Steinhoff and John F. Burgess, in their book *Small Business Management Fundamentals* (McGraw-Hill, 4th ed., 1986), the basic steps for assessing your market and making a forecast are:

1. Determine the market limits or trading area.
2. Study the population within this area to determine its potential spending characteristics.
3. Determine the area's purchasing power.
4. Determine the present sales volume of the type of services you will be offering.
5. Estimate what proportion of the total sales volume you can reasonably obtain.

Step 5 is extremely important. Opening your new business within a given community or market doesn't guarantee additional business volume; it may simply redistribute the business already there.

In conducting your market research, you will be gathering two types of data: primary information that you will compile yourself or hire someone to gather, and, more likely, secondary information already compiled and organized for you. Reports and studies done by government agencies, trade associations, or other businesses within your industry are examples of the latter. Search for them, and take advantage of their content.

PRIMARY RESEARCH

There are basically two types of information that can be gathered through primary research:

1. *Exploratory information*—geared toward defining a problem by questioning targeted consumers, using fairly open-ended and general questions that elicit lengthy answers.
2. *Specific information*—concentrates on solving a problem that has already been defined; usually involves more in-depth questioning than exploratory research. When conducting specific research, the objective is to arrive at concrete courses of action that will resolve a problem defined by exploratory research.

Most companies hire a marketing firm to acquire primary data for them, but this is not always the case. When conducting primary research using your own resources, you must first decide how you will question your target group of individuals. There are basically three avenues you can take: (1) direct mail, (2) telemarketing, and (3) personal interviews.

If you choose a direct-mail questionnaire, make sure your questions are short and to the point. Most people don't like to be bothered with direct-mail questionnaires. If your questionnaire is lengthy, your chances of receiving a good response will drop.

The same is true with telemarketing. Most people are bombarded with phone solicitations these days and have become wary of unfamiliar voices over the phone. This wariness, combined with the fact that you are invading their free time at home, makes you an unwelcome intruder. Many people, however, will provide you with a small amount of their time to answer a few questions. Don't get too verbose, or people will hang up on you.

The best course of action to obtain primary data is to conduct person-to-person interviews. Once you've gained an individual's attention and he or she has agreed to an interview, it is easy to sit down and ask questions that will take an hour or more to complete. The advantage of personal interviews over direct mail and telemarketing is that you're not usually invading the individual's personal territory or time. Interviews are usually conducted at a prearranged time that is convenient with the interviewee. Many interviewers offer an incentive for agreeing to an interview. This might be a small payment such as $10 or a free gift. The important thing is that you are dealing with a willing candidate.

SECONDARY RESEARCH

As previously mentioned, most secondary research information will have been gathered for you by firms outside your company and will be fairly easy to obtain free or at a nominal cost. Secondary research is not as involved as primary research. It doesn't require any interviews to determine problems and develop courses of action. You will need only a knowledge of where to search for resources that have already gathered the information.

Census Tracts

Almost every county government publishes population density and distribution figures in easily available census tracts. They indicate the number of people living in specific areas such as precincts, water districts, or, perhaps, 10-block neighborhoods. Some counties publish reports that show the population 10 years ago, 5 years ago, and currently, thus indicating population trends.

Declining, static, or small populations do not suggest new businesses for an area. Increasing and expanding populations desiring the services you propose to offer are ideal. To judge whether they are potential customers, you must study the lifestyle of the community.

Maps

Maps of major trading areas in counties and states are available from chambers of commerce, industrial development boards, trade development commissions, and city newspaper offices. These maps show where the major business of the subject area is conducted and reflect the population's spending habits.

Look at road maps of any area for information on the ease of access to specific sites. Access is an important consideration in determining market-area limits.

Media Sources

Ask the sales departments of your area's newspapers and magazines for copies of the business profiles used in their sales efforts. They will help determine the financial situation of your potential customers. Advertising managers are another source of information on spending patterns in the community.

Check with the managers of local broadcasting stations. The research they routinely conduct can help you determine whether there is a valid market for your services.

Study the Yellow Pages to see how many businesses of a similar type are already operating and where they are located. This information is also available from Dun & Bradstreet.

Community Organizations

Major cities have chambers of commerce or business development departments that encourage new businesses in their communities. They will supply you with information (usually free of charge) on population trends, community income characteristics, payrolls, industrial development, and so on.

Industry

You must identify the industry in your target area. Payrolls create buying power for your potential customers; unless payroll stability and growth are present, investment in the area may be unwise. Try to locate your business in a community that has substantial diversified and permanent industry, an upward trend in community payrolls, and a minimum of seasonality.

2

PURCHASING YOUR COMPUTER EQUIPMENT— HARDWARE AND SOFTWARE

You will encounter three basic problems when buying your computer equipment:

1. Most likely you won't have an unlimited budget.
2. Office productivity technology is changing so fast it is almost impossible to keep up with it.
3. Just about everyone wants to give advice on what equipment you should buy.

The result is often "buying paralysis," in which the easiest and safest route is to do nothing. Or worse, you end up buying the hardware and software that are most popular, have been advertised the most, or are being pushed aggressively by a salesperson, even if they aren't appropriate for your needs.

This is a solvable problem, however. Start with an overall goal: to acquire the best combination of equipment and software to meet your needs within your budget. Then, by following the steps outlined in this chapter, you can meet this goal and even have some fun doing so.

The more time you spend planning your purchases, the more time, money, and aggravation you will save down the line. You will avoid: wasting time on evaluating choices that don't make sense, listening to sales pitches and other advice that isn't helping, and, most importantly, losing time because of problems with inappropriate hardware and software. You'll save money by buying the best combination of equipment for your needs, and you won't be continually replacing defective or insufficient parts. Finally, you'll minimize the time needed to make your hardware and software work for you, and you'll be able to do the things that will make your business grow and prosper.

The approach you should use is described in general terms below, with more specifics in the sections that follow:

1. Determine your business requirements.
2. Conduct some up-front research.
3. Set a firm budget.
4. Plan your purchase strategy.
5. Evaluate alternatives.
6. Use your business requirements and budget as benchmarks.
7. Buy the basics.
8. Plan for training time.
9. Research your specific needs and then look for solutions.

DETERMINE YOUR REQUIREMENTS

As you identify your business requirements, put them in writing. Sift out what you absolutely *need* to run your business. Confront these key general considerations about your situation:

- What is your budget?
- How important is ease of use?
- What are you familiar with? What software have you used before?
- Do you need a computer to work with at home and at the office?
- Will anyone else be using the computer? Do you have a future plan to network computers?

- Do you (or will you) need compatibility with client or key vendor data?
- Will you be utilizing large volumes of data in your business?
- What support do you have available?

Your answers to these questions will point you in the right direction to start your search. Next, you must get more specific about your business needs. This process comes down to "walking through" mentally, or on paper, how your business will handle day-to-day transactions. For example, envision a sales transaction from start to finish. Answer questions like:

- How will you produce your quotation or sales proposal?
- What does it have to look like?
- Do you need a database to track many prospective customers?
- Will you be faxing your quotes or proposals?
- How important is it to be able to produce an on-the-spot quotation or a demonstration of your product or service?
- When you produce an invoice, how many copies do you need to give the customer, and how many do you need to retain for follow-up?
- Do you need special software that is available only on certain hardware types?

Answers to these questions will be an enormous help in determining your hardware and software requirements. You won't know all the answers to every aspect of your business, but when you must make buying decisions about how much disk capacity to buy, or what type of printer, fax machine, and so on, you will need, you'll be able to make the necessary trade-offs between cost and features/capacity because you have thought through what you really need.

CONDUCT SOME UP-FRONT RESEARCH ON COMPUTER COMPONENTS

The more informed you are, the better your buying decisions. The growth of technology and the vast number of alternatives available in computer hardware, software, and other office equipment can make your research project intimidating, even if you are somewhat familiar with computer technology. The key is to have just enough understanding to make sure that the important issues are covered. After that, everything else falls into the category of features and details that won't make a major impact on your decision.

General Considerations

Start with your computer purchase, before you select any other office equipment. So many traditional office equipment functions have been incorporated into today's computers, you must make sure you don't end up buying a separate piece of equipment unnecessarily.

Many people may recommend determining your software needs before you decide on hardware. That was more of a necessity in the days of the minicomputers. At that time, each manufacturer had its own unique operating system, and software developers had to choose one that their software would work with. Today, personal computers are built to handle primarily one, or only a few operating system standards. As a result, the amount of available software for almost any application has grown explosively. Therefore, unless you have very specialized software needs, other considerations will drive your selection of computer hardware.

Your mission will be to acquire the best balance of computing power, memory, storage space, and printing quality that will meet your needs. You will also need to factor in future expansion capability, service, and support. Let's start by covering the basics you'll need to know in order to perform this balancing act for yourself.

BACKGROUND ON COMPUTER TECHNOLOGY

Computers, in the most basic sense, are electronic machines. Granted, they are more complex than most other machines, but that is their basic description. The difference in many personal computers is in the variety of options available in their components. Consider a stereo system as an analogy. You can buy an all-in-one stereo that has the capacity to play AM, FM, tapes, and CDs. You bring it home, take it out of the box, plug it in, and it's ready to go. Some computers are now sold that way; the Macintosh probably comes closest to the analogy.

Stereo systems can also be purchased component by component. You can pick out a separate tuner, receiver, tape player, and CD player, each with different features and capacities, and then put them together into one system. In essence, that is what most computer manufacturers are doing today with personal computers (PCs). They are mixing the essential components of a CPU, RAM, disk drive, and video monitor with "extras" like CD players, tape drives, and so on, to offer their custom version of a personal computer.

What components make up a personal computer, and how much do you have to know about them to make an intelligent buying decision? You need to know the basics, to avoid making a major mistake. Everything after that is just fine-tuning. We'll start with the basics. The major components of any personal computer are the CPU, RAM, disk drive(s), peripheral bus, video monitor, and keyboard.

What Is the CPU?

The central processing unit (CPU) of the computer is often called the microprocessor or the "chip," because it is made of a small wafer-sized chip of silicon. This part of the computer processes the instructions that direct everything that happens within the computer. Because of its role, the CPU is one of the most important considerations when deciding on the model of computer to purchase. Several manufacturers make CPUs; the largest are Intel, the marketplace leader by far, and Motorola, which makes most of the CPUs for Macintosh computers. Companies like AMD and Cyrix make CPUs that are compatible with those made by Intel.

The model of CPU that is sold the most today is made by Intel and is called a 486. Intel has become more creative with its names of late: the newest, faster (and more expensive) model is called the Pentium. On the Macintosh side, the latest chips made by Motorola are called the 68040 and, more recently, the PowerPC.

Like makers of other computer components, the manufacturers of CPU chips are constantly introducing new models that are faster and smaller. The chips are differentiated mostly by their performance speed, which is sometimes expressed in how fast instructions are executed—millions of instructions per second (MIPS)—but is more commonly measured by the clock speed in which they are processed—millionths of a second, or megahertz (MHz). For example, the range of clock speeds for Intel chips sold today is between 20 MHz and 100 MHz.

Salespeople will tell you to buy the latest and greatest CPU so as to avoid buying an obsolete computer. Proceed with caution: the latest and greatest are almost always overpriced for what you really need. For most business applications today, a 486 or compatible chip in the 33 MHz to 66 MHz speed range will be more than adequate for the next 3 to 5 years. The latest and greatest chip is the Pentium, which is priced $500 higher than a 486. It makes sense to buy a computer with the Pentium when the price falls closer to the price of today's 486-based machines. Remember that the 486 will not be obsolete any time soon.

A Macintosh 68040 chip-based computer, running at 33 MHz, will handle most needs. The same rationale for the Pentium applies to the PowerPC chip-based Macintosh machines: Wait until the price comes down.

What Is RAM?

RAM stands for random access memory, or just memory for short. It is the workspace, much like your tabletop, where all the computer's work is done and is directed by the CPU according to instructions given out by the operating system and application software. Memory is expressed in terms of thousands of bytes (Kb) or megabytes (millions of bytes: MB). How much memory do you need? It depends on the size of computer "desktop" you need to get your work done. Most computers need at least 4 MB to operate software applications at all; 8 MB are needed to run well, and 16 MB are adequate for almost any use. More than that, for most people, would be like working on a conference room table: most of the space would be unused.

What Is a Disk Drive?

A disk drive is a storage place for computer programs and data. Using the analogy of an office, a disk drive is similar to a filing cabinet or set of cabinets. The size of the storage is expressed in millions of bytes (MB). A floppy disk drive is very portable, but has a small storage space, with room for only 1.44 MB. A hard disk drive is usually not portable, but can hold anywhere from 100 MB to as much as 1000 MB or more. (1000 megabytes is usually expressed as one gigabyte (GB).)

Disk drive capacity is a good place to invest your equipment budget. Today's software applications alone will use up a large portion of available space on any drive, before you have saved any data. Don't buy less than 350 MB, with 500 MB being a much better bet.

Bus

You may see advertisements or have sales personnel talk to you about the type of bus a system has. What is the bus and what do you need to know about it? Basically, the bus is the highway along which instructions from the CPU pass to the other components of the system. No matter how fast the rest of your components may be, if you have a slow bus your entire system will perform slowly. The latest bus technology is called local bus, either VL-Bus or PCI. It generally delivers the best performance, especially for video.

Video Monitor and Video Driver

Most monitors sold today are capable of color output, although you can still purchase a black-and-white model if so desired. Monitors are generally priced according to their size, expressed in the diagonal measure of the screen, and their clarity, expressed in dots pitch. For most people, a 15-inch monitor with a dot pitch of .28 is adequate. A 17-inch monitor is a real luxury; prices range near $800 for a reasonable quality monitor of that size.

If you have a monitor, what is the video driver for? The driver is usually on a separate component called a card, or video board, that includes the electronics and memory needed to make the monitor work better. It takes some of the processing load off of the CPU by acting as the interpreter of instructions to the monitor, which serves to speed things up. Thus, the better the video card, the faster your monitor will be able to update on-screen images, up to the limit of its capabilities.

Video cards are sold on the basis of their capability to display and the speed at which they are able to do so; these are functions of the amount of memory they come with and the bus they utilize. Your computer should have a card that uses local bus (either VL-Bus or PCI) with at least 1 MB of additional memory (2 MB is preferred if you have complex needs). Beware of computers built with the video processor integrated into the motherboard instead of using a separate card.

Keyboards and Pointing Devices

Most systems include a keyboard (input system) and a pointing device, usually a mouse, in the price. If the mouse included with your system doesn't work very well, you will need to decide on what type of input system to purchase. For keyboards, the factors to consider are the number of keys and typing comfort. Prices can range from $25 to $200; a good 101-key keyboard is available for around $50. Pointing devices are mostly a matter of personal preference. All manner of pointing devices—mice, trackballs, mouse/trackball combinations, pens, and even finger touch devices—are sold today at prices ranging from $10 to $200. The most important factors are comfort, ability to maneuver the cursor around the screen, and number of buttons to use for selection.

ADDITIONAL TECHNOLOGICAL CONSIDERATIONS

Beyond the basics described above, be aware of a few other factors as you make your decisions: expansion (upgrade) capability and operating systems. In addition, you may wish to look at networking or the future capacity for networking.

Expansion Capability

One way to make sure your computer doesn't quickly become obsolete is to purchase a system that has expansion capability: as components become old or obsolete, you can replace them. If you want to purchase additional components, you can easily do so. The addition of almost any new component (network adapter, CD-ROM controller or sound card, scanner, and tape drive) to your system will require you (or a service) to add a piece to your computer called a board or card that fits into an expansion slot. The more expansion slots you have, the more components you will be able to add later. Buy a computer with at least 5 open or unused slots in which new components can be added.

In the long run, you will be better off purchasing a computer that does *not* have the components integrated into the motherboard. The motherboard, the main electronic component, is the most expensive and complicated component to replace. Integrating the components on the motherboard is a cheaper way to manufacture but it is much more difficult to add or change components without replacing the entire motherboard.

Make sure the computer you buy can accommodate the addition of more memory in the future. Every upgrade of new software seems to require a greater amount of memory than the one before it. If 8 MB will work well today, within a year or two you'll need 12 or 16 MB, so make sure you can add memory on when you want to.

Many machines are sold "CPU upgradable" or, for Intel 486 machines, "Pentium ready." This means that, for a price, you can replace your CPU with a newer, faster model.

Operating Systems

The computer itself is nothing more than a bunch of silicon transistors and other assembled components. To do useful work, the computer requires software programs to instruct it. The operating system is the software program that handles all basic instructions, such as printing and copying files, so that each of the application programs doesn't have to build in replicated instructions for these functions. Over the years, operating systems have evolved to include many utility functions: file listing, text editing, backing up and copying files, indicating available resources, and changing the color of the screen output.

The Macintosh operating system, called System 7, is the only choice of operating system available for the Mac.

If you buy a PC, you have at least three choices of operating systems: DOS, OS/2, and UNIX. The key consideration in determining the operating system to use with your computer is the availability of application software that will work with it. Market share becomes a key consideration because developers of application software will write for the operating system that will help them sell the most software. For the single-user desktop computer market, DOS owns the predominant share. Windows™ is an enhancement to DOS that gives it a graphical interface and other features. You must first purchase and install DOS (approx. $50 from IBM, Novell, or Microsoft) before you can install Windows (approx. $75 from Microsoft). Many computer manufacturers are now selling their equipment with DOS and Windows preloaded, to save you the hassle of doing it yourself.

The other two PC operating systems are OS/2, from IBM, and UNIX, which is available from a variety of suppliers, including Novell, SCO, and others. Each has a very small share of the desktop market and therefore has relatively few applications available. Powerful features may make OS/2 or UNIX the system of choice for some users, but both systems are more expensive than DOS. IBM has recently added the capability of running DOS and Windows applications within OS/2.

Networks

If you have more than one computer and wish to connect them to share files, printers, and other common peripherals, you may consider networking them. In recent years, networking has become easily available, even to computer systems with only two machines. To create a network, you need an additional component called a *network adapter* or *interface card* for each computer, wire to connect them, and network software. The adapters cost about $100 each, and the wire can be purchased with the connectors attached for about 25¢ per foot.

For the network software, all Macintosh computers are sold with built-in networking capability to use LocalTalk,™ Apple's proprietary network system. Three well-known, low-cost networking systems available for PCs using DOS or Windows provide many of the advantages of larger networks:

1. Windows for Workgroups 3.11 (WfWG), from Microsoft, is the simplest and cheapest small network. If you already have the Windows operating system, it will cost you about $50 per

computer to upgrade to WfWG. Add a network interface card (about $100 each) on each computer and you have a network. You will then be able to read and access files on any computer in the network, and print to any printer from any computer.

2. Personal Netware, a scaled-down version of Novell Netware, is another low-cost alternative for use in small networks. Personal Netware costs approximately $60 for each computer or $200 for a set of five. It is able to run and be accessed in Windows or DOS, and is much more efficient in running networked DOS applications than is WfWG. If you think you will eventually need a full-size Novell network, then the upgrade path is much easier. It is a little more complicated for a new user to install and manage than WfWG, so make sure someone who can help is available.

3. LANtastic, by Artisoft, is the other major player in small peer-to-peer networks. LANtastic is often sold in kit form, with all the adapters, wiring, and software necessary to get up and running. A starter kit, with software, cabling, and network adapter cards for two computers, can be purchased for about $200. To add more computers costs about $150 more.

All of these networking products are becoming easier to use, but they are not for novices. Use Personal Netware if you plan to grow into or attach to a Netware network, or if you have a friend who is an expert. Windows for Workgroups is less capable than the other two and doesn't allow DOS networking, but is easier to set up and maintain. LANtastic is somewhere in the middle in terms of ease of use and capability.

SET A FIRM BUDGET

Now that you have a general idea of the cost of the basic computer equipment you will need, you can begin to create a budget. Your primary concern is to end up with the right combination of software and hardware that you need to run your business. Too often, excessive money is spent on more equipment than was necessary, leaving insufficient funds available for the software and peripheral equipment that make a big difference in productivity.

Because of the rapid changes in computer technology and price, there always seems to be a better innovation just around the corner, or an impending price reduction that goes into effect on the day after you buy your equipment. This is somewhat the nature of the computer industry to date. The technological and marketing games of "leapfrog" never seem to stop. Your best buying approach is to utilize a simple rule of thumb: Never buy at the beginning or near the end of a product life cycle. Don't buy the latest and greatest new component that has just been introduced to the marketplace; it will be generally overpriced and undertested for product flaws. Conversely, don't buy the lowest-priced component; it will soon be obsolete—incompatible with everything else you purchase and decreasingly likely to be supported with technical assistance or product upgrades by the manufacturer.

How do you know how far into the life cycle a product is? And how strong is the company you are buying from? A little research in books like this, in computer publications, and through trusted professionals will go a long way. The research time you spend in this area will help you avoid a poor hardware and software investment.

One of the toughest things you will have to do is stick to your budget. Almost every seller along the way will try to get you to add on options and features, escalating your purchase to the neatest, fastest, latest (and most expensive) components available. Avoid spending too much on basics or, by the time you're ready to buy software and other necessities, you will need to cut corners where you shouldn't.

PLAN YOUR PURCHASE STRATEGY

You can buy computer hardware, software, and office equipment through a wide variety of outlets. Each purchasing channel has its pluses and minuses (see Figure 2–1). When you spend less, you often lose other important factors like service, variety of selection, and ease of product return. Which channel you use depends on your degree of computer-purchasing savvy and the amount of time you wish to spend in the purchasing process. The more you know about what you want, the more likely that you can successfully use the lower-price channels. If you don't have the time or inclination to spend a lot of time doing purchase investigations, or if continued service and support are very important to you, you should probably stay with channels that will provide those factors.

The major choices for purchasing computer hardware and software, as listed in Figure 2–1, are:

- *Retail chains*—large national outlets like CompUSA, Egghead, Circuit City, Best Buy, and so on. They sell computer hardware, software, and most office equipment.
- *Mail order*—companies like Dell Computer, Gateway, CDW (Computer Discount Warehouse), Inmac PC Select, and hundreds of others. Almost all can be found in computer magazines

Figure 2–1 Channels for Purchasing Computers

Choice	Pros	Cons	Look Out For
Retail chains	• Can see and use product before you buy • May have service dept. • May offer some purchasing and technical advice	• Limited selection • Prices sometimes higher	• Underinformed sales staff • Pressure to buy the latest and greatest • Poorly constructed systems
Mail order	• Prices very good • Some have limited technical support	• Wide price range • Shipping charges • Can't see product first	• Onerous return policies • Substitutions; know exactly what you want
Local dealers	• Prepurchase advice • After-purchase repair/service	• Higher price • Limited selection	• Steering to higher priced products
Manufacturers	• Technical support • Known quantity	• Higher price	• Delivery time
Local mail order	• Prices good	• Components may be poorly produced • May charge extra for credit card payment • Beware of punitive return policy	• Ambiguity when you order; you must know what you need • Return policy
VARs	• Complete solution • Require less effort	• Generally higher priced	• Reputation; knowledge in your industry

such as *The Computer Shopper,* a massive magazine that is mostly mail-order ads and is carried in major bookstores and other periodical outlets. Hardware, software, and office equipment are all available via mail order.

- *Local dealers*—generally found in shopping malls and in the local Yellow Pages. They sell mostly computer hardware and some office equipment.

- *Manufacturers*—now direct sellers, through organizations like Compaq Direct or Ambra (IBM), of their own product line of hardware.
- *Local mail order*—found in the Yellow Pages or in smaller computer-oriented publications like *Computer Currents* or *Computer Guide,* available by subscription or free in major bookstores and often in shops like Egghead.
- *Value-added resellers* (VARs)—provide a complete solution of hardware and software for a specific business need, often concentrating in a particular type of business.

For buying office equipment, the choices include the retail chains, as noted above, as well as local office supply retail outlets, national office supply chains like the Office Depot and OfficeMax, and some mail-order companies.

One additional note on buying hardware and software via mail order: Be sure you understand in advance the company's policy on returns and on use of credit cards. Many firms charge a "restocking fee" of as much as 20%, plus your return shipping charges, if you decide to return an item for any reason. Many also charge extra for the privilege of using a credit card to pay for your purchase. Near the back of *The Computer Shopper* is a very useful summary of all of the advertisers' hours of operation, return policies, and guarantees and the like, that is worth the price of the magazine if you are going to buy via mail order.

BUYING APPLICATION SOFTWARE

The software you use will have a greater impact on your day-to-day operations than any of the hardware. Once software has been purchased and opened, it generally can't be returned. Yet most people give their software purchase decisions a fraction of the time that they spend deciding on hardware.

Software purchases are more difficult—the sheer amount of software available for business use is beyond the comprehension of any one person—so we avoid the extra work needed to find the right program. Services exist on CD-ROM, looseleaf hard-copy volumes, or on-line services that will provide basic information about each software package and will update that information monthly. The cost of these services (about $1,000 per year) is prohibitive for most companies.

Without the benefit of a buying reference resource, the best way to decide on software purchases is by using the following step-by-step process:

1. Before talking to anyone, write down your top requirements for each application in priority order. For example, in the case of contact management software, your top requirements may be:

   - Ease of use.
   - Ability to export to your favorite word processor.
   - Ability to automatically update client history records after each phone call.
   - Production of mail-merge letters within the program.
   - Tracking of contacts, based on groups you define.

2. Go to as many reliable sources as you have time for. (See step 4 below for suggestions.)

3. Narrow the field by eliminating obvious mismatches for cost, features, ease of use, and support availability.

4. Investigate the remaining choices more carefully. Start with a comprehensive magazine review of all major programs of that type (publications like *PC Magazine* or *MacWorld*, for example), then ask friends, read ads, look for individual articles about the program, call for demo disks, or request more detailed information from the manufacturer.

5. Factor in future growth and needs of the business. You don't want to have to replace all your equipment every couple of years as you grow. Look for software that can be networked and has the capability of supporting somewhat more sophisticated needs than you may have today.

6. Call technical support for each of your finalists. How long do you wait to get through? Can you get through? Never underestimate the importance of technical support.

You most likely will not go through this process for every type of software you buy. You will have covered many of the steps in your prior experience, or you just won't have the time. Whenever you can use this process, you'll end up with better results in the long run. Figure 2–2 provides some guidelines for evaluating software.

EVALUATE HARDWARE ALTERNATIVES

After you have done your research and determined the appropriate buying channel, go back to your original benchmarks—your business requirements and budget. Stack up the alternatives against the benchmarks. No one product will meet all of your requirements, so there will

Figure 2–2   How to Evaluate Software

Source	Cost	Advantages	Disadvantages
Prior experience	• You know	• Great if you liked the product • Lower learning curve	• Missing better alternatives
Word of mouth	• Time	• Low cost • Real experience	• Personal prejudice • Others' use may not mirror yours
Store salesperson	• No cost	• Convenient • Easy	• Generally not well informed
Magazine review	• About $3 per publication	• Low cost • Fairly up-to-date	• Review may not apply to you • Reviewer bias • Time to find and read
Advertisements	• No cost	• Shows differences between their product and others	• Differences are carefully selected to ignore weak areas
Consultant	• Expensive	• Exact fit to your specifications • Time savings	• Cost

be tradeoffs to make. Beware of becoming entranced by whizbang features that look great but aren't what you need.

The following sections lead you through a review of the major tradeoffs and alternatives you'll need to consider as you evaluate your computer needs.

PC or Mac?

First, a definition of terms is in order. The term PC originally applied to an IBM Personal Computer or IBM-compatible computer. At one time, IBM held a very dominant position in the market for personal computers; the PC was the standard that any other manufacturer needed to meet. More recently, IBM's market share has greatly decreased and the term IBM-compatible is no longer an important issue. Still, most people refer to any computer based on a CPU supplied by Intel or compatible with Intel as a "PC."

The term Mac is used to refer to the Macintosh line of personal computers manufactured by Apple Computer, Inc. There are very few suppliers of Apple-compatible computers.

The basic difference between PCs and Macs is in their CPU. As noted above, PCs use mostly Intel or Intel-compatible CPUs, and Macintoshes use Motorola CPUs. All software you might purchase for a Macintosh will not be compatible with a PC and vice versa. The exception is "emulation" programs, available for the Mac, that will run DOS and Windows programs. These programs slow down the speed of the DOS or Windows program significantly; you will be frustrated and unhappy trying to make them work for you other than on an occasional basis.

There are definite advantages and disadvantages with each system. These are summarized in Figure 2–3.

The most important factors involve ease of use and market share. PCs have never had the ease of use out of the box that Apple's Macintosh provides; however, the rigid, and mostly proprietary, standards that have allowed Apple to provide this ease of use have also limited the options for upgrades and add-on components. The result is that when you buy an Apple Macintosh, you get greater ease of use at the cost of being hostage to fewer available suppliers for components, which means fewer choices and higher prices. The benefit is in not wasting a lot of time getting started.

The other issue has to do with market share. Apple has the minority of the market share at about 15%; PCs hold most of the rest. The lower number of Macs out there means that if you need to share data

Figure 2–3   PC vs. Mac: Advantages and Disadvantages

	Pros	**Cons**
PC	• More software available • Larger market share means greater direct compatibility with others • More hardware customization options • Can still use with inexpensive DOS operating system and application software	• More complex to set up • More decisions to make—more confusing
Mac	• Simple setup—works out of the box • Easy to use • Easier to network	• Less available software • Incompatible with 85% of the (PC) population • Peripherals tend to be higher priced

with other people, either vendors or customers, it is going to be more difficult if, as is likely, they have a PC. This sharing is not impossible; there are programs available that will do the necessary conversions for you. The other market share issue is how many hardware and software choices are available for each type of machine. Because of the dominance of PCs, more software developers have chosen to write software for them than have chosen to write for the Mac. There are quite a few choices in most software categories for the Mac, but nowhere near as many as for the PC. The same is true for hardware—CD-ROMs, printers, monitors, and so on. Many more choices are available for the PC equipment. More choices, however, can mean more complexity and less standardization. Adding a component to your PC can be a daunting task.

What can you get for your money? Figure 2–4 provides a rough comparison of a PC and Mac system with a similar configuration of accessories.

You will find that it is very difficult to get an "apples to apples" (no pun intended) comparison of a PC-based and Macintosh-based system. Figure 2–4 shows that they are very close in price and capability and that the peripherals like printers generally cost a bit more on the Mac side. Your decision should be driven by other factors, like compatibility and ease of use, much more than by price.

Macintosh Purchasing Considerations

If you have decided to purchase a Macintosh computer for your business, the next question you need to answer is what type of Macintosh

Figure 2–4   Mac vs. PC—A Comparison

System Components	Mac Quadra		486 PC	
	Feature	Price	Feature	Price
CPU	68040/33 MHz	$1,400	486/66 MHz	$1,600
RAM	8 MB	included	8 MB	included
Disk drive	300 MB	included	300 MB	included
Monitor	15" color	400	15" color	500
Operating system	System 7	included	DOS/Windows 3.1	included
Printer	Laserwriter 360	1,600	HP Laserjet 4P	1,000
Total		$3,400		$3,100

Figure 2–5   Macintosh: General Capabilities and Price Ranges

Model	CPU	Memory Range	Disk Size	Price
Performa 630	68040/33 MHz	4 MB to 32 MB	250 MB	$1,500
Quadra 605	68040/25 MHz	4 MB to 32 MB	160–250 MB	1,700
Quadra 650	68040/33 MHz	8 MB to 136 MB	230–500 MB	2,100
PowerMac 6100	PowerPC 60 MHz	8 or 16 MB to 72 MB	160–250 MB	2,600
PowerMac 8100	PowerPC 66 MHz	8 or 16 MB to 264 MB	250 MB to 1 GB	3,200

to buy. The Mac line ranges from the bottom-of-the-line Performa to the top-of-the-line PowerMac 8100. Figure 2–5 provides general capabilities and price ranges.

Key considerations and price differentiators in purchasing a desktop Mac are shown in Figure 2–6.

Type of PC to Buy

If you have decided instead to purchase an Intel-based (or compatible) computer for your business, your next issue is what type to buy. Computers built on the Intel CPU line range from the bottom-of-the-line 386 to the top-of-the-line Pentium, with variations in the clock speed in each category.

Key considerations and price differentiations in purchasing a desktop PC are shown in Figure 2–7.

Figure 2–6   Macintosh: Considerations in Buying a Desktop Mac

Factor	General Guidelines	Recommended for Mac
Model CPU	• Buy model based on product life cycle (not newest or oldest) • Consider upgrade path, ability to add/improve CPU, components	• Buy at least Quadra 33 MHz • PowerPC is overkill and over-priced for most users
Additional memory	• More is better, up to 16 MB • Buy with at least 8 MB	• 8MB @ $150 per MB
Storage capacity	• Look at cost per MB (incremental cost diminishes as you add)	• Get at least 400 MB • Shouldn't need more than 1 GB

Figure 2–7   PC: Considerations in Purchasing a Desktop PC

Factor	General Guidelines	Recommended for PC
Model CPU	• Buy model based on product life cycle (not newest or oldest) • Consider upgrade path, ability to add/improve CPU, components	• Buy at least 486DX 33 MHz • Pentium is overkill and overpriced; wait for prices to come down
Additional memory	• More is better, up to 16 MB • Buy with at least 8 MB	• 8 MB @ $150 per MB
Storage capacity	• Look at cost per MB (incremental cost diminishes as you add)	• Get at least 400 MB • Shouldn't need more than 1 GB

Because of the wide variation in the number of components included and the quality and features of those components, all prices and configurations noted are intended to provide a very general idea of cost, for your budgeting purposes only.

Desktop and Notebook Computer Considerations

One of the things you'll need to consider as you are looking into a computer purchase is whether it makes sense to buy a portable computer instead of, or in addition to, the traditional desktop model. What is a portable? Generally, you'll see them advertised as a notebook, subnotebook, or laptop computer; the subnotebook is smaller, lighter, and less powerful. In this text, we will refer to all battery operable computers as portables. Among the several good reasons for purchasing a portable computer are the following:

- You travel on airplanes frequently, on business trips.
- You rent an office, can afford only one computer, and need a computer at home.
- You will need to bring a computer with you to your client site.
- You like being able to bring your computer work with you wherever you go.

If you decide you need a portable computer, your next question is whether you can get by with just the portable or will need to buy a desktop as well. The technology contained in the smaller, all-purpose portable or notebook computer has so improved in the past few years that you can get most of the features and functionality you would expect from a desktop machine, albeit at a higher price. Portable computer purchasing decisions are similar to those for a traditional desktop computer, with the following additional considerations:

- *Video screen.* Size is definitely an issue. Most portable screens run from 7" to a maximum of 10½" diagonal, which may be too small for heavy day-to-day use. Color screens on a portable cost more, and the best color resolution, the backlit "Active Matrix" color, is still quite expensive. A less expensive alternative is "dual scan" color screens, which are not as clear or bright but may be adequate for your use. Take a look at the different screens and decide what you need.

- *Battery life.* The range of battery life from different models is anywhere from 30 minutes to 8 hours. If you need to be cordless for any length of time, you will need to get the longest possible battery life and find out how much an extra carry-along battery will cost. Beware of vendor claims on battery life—they tend to be similar to automobile miles-per-gallon claims. If you'll almost always be able to "plug in," spend your money on other features.

- *PCMCIA (expansion) slots.* Don't worry about the abbreviation; just remember that expansion slots will give you room for adding more memory, disk space, modems, and so on. Try to buy a model that has at least two slots, one of which should be a Type II.

- *Removable components.* Many models are built to allow easy removal and replacement of disk drives, batteries, and other components. The more removable components, the easier an upgrade or repair.

- *Placement of the pointing device.* There are several ingenious ways of integrating a pointing device, which is usually (but not always) a trackball, for portable computing usage. Try out a few, to see which is easiest for you to use.

- *Docking stations.* These are intended to provide an easier means to utilize the portable as a desktop machine. They can range in price from $200 to $1,000 and can include the capability of adding a larger video monitor, a larger disk drive, network access, a full-sized keyboard, and other features.

If you are thinking of purchasing both a desktop and a portable computer, you will need to deal with the issue of connecting them to transfer/update/synchronize files. Your choices will be to purchase a software utility program such as Traveling Software's LapLink or Symantec's Norton PC Anywhere, or consider creating a small network that you can use to share data, printers, and the like. The various software utilities for connecting portables and desktop computers often include the cable required to establish the data link.

Figure 2–8 provides the general range of prices you can expect to pay for an Intel CPU-based portable PC. PC portables have a variety of brand names but generally range from the 386 CPU base to a 486/33 MHz on the high end. Pentium chip-based portables are on the horizon.

Add anywhere from $300 to $1,000 for a docking station, each configured with some or all of networking, video boards, math coprocessor, speakers, and so on.

All Mac portables are called PowerBooks. They range from the entry level 165 to the top-of-the-line Duo 280c. Add $900 for a PowerBook docking station with networking, a 1 MB video board, and math coprocessor built in. The 280 and 280c models are subnotebook PowerBook Duo models that weigh about 4.5 pounds. The notebooks weigh about 7 pounds.

Printers

You will need some sort of device to produce printed output from your computer. The amount of money you can spend on printers can range from less than $200 to more than $2,500. The range of dollars translates to whether you select a dot matrix, an ink jet, or a laser printer.

Figure 2–8   PC Portables: General Range of Prices

Model	CPU	Display	Memory	Disk Size	Price
Varies	486DX/33 MHz	10" Mono	4–14 MB	120–340 MB	$1,500
Varies	486DX/33 MHz	9" Dual Scan Color	4–14 MB	120–340 MB	2,500
Varies	486DX/33 MHz	8.5" Active Color	4–14 MB	120–340 MB	3,100
Varies	486DX/66 MHz	9" Mono	4–20 MB	120–340 MB	2,200
Varies	486DX/66 MHz	9" Dual Scan Color	4–20 MB	120–340 MB	2,600
Varies	486DX/66 MHz	8.5" Active Color	4–20 MB	120–340 MB	3,600

Dot matrix printers are the lowest priced and give the lowest quality of print output. They still have utility for anyone who needs to print a multipart form or has no concern about the quality of the printed output. These printers work by striking a tiny set of pins against an inked ribbon to form the pattern of each character. Almost all dot matrix printers offered today use a set of 24 pins to form characters; the print quality is good but not suitable for most business correspondence or sales materials. Print speeds, expressed in characters per second (cps), range from 190 to 400 cps. Prices range from $140 to $800 or more for faster-output, high-volume, wide-carriage models. A good quality dot matrix printer can be purchased for around $200.

Ink jet or bubble jet printers, which work by spraying ink onto the page one line at a time, have the advantage of being very quiet. Ink jet printers produce higher-quality output than dot matrix printers, but sell for similar prices. The speed of ink jet printers ranges from 110 cps to 250 cps (in draft print mode) in a price range of $250 to $400. Ink jet speeds are also often expressed in pages per minute (ppm). A 3-ppm ink jet printer is printing the equivalent of approximately 120 characters per second.

Ink jet printers are now available to produce color output on plain paper. The printers range in price from $350 to $2,300, depending on factors such as print quality, number of typefaces available, and memory included in the printer to speed up processing. One factor to be aware of with bubble jets, especially those that print in color, is the useful life and price of the ink jet cartridges. Black ink cartridges run $20 each. Color printers use at least three additional cartridges at $5 to $10 each.

The prices of laser printers have dropped dramatically in the past few years, allowing more people to enjoy the high quality and print speed of these machines. The major factors that influence their price range are speed and quality. Lasers' speed, always expressed in pages per minute, ranges from 4 to 12 ppm. Print quality is expressed in the number of dots per inch (dpi) the printer puts on the paper. Most laser printers offer output of either 300 dpi or 600 dpi. A typical business letter will look very nice at a 300-dpi resolution, but the higher resolution of 600 dpi may be necessary for printing some graphics, including charts, graphs, and gray-scale pictures.

The other factors that affect the price of laser printers are the amount of on-board memory and font capability. Look for at least 2 MB of on-board memory to help you speed up your printing. Mark especially the time needed to produce the first page (often the only page needed when printing a letter). Laser toner cartridges will set you back $80 to $150 but will last for 5,000 to 10,000 or more pages.

Figure 2–9   Evaluation of Printers: Major Factors to Consider

Printer Type	Print Quality	Price	Speed	Guideline
Dot matrix, 24 pins	Poor	$150–$500	100–300 cps (1–3 ppm)	Fine for multipart forms such as checks and some invoices and internal reports; can get a good printer for $200
Ink jet	Good	$250–$600	4 ppm	Speed slow, color available at a higher price
Laser 300 dpi	Good	$600–$1,000	4–12 ppm	Quality acceptable for most uses
Laser 600 dpi	Best	$1,100–$2,000	4–12 ppm	Best for publishing, pictures, and so on

The market leaders in laser printers are Hewlett Packard for PCs and Apple's own LaserWriter for Macs. Because they are the leaders, they have set the standards for producing print output. If you buy a different brand, make sure it is PCL-compatible for PCs, or PostScript-compatible for Macs. Even better, buy a brand that can print both. The major factors to consider when buying a printer are summarized in Figure 2–9.

SELECTING GENERAL-PURPOSE SOFTWARE

No matter what type of business you are in, certain types of software will be necessary in your business. These "general purpose" applications may include word processors, spreadsheets, databases, presentation software, accounting programs, utilities, and personal information managers (PIMs) or contact managers.

The following discussion is meant to provide general information and guidelines for selecting software in each of the major categories.

All-in-One Programs

Many manufacturers of software have created all-in-one programs that include spreadsheet, word processor, database, and other functions. Examples in this category are Microsoft Works and WordPerfect Works for Windows, Macintosh platforms, and ClarisWorks for the Macintosh.

Each of these programs sells in the $150 range and may sometimes be bundled (included) with the purchase of your computer.

These programs work fairly well for simple home use—writing a quick letter or setting up a simple family budget. For most business use, however, they will eventually (probably sooner than later) frustrate you with their limitations. The old adage about getting what you pay for most definitely applies to this category of software.

Word Processing

There are three major competitors in the Windows world:

1. Word for Windows from Microsoft.
2. AmiPro from Lotus.
3. WordPerfect from WordPerfect (now a division of Novell).

All are in the price range of $250 to $300. For the Mac, Word for the Macintosh by Microsoft and WordPerfect are the major competitors; for DOS users, WordPerfect owns the market.

Each of these programs has tremendous capability to do very sophisticated formatting and other functions, to a point beyond what most people will ever be able to learn or use in their daily work. You can expect a major upgrade once every 12 to 18 months at a cost of about $100 each time. The programs take a tremendous amount of resources, requiring a minimum of 4 MB of RAM to operate, 8–12 MB to work well, and as much as 30 MB or more of disk space if the entire application, with all possible options, is loaded.

If your word processing needs are simpler, and you want something cheaper and less taxing on your system resources, you may consider MacWrite or LetterPerfect for the Mac (both in the $50–$75 range), or Computer Associates' CA-Textor for Windows or PFS:Write for DOS (both about $40). None of these applications has the horsepower of more prominently advertised competitors, but they may be all you need.

Spreadsheets

The spreadsheet software market is similar to that of word processing. Microsoft and Lotus, with their Excel and 1-2-3 products, respectively, are the major suppliers in the Windows environment. Borland, with Quattro Pro, is next in market share. Excel for the Mac (at approximately

$300) is as dominant in the Mac world as Lotus 1-2-3 ($325–$400, depending on the version) is for DOS users, although both do now have some competition. Excel has been joined by Lotus 1-2-3 for Macintosh at a similar price, and Borland's Quattro Pro $49 program has taken some of the DOS market.

There are other alternatives beyond the market leaders for Windows, although not in the DOS or Mac areas. For Windows, Quattro Pro is a full-featured program at a very low price ($49), while Lucid 3D is in the $75 range.

Database Management

The database software area is overcrowded with choices. A word of caution, before listing the major choices: Database software is becoming easier to use but it does not offer the ease of use found in a word processing program. The key factor in utilizing a database that will help your business, instead of being a confusing, time-consuming data mess, is a proper setup. Almost all applications are really a database of one type or another, although the underlying database may be "hidden" from view. Database software can range from a very simple list manager to a very complicated application development tool that only a programmer would be able to tackle.

A number of new products available on the Windows environment have taken a big step forward in ease of use. The top two are Lotus's Approach and Microsoft's Access. Of the two, Approach is easier to use and, at about $100, is less expensive. Access has improved ease of use and is more powerful than Approach in its features and capabilities, but costs about $325.

Other top-quality database programs for Windows (and their respective approximate prices) are: FileMaker Pro by Claris ($125), dBase V by Borland ($350), Paradox by Borland ($140), Microsoft FoxPro ($100), and Symantec Q&A ($170).

For the Mac, the major choices (and approximate prices) are File-Maker Pro by Claris ($270) or Microsoft FoxPro ($100).

In the DOS world, Borland Paradox ($500), Borland dBase IV ($500) and Microsoft FoxPro ($300) are some major choices.

Presentation Software

If you will need to make presentations to prospective customers, or design a presentation for marketing purposes, you will want to invest in a presentation software program. These programs assist you with the headlines, text, graphics, and charts that make for an attractive overhead transparency or slide presentation.

The top programs in this category are:

- Freelance from Lotus Development.
- Powerpoint from Microsoft.
- Harvard Graphics from Software Publishing.
- CorelDraw! from Corel in the Windows environment.
- Aldus Persuasion from Aldus Corp.
- Powerpoint from Microsoft for the Mac.
- Harvard Graphics for DOS.

Their cost ranges from $250 to $500.

Contact Managers and PIMs

This is one of the hottest areas in new software right now; a new program is being introduced almost every month. What exactly is this software category? Contact management programs are database applications that have been built specifically to assist salespersons in doing a good job of staying in touch with clients and prospects. Programs in this category—for example, ACT by Symantec, ECCO Pro from Arabesque, or Maximizer by Modatech (all around $200)—automate the making of phone calls, creator of follow-up notes, generation of follow-up letters, and all sorts of other tasks that should help good salespeople be even better.

Personal information managers (PIMs) offer a variation of the contact manager functions. PIMs have fewer sales features but added productivity features for any office worker: calendar keeping, to-do list management, and project tracking. Some of the leading names in this field are InfoCentral by WordPerfect, Lotus Organizer, PackRat by Polaris Software, Sharkware by Cognitech, and many others, all priced in the $100 range.

Utilities

One of the best investments in software that you can make is the purchase of a general utility program—software that will help you do a number of things to safeguard your system. At a minimum, the program will assist with backups, check for viruses, and, most importantly, fix problems that are sure to arise with your system. The first time you are able to recover a file you thought was deleted, or "repair" a problem that prevents you from accessing a program, you'll be very happy you have a utility around.

The two most popular utility programs for Windows and DOS are The Norton Desktop by Symantec and PC Tools by Central Point Software, both in the $100–$125 range. For the Mac, these same two companies offer MacTools (Central Point) and Norton Utilities (Symantec), in the same price range and perform similar functions. There are many other types of utility programs, many of which are built for one specific function such as backing up a disk, managing memory, allowing Mac files to be read by a PC, or connecting a laptop to a desktop for file transfers.

Accounting Programs

You will need some type of accounting program for your business. Even if your idea of a financial statement is the checkbook balance columns, using an accounting program will ultimately save you time and accountants' fees. This is especially true in the Windows and Macintosh environment with the development of easy-to-use, cheap (in the $40 range) accounting software for nonaccountants—titles like Quickbooks by Intuit and Profit by Microsoft. These programs and others like them use the graphical interface of Windows and the Mac for on-screen depictions of invoices, checks, and similar forms to allow easy data entry.

Make sure that the accounting system you select is capable of handling your company's requirements. If you have inventory or need specialized invoicing, order entry, or other requirements beyond the basic checkbook maintenance, the software you select must be able to do what you need. (See the section on selecting software, earlier in this chapter.)

Other Windows accounting programs include DacEasy by DacEasy Corporation, In the Black by Microrim, Peachtree for Windows by Peachtree, and MYOB by Bestware. All are in the $75–$125 price range.

For the Mac, Peachtree for the Mac by Peachtree or MYOB by Bestware (both about $120) or Quicken by Intuit ($40) are the major choices.

Because DOS is still the stronghold of accounting software, there are many programs from which to choose. Among the best known are:

- Acc Pac BPI by Computer Associates.
- DacEasy 5.0 by DacEasy.

- Peachtree Complete for DOS.
- Quickbooks for DOS.

These programs are also in the $40–$175 range for the most part, depending on whether they include a payroll module.

Suites

Each of the "Big Three" software publishers—Microsoft, Lotus, and WordPerfect (Novell)—has come up with a special way to buy an array of their software at a greatly reduced price. These "suites" of applications go by the names Microsoft Office, Lotus SmartSuite, and Borland Office (soon to be WordPerfect Office). The prices of the software suites for Windows, and the total prices if the individual components were purchased separately, are shown in Figure 2–10.

For the Mac, only Microsoft offers a suite, also called Microsoft Office, which sells for approximately $460 and includes the same software components as the Windows version: Word, Excel, PowerPoint, and a Mail license.

Consider purchasing a suite if you really believe you will use two or more of the included components; otherwise, they are a "great bargain" that gives you no real benefit, unless you like collecting software manuals. A complete installation of any of the suites will involve

Figure 2–10 Office "Suites": Prices and Software

	Microsoft Office Pro	Lotus SmartSuite	WordPerfect Office
Word processor	Word 6.0	AmiPro 3.0	WordPerfect 6.0a
Spreadsheet	Excel 5.0	1-2-3 5.0	Quattro Pro 5.0
Database	Access 2.0	Approach 3.0	Paradox 4.5
Mail	MS Mail	N/A	N/A
PIM	N/A	Organizer 1.1	N/A
Presentation	Powerpoint 4.0	Freelance 2.01	N/A
Total approximate cost	$560*	$450	$380
Cost of components	$1,370	$1,130	$480

* Microsoft Office Professional Edition can also be purchased in a regular edition, without Access, for approximately $480.

several (more than 20) diskettes, 50+ MB of disk space, and quite a bit of your time to install and then learn how to use the suite you select.

If you feel a suite purchase makes sense for you, your choice for purchase depends on the usefulness of the applications contained within the suite. You may want to review the discussion of each of the major software types above.

TELEPHONE/FAX/COPYING EQUIPMENT

Telephone

A telephone may seem initially to be one of your easier choices, but there are more alternatives and considerations than you may realize. Your first decision involves your business phone lines.

The traditional approach has been to order two business lines, one for a phone and one for a fax, but there are other ways to proceed. With *distinctive ringing* (or similar names), a new telephone service available from your local phone company, you may not even need a new line right away. For a nominal setup charge and a monthly addition of around $5 to your phone bill, you can have up to three phone numbers assigned to one phone line. Each number rings with a distinctive sound. You can even go a step further and purchase a $150 call interpreter that identifies each ring and, after one or two rings, routes the call to a phone, an answering machine, or a fax. The downside of this approach is that whenever any one of the three numbers is in use, the other two can't be used.

Another popular alternative for someone with two business phone lines is a fax/data switch that can be placed on the second line to distinguish between fax and voice calls. Thus, if your primary line is in use, a call to the second line could be routed to your answering machine, and any incoming faxes would automatically be routed to your fax machine.

For most businesses, a simple one- or two-line phone, available at any discount retail outlet, will do the trick. You can accommodate up to four lines in off-the-shelf telephones. For more lines, you need to look into the much more expensive alternatives. If you will be spending a lot of time on the phone, invest in a good telephone headset (price range $60–$100).

Your selection of a type of telephone and the number of lines should be governed by your individual communications needs and your budget. Most sales and marketing people advise not to cut corners in this area. The telephone impression you make on potential customers is critically important.

Answering Machines/Voice Mail

The traditional home office approach to message taking has been an answering machine or answering service. Today, the alternatives include voice mail services, voice mail add-in boards for computers, and digital answering machines. The major consideration is the necessity for reliable message taking that allows easy access and response to messages.

Almost all local telephone companies provide business voice mail services, as do private companies like Voice-Tel. For a low setup fee and a monthly charge of $7–$10, you have 24-hour access to voice messages whenever your phone is busy or there is no answer (you pick the number of rings). When you pick up your receiver, a special tone alerts you that a message has arrived. You dial a local area phone number, punch in your password, and can then listen to messages, record greetings, and so on. The advantages of this system are its low cost, reliability, unlimited capacity, and constant availability. The downside features are the hassle of phoning in for messages, limited message save time (usually 2 weeks), and relatively slow message retrieval time.

A digital answering machine is really nothing more than the traditional analog (tape)-based machine with these additional features: multiple outgoing messages, message following (to, say, your mobile phone or off-site location), message alert (to a beeper that would prompt you to call for messages), and time/date stamping. Prices range from $120 to $400, depending on the features selected.

A voice board for your computer essentially uses your computer disk drive for outgoing and incoming message storage, and your screen and keyboard for selection and manipulation of messages. Many voice boards have automatic fax send/receive capabilities as well. Prices range from $100 to $500 or more. These boards can provide all the features of a digital answering machine, plus fax services, and can be run in "background" on your computer. The downside factors include often tricky installation, poor reliability, and the usage of high amounts of disk space. These problems should be ironed out in a year or so, if you want to wait to give them serious consideration.

Fax

Your fax choices are a stand-alone machine using plain paper or fax paper vs. a fax/modem board in your computer, utilizing your printer. The stand-alone fax will send any 8½" × 11" paper and receive and print faxes on either fax paper (price range $300 or so) or plain paper (price range $600–$800). Other factors that may affect pricing include number of memory phone numbers, transmission speed, speed dialing, page memory, and document feeding.

If most of your outgoing fax transmissions originate from computer-generated output from your word processor or other program, you may wish to consider using a fax/modem board on your computer instead of a separate machine. For about $100–$150, you will be able to receive any fax and send faxes directly from your computer as if you were printing them. Fax software, generally included in the price of the board, will allow you to include a cover page, log all outgoing and incoming faxes, and view them on the screen before deciding whether to print them. You will not, however, be able to send a fax of anything that has not been generated by your computer. You would have to first scan it with a scanner, which is time-consuming, cumbersome, and more expensive.

Copiers

The need for a copier is no longer definite, depending on the type of business you are in. For some businesses, judicious use of multiple copies from a laser printer and bulk printing at a nearby copy center will be sufficient. If you choose to purchase, the good news is that copier prices are way down from what they were a few years ago. Prices for home or small office copiers range from a low of $300 to $5,000 or more. The difference has mostly to do with the copy capacity, speed, and features.

Copy capacity is defined as how many copies the machine is rated to be able to handle. If the machine is rated for 300 copies per month and you try to use it monthly for 1,000, the machine will not last very long. Copy speed ranges from 6 per minute on the low end to 18 or 20 per minute on the high end. Features have mostly to do with ability to produce reductions and enlargements, paper tray capacity, and the size of original that can be copied.

The machines on the low end, from companies like Canon, Sharp, and Xerox, will run 6 to 10 copies per minute at an initial cost of $600 to $1,000. Beware of toner and drum replacement for these machines: these consumables will cost $100 to $150 every 1,500 to 3,000 copies. On the higher end, the same companies have machines that will provide 12 to 18 copies per minute and 5,000 to 10,000 copies per toner cartridge.

Estimate your monthly copy volume and purchase a machine that will handle it. Project the cost of drum and toner replacements to come up with your estimated cost per copy.

Office Equipment Summary

As technology changes and constantly advances, the choices available for telephone, fax, answering services, and copiers are growing and changing. Some of the functions traditionally associated with those machine names are changing or being combined into a single machine or into computers.

Be careful when evaluating machines that combine functions. They are generally fairly high priced but deliver lesser functionality for any one feature than a stand-alone machine would. Once you buy one of these all-purpose machines, you may feel stuck with it because of the cost.

Buy, Install, Start to Work!

When you have these basics to get your business operations going, stop buying for a while and get used to your new system and software. There may be a great temptation to purchase some of those great software programs or extra peripherals that are guaranteed to save you money. Resist the sales pitches for a few months. Invariably, once you are operational for a while, you will discover new needs you didn't know you had when you started. Save some money in your budget by adding only a key piece of software or hardware upgrade that will make a difference.

Take some time to skim through your user manuals. Very few people read them from cover to cover, but a quick review will save you a great deal of time and frustration in the early going. Take the time to send in the registration cards. They may produce a certain amount of junk mail, but they really do guarantee that you will get notification of upgrades and, occasionally, free upgrades or maintenance releases.

PLAN FOR TRAINING TIME

Software Support Issues

Software support is now a much more important consideration than it was a few years ago. As competition has driven down prices, the software developers have adjusted by increasing the cost of their support programs dramatically. What is at issue for you as a buyer is not only the cost of these services, but their availability and quality. As vendor support pricing has started to become very similar, the quality and availability issues become even more important.

Here's the deal you will probably get on service from most software purchased off-the-shelf or by mail order. The first 60 to 90 days from the date of your first support call will be free. If you install the software right away but then don't use it until you get around to having time to learn it, beware of the support call you make to get help with the installation. After the free support period, your options are only how much and how often you will pay. Most vendors have a $2 per minute 900 number you can call, with a minimum charge of $25 or so per call (some have maximums per call as well). Service plans are also becoming more popular: for a mere $100–$200 in advance, you purchase a software support "contract" that will give you (usually) unlimited support access for a year. For a higher amount of money, you can usually get access to an 800 number for support as well, so whatever time you spend on hold will not be added to your phone bill.

If you are the kind of person who relies heavily on telephone support, by all means sign up for one of the support plans. Otherwise, proceed with caution. For the most part, software customer support works well for routine questions, most of which can be found in the written documentation. If you have a more complicated question, the chances of getting an answer you'll be satisfied with become lower, depending on which service technician happens to get your phone call.

Under quality of support, we include all aspects of the vendor: the software support program, including the readability and comprehensiveness of both hard copy and on-line documentation; context-sensitive help and "tips"; and the likelihood of getting a correct answer when you call the support hotline. One of the best services provided by magazine reviewers is coverage of the quality of technical support in all of these areas. It is worthwhile to read the recent reviews just for this information. Be sure to take into consideration the type of support that works best for you. If a software vendor writes high-quality manuals and you are a learn-as-you-go kind of person, that great documentation isn't going to do you any good.

Availability covers the hours of operation of the support center, how long it takes to get through to a technician, the comprehensiveness of any fax-back support programs that are available, how many (if any) on-line services the vendor belongs to, whether an electronic bulletin board service is available for downloading program corrections and getting technical questions answered, and the comprehensiveness of the affiliated certified consulting program, if any.

It is worth your while to call the technical support center before you buy, and ask what you think is a simple question. Test out how long it takes to get through, how polite the technician is, and how good the answers seem to be. If you are able to get access to CompuServe or any of the competing services, see whether the vendor has a forum on that service. It also makes sense to spend more time with the manual and any other training materials that come with the software. Software companies continue be amazed at how many of the questions that they answer by phone could have been easily found in the book.

Training

Everyone's learning style is not the same; thus, there are many different types of training available, especially for the first stages of learning how to use software. Classroom training in some of the very popular applications will probably be available at a local community college. Many companies specialize in software application training that you can attend on-site, with computer usage included, for around $200 per day. Don't be afraid to ask for references. Video and audio tapes are also available; many are listed in most computer publications. You may benefit from a tutorial that comes with your software. For other trainees, just sitting down and testing out the program works. Whatever method you choose, don't forgo this activity because you don't have time. You will save much more time over the life of the program by knowing how to use it properly.

EVALUATING SPECIAL COMPUTER HARDWARE FOR YOUR SPECIFIC NEEDS

Beyond the basic computer hardware, software, and office machinery setup, your business may have additional requirements that are not met. For add-on hardware components and software programs, you will need to do more research to make sure your purchases will last a long time. You can add several accessories to your computer, limited only by the number of expansion slots available and your pocketbook. Following is a brief description of some of the hardware "extras" you can buy.

CD-ROMs

A CD-ROM is a device that reads data from, but cannot write data to, a compact disk. The compact disk is the same as the one you use to play music, only it holds a tremendous mount of nonmusical data: entire encyclopedia volumes, dictionaries, or graphical icons called clip-art, for example. The main usage of CD-ROM players in computers today is home entertainment. You can hook a pair of good speakers to your computer CD-ROM and play thousands of games that are available for $10–$50 or more. For business, the best and most likely usage would be either research or a multimedia presentation development. Within a couple of years, CD-ROMs will probably have greater utility in the business world for software distribution, graphic image storage, and reference material.

The price of CD-ROMs is affected most by their data transfer rate, measured in kilobytes per second (kps) throughput and access, or their seek times, measured in milliseconds (ms). The faster the CD-ROM spins, the better the throughput and the shorter the seek time. You'll see CD-ROM machines advertised by 2X or 3X and, more recently, 4X, all of which refer to how much faster they are spinning when transferring data. Expect to pay around $200 for a 2X machine, $300–$450 for a 3X and over $500 for a 4X.

Scanners

Why would you want a scanner? A scanner is generally used for importing pictures into a text or presentation file and, occasionally, for mass conversion of text that cannot be input any other way. In the latter case, an optical character recognition (OCR) program must be used to convert the scanned image to actual letters and other characters that can be edited. Often, OCR programs are included in the price of the scanner—read the labels or check with the sales representative if you are unsure. At the low end of the scale, a handheld gray-scale (black-and-white) scanner can be had for around $200. A scanner with a flat surface to rest the document on (flat bed scanner) is easier to use but will run you $600 for gray-scale or $1,200 and up for color scanning.

UPS (Uninterruptible Power Supply)

A UPS performs two essential functions. The first, protection from electrical line spikes and surges, can also be attained with any variety of surge protectors available in the $10–$40 range. However, the second function, keeping your computer equipment operating on battery power for 5 to 20 minutes when power is lost, is not otherwise attainable. For many people, having a UPS means having the opportunity to gracefully complete their work and shut down the computer vs. experiencing a sudden stop that almost always means the loss of whatever they were working on and had not yet saved. This type of insurance policy is worth its one-time cost of between $115 and $200.

Input Devices

For most people, a keyboard and, for the Mac and for Windows, a mouse, are all the input devices they will ever need or even think about. Alternatives are available that may save you time and/or improve your productivity. For example, keyboards with built-in trackballs or more function keys are available for $100–$200, and ergonomic versions of keyboards are available in the $300–$500 range.

The alternatives for pointing devices are expanding constantly. From the basic mouse (in several sizes and shapes) to the latest touch-sensitive, use-your-finger devices, the choice is yours. A personal favorite is the Logitech Cordless mouse. For about $100, you get rid of that darned cord and get a comfortable three-button mouse that is very responsive and can be set to provide a double click with one button, or a larger pointer on the screen.

Modem

A modem is a device that allows computer information, including fax images, to be transferred over telephone lines to any location where another modem exists. Most modems sold today now include fax transmission and reception capability and are sold as fax/modems. Modems are becoming such an essential computing component that many manufacturers often now include one with their machine.

If yours doesn't, plan to spend $100 to $150 for a fax/modem of reasonable speed that will usually include software for faxing as well. What is reasonable speed? A modem that could transmit data at 2,400 baud (bits per second) used to be great, but now 9,600 baud is the minimum, 14,400 is the norm, and 28,800 baud is widely available. For most uses, 9,600 or 14,400 will work fine. Manufacturers of fax/modems include Hayes, Intel, and many others.

Backup Devices

Don't forget that you will need to regularly back up your data to be prepared for a disaster like a hard disk failure, a theft, or a natural disaster that could destroy all your data. Tape backups are becoming cheap enough to be rated as the predominant method of backup for most small systems. A tape drive that fits right into your computer case (internal drive) and can back up 120 MB of disk space can be obtained for as low as $120. As you add capacity, the price goes up. A 250 MB tape drive will cost $220, or can go up to $350 if you want an external model that you can plug in like a printer vs. installing it inside the computer. Devices that will back up 1 GB at a time start around $1,000.

An alternative for tape backups is to use floppy disks in conjunction with some type of backup utility. Backup utilities like MS Backup (included with Microsoft DOS versions 6.0 and above) and Norton Utilities from Symantic will compress your backup disks so that you may be able to squeeze almost 3 MB on each floppy. Depending on the amount of data you have to back up, this may be feasible for a while. You can choose to back up only your data, thus limiting the number of required diskettes and associated backup time. By not backing up your programs, you risk the time and hassle required to reload all your programs on a new hard disk in the event of a failure.

The key factors in buying peripherals, and their approximate costs, are summarized in Figure 2–11.

OFFICE EQUIPMENT EXTRAS

Some of the extra toys you can buy include a electronic personal organizer, or, more recently, a personal digital assistant (PDA), typewriter, overhead projector, and cellular phone. Of all of these, a basic electric typewriter at about $90 is your best bet. There are still situations in which typing out a label or an envelope is a quicker and cheaper alternative than trying to do the same task with the computer. A typewriter also serves as a last-resort disaster backup.

Figure 2–11   Key Factors in Buying Peripherals

Peripheral	Cost	Key Factors	Recommendation
CD-ROM	$200–$500	Speed, internal vs. external	2X speed adequate; not yet a necessity
Scanner	$200–$600	Flatbed vs. handheld Color vs. gray-scale	Save up for flat bed (ease of use) Do you really need color?
UPS	$100–$300	No. of lines covered	Buy ASAP
Mouse	$30–$150	Personal—ease of use	$100 cordless mouse is convenient
Modem	$100–$300	Speed	Buy combination fax/modem at least 14,400 bps
Tape drive	$200–$350	Capacity, internal vs. external	Buy ASAP; external can be moved to different machines easier

Electronic personal organizers like the Casio Boss and Sharp Wizard can be purchased starting at $150 and going up to $500.

The decision on a cellular phone boils down to how much time you spend in your car. If you drive a lot and need to be reached, anticipate a $100 to $250 up-front investment and at least $40 a month in airtime bills—much more, if you use the phone a lot. Remember that you pay airtime charges for both inbound and outbound calls.

SOFTWARE EXTRAS

Thousands of software programs are available for purchase. You can spend as much money on software extras like screen savers and replacement desktops as you have in your bank account. Try to always ask yourself: Do I really need it? Remember that any program you buy will cost much more than its original price when you start tallying the annual upgrades, support fees, training costs and training time, and disk space utilized. Stay away from the screen saver and cursor enhancing utilities. They are programs that are constantly in use, eating up memory that could almost always be better utilized for your business applications. They sometimes cause memory conflicts or other problems with other software as well.

INDIVIDUAL SOFTWARE BUSINESS NEEDS

This section covers the hardware and software requirements of each of the 24 businesses listed in Chapter 1 (see Figure 1 3). If software generally available in major retail and mail-order channels is needed, the software *category* has been listed, without reference to a particular brand name. If specialized software is required, a few titles have been suggested. Phone numbers for the publishers of specialized software are listed in the Appendix. You most likely will need to supplement the information given here with a search of your own, using industry resources, on-line searches, and the like.

The software listed for each business is meant to be only representative of programs that are available for purchase. For your specialized needs, you may wish to sign up for an on-line service that will provide you with software search capability as well as a possible user forum. On CompuServe, for example, you can get access to Ziffnet's (from Ziff-Davis, the publisher of *PC Magazine, PC World,* and others) Computer Library, which will give you key word search capability for thousands of software titles, along with brief descriptions, magazine review, and company profiles.

One additional note about specialized software: *Buyer, beware.* There are literally thousands of software development companies out there, and they come and go out of business daily. It is very difficult to tell how large and how stable a particular company may be from outward appearances. An 800 number is easy to get, and advertisement size or brochure size is no certain indicator of company viability. Your best bet is to try to get references from the vendor and/or do some library or on-line research.

1. Architect/Computer-Aided Design

You will need to buy computer-aided design (CAD) software, such as DesignCAD 2D from American Small Business Computers ($200) or DrafixCAD Professional for Windows, from Foresight Resources Corporation ($250).

2. Bulletin Board Service

For this business you will also need one or more high-speed modems to allow your customers easy access to your bulletin board. A large disk drive, perhaps 1 GB or more, will also most likely be necessary to provide adequate room for bulletin board listings from your customers.

3. Business Consulting

In general, a consultant will require a fairly sophisticated desktop computer and a laptop computer, as well as presentation software, word processing software, and a spreadsheet. Consultants may also require more industry-specific software, depending on their fields of expertise.

4. Business Plan Writing

A standard 486-based PC or portable should be adequate for this business, along with the spreadsheet and word processing programs of your choice (see the section on selecting general-purpose software). Hundreds of specialized business planning software programs are available, including PlanWrite from Business Resource Software, Starting Your Business from DMACS Software, and Success One from Dynamic Pathways Company—all for Windows.

5. Computer Consulting/Training

No matter which alternative you choose, you won't need a superpowered computer to do your work. You'll want a portable computer with an active matrix color screen that can be viewed from most angles. Beyond that, plenty of disk space to load software programs and tutorials will be helpful. As your business grows, you'll want to network multiple computers for training classes. Any 486 PC or Macintosh with 8 MB of RAM and a 300 MB or larger disk drive should be sufficient.

You'll also want a modem and software to remotely connect programs like pcAnywhere from Symantec or Carbon Copy from Microcom to your client's systems.

6. Computer Repair/Maintenance and Programming

There are many different approaches to this business as the development of software continues to evolve. Many programmers still use the standard programming languages—COBOL, C, Basic, and others—but fourth-generation development languages are simplifying some of the tasks. Your best bet may be to learn to program using the extensive development tools of a database like Microsoft's Access or FoxPro, Borland's dBase or Paradox, or Alpha Corporation's Alpha 4. Another emerging alternative is Microsoft's Visual Basic.

No matter which alternative you choose, you won't need a superpowered computer to do your work. Any 486 PC or Macintosh with 8 MB of RAM and a 300 MB or larger disk drive should do the trick. You'll want to have a good backup system and probably a UPS unit to make sure you don't ever lose any of your hard work.

7. Data Detective

You will need to purchase data security software, which will allow your clients to protect computer files by using passwords and encryption. Here are three data security packages: RSA Secure ($99) from RSA Data Security Inc., FolderBolt-Pro ($129) from Kent-Marsh Ltd., and ultraSHIELD ($149) from usrEZ.

8. Database Management/Mail List Service

Your most important piece of equipment will be list management software, such as ArcList from Group 1 Software Inc., Now Contact from

Now Software, and OmniMailer from Janac Enterprises. Expect this kind of software to range from about $500 to about $750. You might also make use of some of the database management software discussed in this chapter.

9. Electronic Clipping Service

For this business, you will need a high-speed modem for access to on-line services like CompuServe, and communications software like ProComm Plus from Datastorm, Smartcom from Hayes, or Delrina WinComm Pro to assist in the communication process to the services and to your clients.

10. Freelance Writing

As a writer, you'll need a word processing program that you are very comfortable with and a high-speed modem to send off your work when completed. A laser printer may be needed at times as well.

Your choices for computer equipment should include a middle-of-the-road 486 PC or Mac with 8 MB of RAM, and a monitor size you are comfortable with (at least 15").

11. Graphic Design

In this business, a Pentium or PowerPC-based computer system with at least 8 MB (preferably 16 MB) of RAM is a good investment, but it's only the start. You will also want a larger (17") monitor with graphics accelerator, a color scanner, a high-resolution (600 dpi) laser printer, and, possibly, a color ink-jet printer. A modem makes sense as well, for receiving information from 'customers. Many graphic designers use a Mac with programs like Aldus Freehand 4.0, Adobe Photoshop, or Quark Express by Quark. On the PC side, Corel Draw by Corel, or FrameMaker or QuarkXpress for Windows will be your most likely alternatives. All of these programs will take a great deal of disk space and memory and will set you back $500–$650.

12. Home Inventory Cataloging/Organizing

The key ingredient is a database program to allow categorization and tracking of inventory items. Among programs available on the market are Home Insurance Inventory from DynaComp, Inc. and Inventory Pro form Hi-Tech Advisers, both for DOS, and Value Vision for Windows from Fusion.

No special computer equipment is necessary unless you find a way to use bar coding equipment to produce bar codes for the inventory and track the items that way.

13. Information Broker/Research Service

For this business, you will need a high-speed modem for access to on-line services like CompuServe, and communications software like ProComm Plus from Datastorm, Smartcom from Hayes, or Delrina WinComm Pro to assist in the communication process. A higher-speed (2X minimum) CD-ROM drive to use for additional reference research would be a good investment as well.

14. Inventory Control Services

To run this business efficiently, you will need a PC computer system with a large disk drive and tape backup. A Macintosh would generally not be a good investment just because there are so few accounting software systems available for the Mac. The large disk drive is for holding all the client data, and the tape drive will allow you to back up the data on a daily basis. There are numerous good accounting systems that handle multiple clients' data, although most of them are available only for the DOS operating system. Some of the better known low-cost systems include DacEasy by DacEasy Corporation, Accounting Works by One Write Plus, and Peachtree Complete 7.0 by Peachtree Corp.

15. Mail Order

For mail order, you'll need software for inventory tracking, billing, order entry, and catalog printing. In addition, you'll want to pay extra attention to your phone system to make sure you have enough lines always open and available for orders being called in.

The standard accounting systems will be able to handle most of the inventory and billing requirements. You may choose to look at some of the specialized software for this business, including Mail-Order and Business Control for the Mac from Engineering Consulting, Mail Order Management from Dydacomp, and Catalog Creator from ProHelp Software,—all for DOS.

16. Multimedia

Your most important investment in this business is a CD-ROM—at least a double-speed if not a triple-speed variety—plus a good sound card and speakers. Your choice of PC or Mac doesn't matter too much, but you'll probably want to purchase a large, high-clarity monitor to show off your multimedia work.

On the software end, you'll need a current Windows or Mac-based presentation software package along the lines of Harvard Graphics 2.0, Micrografx Charisma 4.0, Aldus Persuasion 3.0, Microsoft PowerPoint 4.0, or Lotus Freelance 2.0, all in the $400–$500 range.

17. Newsletter Publishing

To design and publish a newsletter, you'll need desktop publishing software and a high-quality (600 dpi) laser printer. Desktop publishing software is fairly widely available in Mac or Windows versions in the $300–$600 range. Supplier products include: for Windows, Aldus Pagemaker, Frame Technology's Framemaker, and Microsoft Publisher; for the Mac, Aldus Pagemaker or Quark Xpress.

You'll need a higher-powered computer, either a fast (66 MHz or higher) 486 PC or a 68040 Mac, 8 MB or 16 MB of RAM, a larger monitor (17"–20"), and a 600 dpi laser printer.

18. Personalized Children's Books

To design and publish personalized children's books, you'll need desktop publishing software and a high-quality (600 dpi) laser printer. Desktop publishing software is widely available in Mac or Windows versions in the $300–$600 range. Supplier products include: for Windows, Aldus Pagemaker, FrameMaker, and Microsoft Publisher; for the Mac, Aldus Pagemaker or Quark Xpress.

You'll need a higher-powered computer, either a fast (66 MHz or hither) 486 PC or 68040 Mac, 8 MB or 16 MB of RAM, a larger monitor (17"–20"), and a 600 dpi laser printer.

19. Referral Service

For this business, invest in a high-speed modem for access to on-line services like CompuServe, and communications software like ProComm Plus from Datastorm, Smartcom from Hayes, or Delrina

WinComm Pro to assist in the communication process to the services and to your clients. A higher-speed (2X minimum) CD-ROM drive will be helpful for additional reference research.

20. Sales/Marketing Service

A good word processing program and, most likely, a high-quality (600 dpi) word processor are your only necessities in hardware and software for this business. Your life will be easier if you buy a comfortable keyboard and mouse (if using a Mac or Windows), a larger (17" or more) screen for full page editing, and, possibly, a fax/modem for sending/receiving copy. A second word processing program, a program for converting formatting from other types of word processors, and a MAC to DOS/Windows conversion program would be useful extras.

21. Sign Making

Begin with a 486 or Quadra computer. You will also need a scanner, so that you can take images supplied by your clients (such as logos or other graphics) and place them on the signs you make. You will also need a signcutter or plotter, which will print a sign onto vinyl and cut the vinyl to the appropriate size and shape. Two of the leading signcutter manufacturers are Ioline Corporation and Roland Digital Group. Ioline's signcutters start at about $5,000. You will also need illustration or draw software, such as Canvas from Deneba Software ($400) or CorelDraw from Corel Systems ($595), as well as paint or image editing software, such as Adobe Systems' Photoshop ($895) or Electronic Arts' DeluxePaint IV ($170).

22. Software Design/Custom Software

In this business, you need the ability to mass duplicate disks and manuals for assembly and shipment to your distribution channel. The most important software will be a system to help you produce invoices and keep track of shipping and inventory. You will need to do a thorough search for the right software, which may include the need for bar code tracking. DacEasy 5.0 from DacEasy Corporation is a lower-cost accounting system that can handle order entry, bar code, and inventory tracking.

There are no extraordinary software requirements for this business, so a standard 486 PC or 68040 Mac will be adequate. You most likely will need a dot matrix printer to allow you to easily produce multiple copy shipping documents and invoices.

23. Utility Bill Auditing

A portable computer may be handy in this business if you want to do your work on-site. A standard 486-based PC or portable should be adequate, along with a spreadsheet program of your choice (see the earlier section on selecting general-purpose software). At least one specialized audit program, appropriately named Electric Utility Rate Analysis, from General Energy Technologies, is available for DOS.

Some of the specialized software available in this area include RL54 from MC2 Engineering Software, Heat Loss from Dynacomp, Audit from Elite Software Development and Energy Conservation, and Analysis Software from General Energy Technology—all for DOS.

24. Word Processing

The only necessities in hardware and software for this business are: a good word processing program and, most likely, a high-quality (600 dpi) printer. Other equipment will make your life easier: a comfortable keyboard and mouse (if using a Mac or Windows), a larger (17″ or more) screen for full-page editing, and possibly a fax/modem for sending/receiving copy. Extra software could include a second word processing program, a program for converting formatting from other types of word processors, and a MAC to DOS/Windows conversion program.

3

24 COMPUTER-BASED BUSINESSES

Think of this chapter as one crammed full of ideas that you can adapt, hone, or expand on to suit your business needs. We include an overview of several businesses, aspects of prospecting for customers not covered earlier, and unusual pricing considerations. Refer to Chapter 2 for more specific information about hardware and software for the business you select. Thousands of specialty software packages are on the market, several of which will be mentioned in reference to the particular industry to which they apply. To obtain the software that is most appropriate to your individual business and hardware, consult a reputable software dealer who can recommend the package best suited for your purposes, or, if necessary, advise you on how an existing package might be customized to meet your needs (although this can be very expensive).

The following businesses are highlighted in this chapter.

1. Architect/Computer-aided design.
2. Bulletin board service.
3. Business consulting.
4. Business plan writing.

5. Computer consulting training.
6. Computer repair/maintenance and programming.
7. Data detective.
8. Database management/mail list service.
9. Electronic clipping service.
10. Freelance writing.
11. Graphic design.
12. Home inventory cataloging/organizing.
13. Information broker/research service.
14. Inventory control service.
15. Mail order.
16. Multimedia.
17. Newsletter publishing.
18. Personalized children's books.
19. Referral service.
20. Sales/Marketing service.
21. Sign making.
22. Software design/custom software.
23. Utility bill auditing.
24. Word processing.

You'll find that some features of these businesses overlap and converge. However, as mentioned in Chapter 1, it is important to select only one and specialize—at least during start-up and the first several months of operation—before branching out into add-on services. With this strategy, you'll keep your start-up and operating costs to a minimum.

The information provided here can be adapted to fit your business. Remember: It's possible that the most important computer-related business of the 20th century has not yet been conceived. That's where your ideas may come in. Our purpose is to point you in the right direction.

1. ARCHITECT/COMPUTER-AIDED DESIGN

To be successful in this type of enterprise, one of the more specialized skills/businesses highlighted in this book, architects and computer-aided designers (CADs) must have both architectural education or training and advanced computer skills. There is plenty of software on the market to help even novices design their own homes, but running a home-design business this way is difficult. For one thing, the business relies almost 100% on referrals and networking. "There's a canon of ethics in the architectural field against direct marketing," said one entrepreneur. "Personal referrals work best."

If you have the necessary architectural and/or engineering background, however, the business is lucrative. Today's computer systems astound clients, showing them exactly what they can expect from your design skills, and allowing you to work with them to create the perfect, custom home that they desire.

Start-up costs will range from $7,000 to $10,000 on average, depending on what equipment and supplies you already have (i.e., drafting table, computer, and so on). Most architects/CADs charge by the project, so your estimates of job time are important.

Other necessary expenses, besides a computer, will be letterhead stationery, business cards, a business telephone, office furniture (including visitor chairs and, preferably, a small meeting or conference table), and a letter-quality printer. Optional items include a fax machine and high-quality laser printer, as well as various CAD software programs. The software is listed as optional because there are home-based architects who have not yet chosen to invest in the programs and still make more than $50,000 annually.

A professional-looking home office is essential for making the right impression. Your market will likely include upper-bracket, two-income families who are buying or renovating a home, and landlords who own small commercial buildings in select neighborhoods. Monthly operating costs will run from $800 to $2,000 and up, depending on whether you hire personnel to help you. These costs include drafting paper and supplies, blueprint production, phone/utilities, marketing, and travel/transportation costs.

Daily operations will involve meeting with clients/visiting sites; hands-on drafting and design; scheduling new projects; and marketing. Bookkeeping can probably be kept to twice a month.

2. BULLETIN BOARD SERVICE

As Kevin Behrens, owner of Aquilla BBS, Inc., based in Aurora, Illinois, puts it: "You don't have to be a tech weenie to run a BBS, but it doesn't hurt." To get your service going, "you need to configure modems, read manuals, follow step-by-step instructions, and be well-shopped in terms of software." Actually, the volume of software available to help you get started makes the job easier.

Start-up costs will range from a minimum of $5,000 to $10,000–$15,000 on average, depending on how many subscribers you estimate having, based on market research for your BBS offering. The reason: the number of phone lines needed to accommodate "callers" to your BBS (at a minimum, five phone lines are recommended for a new BBS, though you can get by initially with one dedicated computer and one phone line).

You will need a separate computer to handle your own business tasks, because you will not want to risk tying up your BBS computer. Other necessary expenses include software, resource materials, basic business supplies, furniture, a high-quality printer to print messages from subscribers, and a separate business line to offer customer service (an 800 number is recommended). Optional items include a fax machine (which you can forgo if you purchase automatic fax capabilities software for your computer).

Monthly operating costs will run from $1,000 to $5,000, to cover phone/utilities, advertising, on-line subscription and research costs, and similar outlays. (Aquilla BBS spends approximately $1,000 per month on phone bills alone, for their 42 phone lines.) Phone lines used for your BBS should not have call forwarding, call waiting, or other features that might interrupt the line.

Daily operations will involve: BBS maintenance and updating; answering e-mail and service calls; adding new subscribers; bookkeeping and marketing; and regular and ongoing market research.

3. BUSINESS CONSULTING

If you've got a strong background in business and some expertise for getting specific company projects underway, business consulting can be a financially and personally rewarding venture. Business consultants are hired to complete myriad tasks, from reorganizing and refocusing a company to creating a new marketing approach for 1996, or helping to train management and/or other employees. As mentioned in Chapter 1, the tasks completed by business consultants generally could be done by existing company personnel. The problem is that staff cutbacks or shifting business priorities leave a gap between projects that company executives want completed, and the number of people who can dedicate time to completing them.

By hiring a consultant, businesses can see a worthwhile project completed by a knowledgeable person who can dedicate *all* of his or her time to a project until completion. It is important to be aware, however, that consultants can make existing employees—who would normally be given jurisdiction over the project—nervous or angry. Projects for which consultants are hired are generally more interesting than day-to-day company operations, so there can be resentment. Additionally, though an employee who performs other vital company functions truly may not have the time to complete the project given to a consultant, the employee may fear he or she is being supplanted.

Thus, this is a business for people with strong communication and human relations skills, and experience in corporate settings. You will need strong referrals, especially when you first begin, from people who will attest to your expertise and business savvy.

Start-up costs for consulting range from $8,000 to $20,000 on average—slightly higher than for some other home-based business options. Start-up costs for consultants include not only a high-end computer setup and extensive software packages (for presentations, marketing, hand-outs, and so on), but also a reliable laptop computer, fax machine, modem, and—most importantly—operating capital. Clients can be asked for deposits up front, but you will likely not push this with your first client. If you opt to be paid an hourly fee for the length of the project, with payment due at weekly or biweekly intervals, you will still have a gap between your start date and receipt of the first check, because of normal corporate payment schedules. It's important not to seem desperate for the cash; companies want to know they have hired a steady professional. Your appearance, dress, briefcase—everything—must be first-rate.

Other necessary expenses will be letterhead stationery, business cards, a business telephone, and basic office furniture. More than likely, your clients will never need to come to your home.

Look to companies that are downsizing or are ready to launch a new product or program. Stick to a single field (insurance, banking, health care, securities) or a single specialty (human resources, MIS, marketing) to get the best referrals and results. Remember, your key selling points will be (1) your expertise and (2) the results you produce.

Monthly operating costs will run from $1,000 to $2,000 and up, depending on whether you hire personnel to help you. Your costs will include supplies, phone/utilities, marketing, and travel/transportation.

Daily operations will involve: meeting with clients or other key company personnel for the project you are handling; direct project work; maintaining your work log (for yourself, your billing records, and your client reports); and returning calls. Set aside time each week to dedicate to your own business marketing, networking, bookkeeping, and management. (More time than this may be difficult to give to your own business, because you are on-site with clients for long periods—often full workdays. However, make time, or you will find yourself with gaps in between projects.)

4. BUSINESS PLAN WRITING

This business is geared toward business-savvy individuals who find financial projections, profit-and-loss statements, and marketing plans a pleasant challenge. A strong economic and/or business management background is important. Your clients will not look to you for basic word processing, but will need you to help them analyze their business from every angle, target their market, and make crucial decisions regarding operations and services.

As mentioned, your clients will include both hopeful entrepreneurs and business owners looking to expand. The majority will come to you because they need a professional and well-founded business plan that will get financing for them. Others will look to your expertise to guide them through critical start-up or expansion.

Start-up costs for this business will range from $7,000 to $10,000 on average, including computer, fax, modem, laser printer, and basic business supplies: letterhead stationery, business cards, telephone, and furniture. You may also want to invest in a notebook computer, transcription equipment, and a dedicated phone line just for faxing and modem connections.

Your options include visiting your clients, having them come to you, or working through phone/fax/modem/mail to get a satisfactory finished product. Once your reputation is established, you may hardly have to leave your home to get business and gather information. (This means, also, that you can serve clients across the country.) Business-specific information will come from your clients. Other necessary information is easily obtained from a variety of sources: the Small Business Administration, a local business library, the business section of a major metropolitan library, and market surveys. Using these resources to study specific industries and types of businesses within those industries will provide a wealth of valuable information. Much of the legal and recordkeeping information supplied in this book is applicable to many businesses; for example, all businesses must have a legal form of operation, must apply for a taxpayer identification number, and must establish a method of maintaining important records. Your job is to tailor this information to fit the client's specific needs, and to compile it in an easily understandable format.

Monthly operating costs will run from $1,000 to $2,000, including supplies, phone/utilities, marketing, and travel/transportation.

Daily operations will involve talking with new clients about their business; research and other direct project work; scheduling; and networking. New clients will come largely from referrals and networking, but advertising is still a good idea. Especially in metropolitan areas, the number of fledgling entrepreneurs is likely to be large enough to justify Yellow Pages and local newspaper (classified) advertising.

Direct mail marketing to local businesses can also pay off if a town has recently experienced economic or population growth that would make business expansion lucrative.

5. COMPUTER CONSULTING/TRAINING

As mentioned in Chapter 1, computer consulting and training covers a broad spectrum of opportunities, from having individuals learn basic computer programs in your home to helping select the right hardware/software/accessory packages for growing businesses.

Though this should be self-evident, you need to be very knowledgeable about computers to provide any of these services. As the teacher and expert, there should not be any—or at least not many—questions you can't answer. When you are stumped, you should know where to go for the information.

Many entrepreneurs in this business have computer science, information management, or other computer-specific backgrounds. A few are self-taught computer enthusiasts who stay current on emerging technologies. Some are community college or university instructors who operate their own businesses part-time.

Start-up costs when training from home or working with companies that provide facilities and equipment for group training will range from $7,000 to $10,000 on average; if you offer computer consulting services, expect to spend a minimum of $20,000 to $23,000 at start-up, because of the great amount of hardware, software, and accessories you will need to stay on top of. Expect to pay a minimum of $3,500 to $4,000 for a business computing system alone; $6,000 may be a safer figure if you plan to expand your programming significantly. Some consulting shops have invested tens of thousands of dollars in equipment for their offices, with a great deal of the money going into software, accessories, and hardware. Your only other expenses besides a computer set up will be letterhead stationery, business cards, a business telephone, and simple but functional office furniture. If you train in your home, your office decor should reflect professionalism and put your students at ease. Be sure the furniture is comfortable enough for the students' long sessions seated at the computer station.

If you decide to expand your service to include community training, you will need enough computers to handle a class. A good way to save money, at least during the start-up phase, is to make arrangements to teach classes in a computer store, where hardware is readily available. The retailer benefits because, through use of the machines, the students may be persuaded to buy hardware at the site of their lessons. Another option, discussed in Chapter 1, is to work out an arrangement with local schools or civic organizations. In these cases, however, you will have to come up with the hardware and software—a costly proposition.

Monthly operating costs for a computer training/consulting business will run from $800 to $2,000, including supplies, phone/utilities, marketing/advertising, travel/transportation, and subscriptions.

If you are consulting, plan on being away from your office 60% to 70% of the time. Daily operations will involve scheduling; talking with new clients about their business and expected system needs; meeting with key personnel who will use the systems daily; research and other direct project work; and maintaining your work log (for yourself, your billing records, and your client reports). As with business consulting, set aside time each week to dedicate to your own business marketing, networking, bookkeeping, and management. It may be difficult to give time to your own business when you are away most of the time, but it is essential.

Computer training may involve similar operations (if training company personnel) or be vastly different if you're training in your home. For at-home training, daily operations will involve scheduling new clients; class preparations; actual system training; bookkeeping; and marketing.

There are several organizations for computer consultants. One such organization is the Independent Computer Consultants Association (ICCA) (see the Appendix for the address). You might also ask your local chamber of commerce for the names of similar organizations in your area. Subscribing to computer and trade magazines is a must for both consulting and training. In addition to those listed in the Appendix, seek out others that may be more specific to the type of consulting and training you do. Don't forget to check with the better computer stores. In addition to being great sources of new clients, they can help you access the grapevine.

Remember, most people who take computer classes want to know how to use the keyboard and master the basics of running a computer, not how to refine their high-order bits. Cover the basics of operating systems, the most popular types of software, and, in broad terms, relational vs. hierarchical programs. Focus heavily on hands-on practice with computers.

6. COMPUTER REPAIR/MAINTENANCE AND PROGRAMMING

As with consulting and training, you need to be knowledgeable about computers to be successful in the computer repair/maintenance and programming racket. A background in computer science, information management, or similar areas can be helpful, but essentially you just need superior know-how and familiarity with numerous systems and how they operate.

Your market can be unlimited, including local retailers, law offices, doctors' offices, publishing firms, CPAs—and, of course, home-based businesses. The majority of people who own computers will need services like yours at one time or another, because most computer owners are happy just to know how to run their software. If their screen suddenly goes black, or they purchase a new, high-end software applications system with 17 disks and a huge "how-to" manual, they'd much rather call an expert to come and get things going for them.

Start-up costs will range from $15,000 to $25,000 minimum: this business requires tools and some inventory for computer repair and programming. Most business owners keep two computers of their own—one for business management and one for practicing and testing their repair and programming skills. You will also need letterhead stationery, business cards, a business telephone, a fax machine, and basic office furniture, as well as a reliable and roomy vehicle for making service calls and carrying your equipment. If you do not currently own a vehicle that will meet your company needs, plan on spending a minimum of $7,000 to $8,000 more to invest in a used, roomy business van for your company.

Monthly overhead operating costs will run from $800 to $1,600, including supplies, phone/utilities, transportation (gas, oil, vehicle maintenance), and marketing/advertising. Costs will be higher for extensive travel if you are not located close to your clients, and you may need to figure in the costs of a loan if you purchase a vehicle for your business. You will also have to keep your inventory stocked.

Daily operations will involve scheduling new jobs; making service calls; purchasing needed supplies; and daily bookkeeping. Remember to build strong relationships with your suppliers; they can be an automatic referral base for new clients. Set aside time each week to dedicate to your own business marketing, networking, and management. It may be difficult to give time to your own business when you are away most of the time, but it is essential.

As with consulting and training, subscribing to computer and trade magazines is a must in order to keep on top of the newest technology and advancements in programming and repair. In addition to those listed in the Appendix, seek out others that may be more specific to your market.

7. DATA DETECTIVE

If you are a skilled, high-tech programmer who can find a way through the most complex of systems, being a data detective can be profitable and fun. Your job is to find important information on computers, either for disclosure or to ensure it's protected from others.

Services provided by data detectives include:

- *Security*—of increasing importance as the need to protect data and programs is felt by companies.
- *Systems audits*—to ensure computer security and systems controls are adequate.
- *Litigation*—to determine whether information exists on computer that can help your lawyer/client; to gain the proper authority to go after the data; and to find the data and present it.

You will probably be paid on a contract basis for your services. For example, a small firm may pay you quarterly or annually for regular systems audits of its computers and updates of its software needs. Alternatively, you may sign a contract stating an hourly rate for services. This arrangement will be especially found when working with law firms.

A word of caution: experts say that this is a business that must retain the constant services of a lawyer—full-time. This retainer can add substantially to start-up and operating costs, but will save you money and problems in the long run. If you market your services to companies, which is somewhat easier, there is a potential that your security will not be able to withstand the interrogation of another skilled data detective. A lawyer can help you design proper contracts, communication, and necessary disclaimers (your business cannot realistically offer a foolproof guarantee). Also, if you plan to work for lawyers and law firms, remember that they have no expenses when it comes to suing you. This does not mean that the business should be avoided at all costs, but it does require that you not enter into it with seat-of-your-pants planning.

Start-up costs will range from $50,000 to $100,000 minimum, because of the great amount of hardware, software, and accessories you will need to perform your services and the costs for legal services throughout start-up and operations. Depending on the services you offer, monthly operating costs will run from $15,000 to $25,000, including supplies, phone/utilities, marketing/advertising, travel/transportation, and purchase of software.

Daily operations will involve scheduling; talking with new clients about their business and expected needs; research and other direct project work; maintaining your work log (for yourself, your billing records, and your client reports); purchasing needed supplies; and daily bookkeeping and marketing.

8. DATABASE MANAGEMENT/MAIL LIST SERVICE

When looking at your operations for a database management/mail list service, your first consideration is the scope of services you will offer:

- Providing initial list input, updates from materials supplied by the client, and printing of lists (onto labels and hard copy).
- Providing mailing services, including bulk mail sorting and mailing.
- Receiving "bingo" cards directly and updating databases from the cards received. (The cards are used as advertisements. Readers or purchasers send them in to receive a free gift and/or more information.)

Typically, business-oriented lists contain names, titles, company names, addresses, and telephone numbers. If you're managing sales-record lists, there may also be commissions, orders, and other sales-related information. The lists may be used to personalize mass mailings, to generate sublists, and for similar functions. For this purpose, the database can be integrated with a word processing package.

The initial design phase of a mail-list database is your most important concern. If you create a database containing hospitals and their resident doctors, you have to realize that you may later want to send information only to the pediatricians. You'll have to be careful enough when you set up the data to be able to sort the names according to each doctor's specialty. If you don't want just a list of doctors in your application, you'll have to interface with the client to include a number of data fields.

As an entrepreneur, your best bet would be to design specialized systems for each client. In this way, all possible permutations of a list can be covered, and the client will be able to sort the material differently for each project. You might also design a prepackaged specific management tool to collect the information yourself and then sell it to various customers.

Some clients may already have machine-readable lists they want you to store, manage, and/or update. Using their system, you serve whatever list-generating/reporting needs they may have. They may want to do a completely new mailing to a completely new list. You would then deal with a broker to generate the list on their behalf, becoming, in effect, a subbroker, though subject to the same restrictions on list use as the client doing the mailing.

The toughest part of mailing lists is maintenance. People move, there are names almost but not quite identical to each other (Dr. Smith and Mr. Smith/Chuck Smith and Charles Smith). Doing a good job is difficult. Not doing a good job will put you out of the marketplace. You'll need to try as hard as possible to develop a regular schedule of mailing-list updates with clients.

Usually, there is a per-hour charge for the entries, a storage charge for the information, and a per-page charge for the reporting. If you're generating letters or labels off the list, there would be a per-unit charge as well. There could also be a separate charge for maintaining off-site backup of the material.

Database management and word processing (list, label, letter creation) are two different applications, yet they go together. A number of integrated packages are on the market, and some systems will permit you to convert word processing text into a database of sorts. If you aren't using an integrated package, at least make sure the word processing and database software are compatible. The word processor needs to be able to accommodate inserts and to handle "variables," such as names and address designations. Again, for this stage of the operation to run smoothly, you must carefully design the database in the first phase. You may need to invest in more than one type of database or word processing program to meet the specialized needs of certain clients.

Different clients will have different needs. If they are straightforward, with a minimum of complicated variables, there will be a minimum design time as well. You could probably design and set up a test for reporting and generating in 10 to 20 hours. But some designs take several months to set up because of the variables. If you're doing international mailings, you'll have one set of criteria; if including a different number of categories, there will be another. Planning the design is the key to this business, and your ability to *sell* your design ability is going to play the largest role in getting and keeping clients.

Start-up costs for your business will range from a minimum of $23,000 to $28,000 on average, because of the amount of hardware, software, and accessories you will need. Expect to pay a minimum of $7,500 to $9,000 for a database management/computing system alone, and buy a high-volume, high-quality printer. As with computer consulting and other computer-intensive businesses, some entrepreneurs have invested tens of thousands of dollars in equipment for their offices.

You will need a separate computer to handle your own business tasks, because you will not want to tie up your main client computer. Other start-up expenses include letterhead stationery, business cards, a business telephone, a fax machine, and office furniture. If you will provide expanded services, such as bingo-card receiving and bulk-mail services, you will also need sorting bins, postage meters, extensive client files, and other miscellaneous shipping supplies.

Monthly operating costs will run from $1,500 (for a one-person operation) to $5,000 and up (as personnel requirements dictate). These costs include phone/utilities, advertising, operating inventory (labels, postage, stationery, toner, and so on), and personnel, depending on the number of clients and lists you are working on.

Daily operations will involve meeting with new clients to design their database; client list input, maintenance, and updating; answering new business calls, as well as regular calls from clients; scheduling jobs (especially those involving mailing); bookkeeping; and marketing.

9. ELECTRONIC CLIPPING SERVICE

This business requires a computer, a modem, and subscriptions to various on-line databases—and/or subscriptions to numerous publications—that will meet the clipping needs of your market.

The SDI (selective dissemination of information) feature of electronic databases allows subscribers to request regular updates on specific topics, making your job that much easier. These updates can provide bibliographic information or full text of published materials. The mechanics of this service would most likely be that you, as subscriber to a database such as Dialog, would request SDIs on specific topics, as directed by your client. When the SDI items arrive in hardcopy form, you pass them along to your client, at an appropriate rate. You might want to consider using SDI services in conjunction with traditional on-line research and clipping. The principal advantage in this type of service would be that it allows you to decrease the labor-intensive aspects of information searches.

Clients are generally billed either monthly (for ongoing clipping needs) or per project, with a deposit and the balance paid upon completion. With regular accounts, you may be able to determine an average cost of providing regular clips, attach your own time and overhead costs, and allow them to pay you on monthly retainer. This is great for your business budgeting and bookkeeping, but be sure to keep accurate records and devote sufficient time to such valuable clients.

Start-up costs for this business will range from $8,000 to $12,000 on average, including computer, fax, modem, laser printer, on-line subscription costs, and basic business supplies. You may also want to invest in a dedicated phone line just for faxing and modem connections.

You have the option of visiting your clients, having them come to you, or working through phone/fax/modem/mail to get an idea of clipping service needs—meaning that you can serve clients across the country. However, until you build a name for yourself and your service, you should market aggressively to local businesses, public relations firms, universities, and others through direct mail, Yellow Pages, newspaper, and trade magazine advertisements. Networking, as always, is important to client growth.

Monthly operating costs will run from $2,000 to $4,500, largely because of the amount of money you will spend performing research and clipping on-line. Though these expenses will be reflected in your client billings, you will still need to be able to budget properly for them. Other expenses included in monthly operating costs are: office supplies, phone/utilities, marketing, and subscriptions. Eventually you may add personnel—at least a part-time assistant to handle job scheduling, bookkeeping, and client communication.

Daily operations will involve talking with new clients about their information needs; research and other direct project work; scheduling; networking; and bookkeeping. You will also need to set aside time each day (or each week, if client information needs are not same-day-sensitive) to package and send the gathered clips to your clients.

10. FREELANCE WRITING

They'll tell you in journalism school not to plan to make money being a writer. As with all businesses, making money can be a challenge in the beginning. As a freelance writer, it is important for you to approach your craft as a business, not a hobby. You must invest in a sophisticated computer system, ample filing space, necessary research materials, and similar resources, if you are to be successful.

Many people don't realize what a large part research plays in being a successful writer. Both at the query stage and during the writing process, you must be well-informed about your topic or a lack of expertise will show in what you write. Stay up-to-date on current events and trends, especially in those areas where you choose to specialize.

Here are some tips for improving your chances of selling an article:

- Don't solicit blindly; know your market (a.k.a. client) and make this knowledge evident.
- Don't pitch "old news"; its obsolescence will be remembered later. If you have a new twist on a much-reported topic, be sure it's new; if a topic was once "hot," don't assume it will sell indefinitely.
- Always spell-check your work, proofread your manuscript, and send it to your client in the proper format (i.e., hard copy plus diskette formatted for their system).

- Photos can help sell your story, especially to budget-conscious clients. If you are doing an interview piece, ask for photos or take some yourself. Even if they are not used, your extra effort is likely to be noted.
- Don't get too particular over your client's edits or you will likely not be used as a writer for them again. Remember, as a freelance business operator selling your writing, your goal is to please the client so that your business will prosper.

Start-up costs for this business will range from $7,000 to $10,000 on average, including computer, fax, modem, laser printer, on-line and periodical subscriptions, writers' reference materials (dictionary, thesaurus, style books, atlas) and basic business supplies: letterhead stationery, business cards, telephone, and furniture.

Monthly operating costs will vary based on the number of long-distance phone interviews conducted and the amount of time spent in on-line research. Remember to negotiate for article-related expense reimbursement. Not all clients will agree to pay for expenses, but many will. Those who will not may agree, instead, to purchase simultaneous submission rights instead of first North American serial rights, or to provide you with several copies of your published article for your marketing efforts. Expenses, which will run approximately $500 to $1,200 per month, include office supplies, phone/utilities, marketing, and subscriptions.

Daily operations include writing and sending query letters; talking with new clients about their article needs; research and writing of articles; networking; and billing/bookkeeping. This is the perfect business for entrepreneurs who enjoy working in solitude. You will rarely have to meet with your clients, except perhaps at introductory sessions with business clients. However, remember to be disciplined. The first time you miss a deadline could be the last time you serve that client.

11. GRAPHIC DESIGN

You do not have to be a skilled illustrator or artist to be a successful graphic designer (though talented illustrators and artists do quite well in the business, of course). The reason: today's advanced computer technology. Anyone with a good sense of design, color, and marketing can find his or her services much in demand as a graphic designer.

Today's software includes such wonders as Quark and Photoshop, which make it a breeze to bring art and design on-screen. Using computer technology, you can produce impressive logos, product packaging, brochures, and other pieces in a fraction of the time once required for freehand graphic design. In addition, you may offer overhead or slide presentation services, where you provide the graphic design and produce the actual overheads/slides for your clients. Get to know printers and typesetters in your area well. Besides their standard services, they can be good contacts for finding overnight slide production or other needed services—including freelance artists, should you require custom art for a client's design.

Start-up costs for this business will range from $9,500 to $30,000. The variation depends on the sophistication of your computer hardware and software packages and the other equipment required for the full range of services you offer (for example, overhead slides needing a high-quality color printer). You will need a drafting table, art supplies, a scanner, a fax, and basic business supplies: letterhead stationery, business cards, telephone, and furniture.

Monthly operating costs will likely run from $800 to $2,500, including supplies, phone/utilities, marketing, and vendor bills. Bidding projects sufficiently is important, though it may take you some practice to get good at doing so. Besides figuring in your time (which is easy to underestimate), you also need to calculate your supplies, which are not cheap: color printer film, camera-ready reproductions of your pieces, CD-ROM and other design sources, overhead materials, and so on.

Daily operations include networking and marketing; meeting with new clients; direct project work (design); shopping for supplies; billing; and bookkeeping.

12. HOME INVENTORY CATALOGING/ORGANIZING

Home inventory cataloging and organizing are natural complements that can offer a steady income once you have established yourself and your business. Your marketing strategy should slant your appeal toward the need to safeguard possessions by having them catalogued carefully; separately, you need to push your expertise as an organizer.

As mentioned in Chapter 1, networking is vital to your success, so a great deal of your time should be spent cultivating and maintaining contacts with real estate and insurance agents, general contractors, and other family-service providers. From there, offering local seminars or a free newsletter on organization will help to attract new clients. Your reputation will be built on your thoroughness and professionalism. Inventories should be complete, including *every* valued item in the house, and catalogued to indicate cost, location, age, description, and, if available, model, make, and serial number. Organizing should be done to meet the space and daily needs of the client with regard to lifestyle and personal preferences. Above all, you must build a reputation for being discreet. Your clients will not stay long if they fear their economic or other position will be shared with the community.

Start-up costs are relatively minimal, ranging from $5,000 to $8,000, including computer setup, letterhead stationery, business cards, a business telephone, basic office furniture, and a letter-quality printer. Optional items include a fax machine and high-quality laser printer. You will also need ample secured files for your client records.

Monthly operating costs will likely run from $500 to $1,500, including supplies, phone/utilities, marketing, and travel/transportation. You should charge an hourly rate for your services, and give clients an estimate up front. Daily operations will include networking and marketing; meeting with new clients; direct project work (inventory and organizing); shopping for supplies for your business and your clients; billing; and bookkeeping.

13. INFORMATION BROKER/RESEARCH SERVICE

The possibilities for making money doing research and providing information for business, professional, and other organizations are enormous. Depending on your specialty, there may also be a large consumer market, such as offering in-depth medical reports to people who have recently been diagnosed with a chronic or serious condition. Because of today's advanced technology, you have the option of visiting your clients, having them come to you, or working through phone/fax/modem/mail to get an idea of their research needs.

However, information brokering is more than just researching—it's knowing how data are stored and classified and being able to manipulate and discriminate among sources of information to obtain the facts your client needs. As Cookie Lewis, owner of Informania in California, says: "Anybody can take things off of a computer. What distinguishes my business and puts me ahead is being able to evaluate and analyze the data and information I gather. Just because information is on the computer doesn't mean it's correct. Just because a study was done and cites statistics doesn't mean that it's so. . . . A lot of things that get filtered into magazines and newspapers are old news [or] are taken out of context."

Use every information source at your disposal: libraries, interviews with experts, subscriptions to periodicals and newsletters, online services, and so on. It's possible to get information from U.S. data banks and from most areas of the world, by accessing many of the large timesharing computers located outside the United States and Canada. Dialog, owner and operator of one of the largest collections of databases, has published two documents describing the procedures. Talk to your local software dealer about packages for small businesses similar to those used by libraries and research institutions.

Remember, this business is more than a clipping service. You provide not only ready-made information in the form of clips, but analyses and compilations of information. In essence, you are the eternal term-paper writer—only more than a grade is at stake. Your ability to gather information, analyze it, and, just as important, *present* it to your clients defines your success. If your writing skills are lacking, you will need to hire someone to help you with the presentation stage.

Start-up costs for this business will range from $10,000 to $15,000 on average, including computer, fax, modem, laser printer, on-line subscription costs, and basic business supplies: letterhead stationery, business cards, telephone, and furniture. You may also want to invest in a dedicated phone line just for faxing and modem connections, and you will need to have a minilibrary, in your home, of sources published in your area of research.

Depending on the number of clients (i.e., projects) you begin with, monthly operating costs can easily run from $2,000 to $10,000 in the first year. The vast range is largely due to the varying amount of money needed to perform on-line research and the number of people it will take to get your clients' projects completed quickly. Beyond personnel and on-line costs, you will also need to budget for office supplies, phone/utilities, marketing, and subscriptions. Office expenses should include professional packaging for your information reports to clients.

Daily operations will involve talking with new clients about their information needs; research and other direct project work; scheduling new projects and ensuring you have enough personnel to meet deadlines; marketing/networking; and bookkeeping. You will also need to set aside time to professionally package your reports and send them to your clients.

14. INVENTORY CONTROL SERVICE

Many small business owners fail to realize the importance of inventory control. An adequate stock control system will tell clients what merchandise is in the store, what is on order, when it will arrive, and what has been sold. With such a system, clients can plan purchases intelligently and quickly recognize fast sellers that need reordering and slow-moving items that should be marked down or given special promotion.

You, as the expert, need to be able to design a system that works best for each particular client. With each new business, you must establish a foundation—or frame of reference—regarding the business's inventory. To make an accurate calculation of basic stock (or minimal inventory requirements), you must review actual sales during an appropriate time period, such as a full year of business. If your client is a new business owner without a year's worth of records to guide you, you must calculate what is known as the "open-to-buy" assessment, determining the amount of sales needed to pay store overhead and cover the owner's personal needs, and the amount of stock needed to meet these sales projections.

Basic stock of a business must fulfill two functions: (1) provide customers with a reasonable assortment of products and (2) cover normal sales demands. Lead time—the length of time between reordering and delivery of product—must also be included when calculating basic stock. If product reorders are not made until the stock is actually needed, the basic inventory will experience a shortfall and your client will lose sales. On the flip side, excess inventory that sits in your client's storeroom creates extra overhead and costs money by generating losses that will shrink the business's bottom line.

Though you will use your home computer to track client records, you will want to be flexible in working with clients to establish their on-site tracking. Some retailers find that tracking inventory via a manual tag system is effective, and it saves them money during their first several months of business. A manual tag system can be updated daily, weekly, or even monthly, and is based on the tags removed at the point of purchase. The tags are cross-checked against physical inventory to determine what has been sold and in what quantities. Information gathered by stock clerks or others performing this tracking will be given to you for input and analysis.

Most retailers today use computers to record inventory by type, volume, cost, and profit. Such systems show the amount of money invested in each merchandise category, and they can log the time of orders and sales, providing help in determining when to reorder. Cash registers can also serve as computer information gatherers: sales receipts are matched with delivery receipts to determine a retailer's gross profit margin.

To keep inventory flowing through the business at optimal levels, your client must purchase wisely and in a timely fashion. The purpose of establishing and maintaining your inventory control system is to have your client know *when* to purchase replacement inventory, *what* to purchase (as well as what *not* to purchase), and *how much* to purchase.

In the course of operating a real business, both inventory shortages and excesses will occur. A business owner may come to you for help at this stage.

If a shortage occurs, you can guide the business owner to:

- Review production to locate any bottlenecks.
- Change production schedules or policies to correct them.
- Place a rush order.
- Employ another supplier.
- Employ substitute materials (if necessary).

If the problem is excesses or overstocking, recommend:

- Reducing prices.
- Returning excess stock to suppliers.
- Increasing sales incentives.
- Creating a promotion to stimulate demand.

In either case, the first order of business you must address is an *analysis* of the client's reordering system.

If purchasing and reordering are conducted correctly, excesses and shortages should not occur. Be sure that inventory is counted as often as needed (every week, or two weeks, or four weeks), and recommend that your client work with suppliers to improve delivery efficiency.

Your most effective tools in tailoring inventory control systems to clients' needs will be commercially available inventory control software packages that enable you to track clients' inventory easily and generate customized reports. Many such packages are available. Carefully assess your needs, and those of your potential customers, before buying a package that has features you will never use or one that does not fulfill all your requirements.

Start-up costs for your business will range from a minimum of $15,000 to $20,000 on average, because of the sophisticated hardware and software you will need to track extensive inventories for several clients. Expect to pay a minimum of $7,500 to $9,000 for your computing system alone, including a laser printer. Other start-up expenses include letterhead stationery, business cards, a business telephone, a fax machine, and office furniture.

Monthly operating costs will run approximately $800 to $1,800, including phone/utilities, advertising, supplies, and travel/transportation. Your pricing structure is based on one-time consultations, monthly or quarterly updates, or annual or six-month fees, depending on the customer's needs.

Daily operations will involve meeting with new clients to design their inventory systems; inventory information input, maintenance, and updating; answering new business calls and regular calls from clients; scheduling jobs (especially those involving large inventory warehouses); bookkeeping; and marketing.

15. MAIL ORDER

The mail-order business has been around for more than 100 years. Aaron Montgomery, of Montgomery Ward fame, started out in the 1880s by mailing a one-page catalog that featured such items as bed ticking and hoop skirts. Today, ordering through the mail has become busy consumers' most convenient way of shopping. They can purchase all the items they need without the hassle of crowded shopping malls or the headaches of lugging home bags and boxes.

Essentially, your business entails three main operations once you have selected the products you will offer: (1) producing the catalog, (2) mailing the catalog to your target market, and (3) servicing customer orders. If you plan to produce the catalog in-house and send out only for printing, your equipment needs will include a quality computer setup with a large video monitor; software that includes a photo layout program like Quark and Photoshop; a high-quality laser printer; and a color scanner. Alternately, you can design the catalog layout, provide the photographs and use a printer with photo capabilities to finish the final production. This approach takes considerable organization because the number of photos being used is likely to be significant. Be sure to provide very clear "dummies" of the catalog with numbered references for each photo, and all necessary captions and order numbers clearly marked and triple-checked for accuracy. Ask to see a proof after the pages are stripped up and before the catalog is printed.

Next, you must consider catalog mailing and order fulfillment. Will you provide both from your home-based business, or will you contract out for database management, mailing, and fulfillment services? The choice will largely depend on the available space and the size and quantity of products being offered. Collect prices from available vendors, and weigh the pros and cons of doing both before investing in the equipment and space to perform a full-service operation. Bruce Holmes, a creator of software for the mail order business, developed his software package, *Mail Order Wizard,* after running his own mail order company, and was able to operate out of his home until his business grew to 16 employees. His software now helps other mail-order businesses run successful operations, even from home: "We have a program called the *Mail Order Wizard* which runs mail-order companies. It processes their orders, does their accounts receivables, keeps track of their inventory, keeps track of their back-orders, does their charge cards for them. It does their printout of their manifest for UPS or the Post Office, so that they can get a thousand packages out a day and not have to go crazy over it," says Holmes. And that's not all. "The program analyzes ads so that you know which ads are succeeding and which are costing a ton of money. It analyzes products and tells you which product on which page of the catalog is doing great and which is losing a ton of money so you better get rid of it. It keeps track of mailing lists, and helps you do selections of who you want to mail to at any one moment." (See "Database Management/Mail List Service," above, for more tips on running this side of your mail-order company.)

Finally, you need to decide whether you will accept only mail-in orders or will also offer an 800 number for telephone orders. The decision will significantly affect your start-up and operations. Regardless of what route you choose, you must offer a toll-free customer service line to handle customer queries and complaints regarding orders.

Start-up costs for your business will range from a minimum of $20,000 to $70,000 on average, because of the great amount of hardware, software, inventory, and equipment you will need. Expect to pay a minimum of $7,500 to $9,000 for a database management/computing system, and add a high-volume, high-quality printer if you will be running a complete operation. You will also need a separate business computer for taking orders and managing your business (plus several computer workstations if you plan to hire employees to take and process orders). Phone lines and utility costs must be figured in. Other start-up expenses include letterhead stationery, business cards, a business telephone, a fax machine, and office furniture. If you will handle all catalog mailing and fulfillment in-house, you will also need sorting bins, postage meters, extensive client files, shelving, and miscellaneous shipping supplies. If you will design the full catalog in-house, you will need a drafting table, art supplies, a scanner, a fax, and layout/design supplies.

Monthly operating costs will run from $1,500 to $50,000, depending on volume and personnel; you may find your expenses increasing rapidly as your catalogs hit their mark, or peaking during seasonal periods and then going through a slow period. Business management is crucial to success—watching your business closely, anticipating staffing and inventory needs, and reacting quickly when you miss the mark.

16. MULTIMEDIA

Novice computer users, beware; but if you are among those who have a good understanding of technology and can operate not only your computer but video and CD-ROM accessories, then multimedia services can bring you success. Business owners offer a wide array of services, from training and informational videos to custom, interactive CD-ROM products and even high-tech "virtual reality" presentations that lawyers use in courtrooms to reenact crime or accident scenes. Essentially, your skill is being able to combine sound, music, graphics, and video into presentations that can be shown through a computer or video screen and meet specific client needs.

With this business still in relative infancy, opportunities abound for the creative and skilled computer whiz who sees no limit to what can be produced for clients. Most clients will not know what they want, because multimedia will be a new concept for them. They *will* know that:

- They want to blow away the competition at the next open product demonstration/sales presentation they give to a major client prospect.
- They want to save money on production errors by creating for their employees a thorough interactive training video that provides regular testing of skills at scheduled intervals.
- They want visitors to their store or organization to be able to find what they are looking for quickly and easily, and to receive a pleasant sales pitch and "thank you for visiting" message.

Besides advanced computer skills, you need to know where your limitations are. Earl Tyson, owner of Interactive Multimedia in Marietta, Georgia, says a key to success is knowing when to contract out to others to help complete a project. "I contract out as needed. For example, a project may require these skills: being a graphic designer, an application designer; if it contains video, then I'll need a video talent, and a programming talent. On each particular project, I contract for various forms of talent, depending upon the need." Tyson adds that he contracts for such services for up to a year, as needed, to complete a multimedia project.

Start-up costs will range from a minimum of $16,000 to an average of $60,000, depending on what equipment you already have and what components you'll need to purchase, as well as how much you'll have to spend on outside contractors to complete your first projects. As mentioned in Chapter 2, your most important equipment need (on top of a good computer system) is a CD-ROM, at least double if not triple speed, and a large, high-clarity monitor to show off your work.

Other necessary expenses, besides your computer setup, will be a fax machine, letterhead stationery, business cards, a business telephone, office furniture (including visitor chairs and, preferably, a small meeting or conference table), and a laser printer.

A professional-looking home office is essential for making the right impression. Your product does not come cheap, and you must instill confidence in your clients. Though you may be able to conduct some meetings at their offices, they will inevitably need to come to your home to see their work in progress, on-screen, with your equipment.

Monthly operating costs will run from $2,000 to $8,000 and up, depending on client project costs; established business may well spend significantly more. Daily operations will involve meeting with clients; hands-on drafting; design and project work; scheduling work for subcontractors and new projects; and marketing/advertising. Bookkeeping can probably be kept to twice a month.

17. NEWSLETTER PUBLISHING

Many entrepreneurs have been successful in publishing newsletters, whether for a specific company or organization, or for a segment of the general market. A newsletter is a specialized information service concentrating on in-depth coverage of one subject. Newsletter publishers can either market their product to subscribers for whom the newsletter's information is particularly valuable, or offer their computer and production expertise to put out a professional newsletter for groups and companies that do not have the staff or equipment to do so themselves.

There are three ways to approach revenue generation in newsletter publishing: (1) charge a subscription rate to readers; (2) charge a production rate to clients whose newsletters you produce; or (3) sell enough advertisements to pay for the costs of production, overhead, and profit, and deliver the newsletter to targeted readers at no charge. The latter is successful for entrepreneurs who find a niche of content that is attractive to readers and thus draws a wide audience that advertisers will want to reach. For example, a newsletter for children and families in your community will attract day care centers, dance studios, dentists, pediatricians, orthodontists, pizza parlors, toy stores, and other advertisers. You can actually give the newsletter away for free in the community, and let the advertising revenues pay your business costs and yield a profit.

Another option is to approach businesses and organizations that already publish newsletters—or market products or services that lend themselves to interesting newsletter topics, like pharmaceuticals, medicine, law, or entertainment—and show them how much better they can be produced through your service. Your business can offer writing, editing, design and/or layout, and production, working with in-house staff or handling the entire project from concept through completion. You might handle the printing and delivery of the finished product, and, if desired, can offer mailing, bulk mail sorting, and mail list services as well. Diane Averill of Averill & Associates in New York used "before" and "after" samples of newsletters she had redesigned to attract new clients to her business.

Finally, if you enjoy research and writing, you can become publisher of a subscriber-based newsletter that offers "inside information" on a unique topic with a large potential audience. Your market will be defined by the topic you choose, but can include both consumers and businesses, so don't overlook the potential to penetrate both segments. For example, a newsletter on organizational tips can appeal to homemakers, home office workers, company office managers, and nonprofit and community organizations. A newsletter on antique furniture may appeal to homeowners in select neighborhoods and to home improvement stores, magazines, and museums.

Start-up costs for your business will range from $17,000 to $40,000, because of the extensive equipment you will need (and depending on the type of newsletter you publish). A subscriber-based newsletter requires extensive market research, mail lists, and advertising to get properly launched. Equipment costs will include a quality computer setup with a large video monitor and software that allows a large number of fonts for a creative design; a high-quality laser printer; a color scanner; and a modem. Other start-up expenses include letterhead stationery, business cards, a telephone, a fax machine, and office furniture. Optional items are a color printer and CD-ROM accessories.

Monthly operating costs will run from approximately $1,000 to $5,000 and up, depending on circulation and the type of newsletter produced. To keep costs in line, you must weigh all the variables against the benefits they provide. For example, does your newsletter warrant four-color printing, or can you get by with two or three colors? What type of paper stock is needed—heavy professional bond, newspaper/tabloid quality, or something in between? Will your readers notice the difference? Will they pay for the newsletter, or get if for free?

Daily operations for all newsletter approaches involve: newsletter design and formatting; gathering information, stories, and art elements; inputting or converting text; scheduling jobs and production schedules; bookkeeping and marketing. You may also need to dedicate time to mail list maintenance, advertising, writing/editing, and sales. As Charles Fletcher, publisher of *Lower Columbia Business*, emphasizes: "You have to know how to sell. Lots of people think, 'I know how to make widgets, but I don't know what to do with them once I've made them.' The most important skill I have is being able to generate income through sales. I thought I was a terrible salesperson, but I needed to learn. I took a sales course." Sound advice.

18. PERSONALIZED CHILDREN'S BOOKS

Publishing personalized children's books for gifts and keepsakes is surprisingly easy, compared to start-up needs in many other computer businesses. The reason is the high number of software packages available that work with your desktop publishing system to create customized books without the need for writing or artistic skills.

Professionalism and marketing know-how are essential. You must have the ability to go out and get people to showcase your books for you, to increase awareness of your business. You should make cold calls at bookstores, gift stores, mail-order firms, and other outlets, to see whether they will carry your product. If you *are* a good writer or artist, your opportunities can expand to creating your own line of books, or even setting up and selling your own personalized children's book packages, ready for customizing by other entrepreneurs.

As mentioned in Chapter 1, county fairs, holiday boutiques, special community functions, and other gatherings where parents and children are found make perfect marketing and selling opportunities. You should also get out into the community and network. And, if you prefer having a home office to actually working from home, you can "set up shop" with a cart or kiosk at a local mall or strip center—especially during the holidays.

Start-up costs for this business will range from $15,000 to $25,000 on average, including your computer hardware and software packages, a color printer and book covers, art supplies, and small display items. You will also need letterhead stationery, business cards, brochures, flyers, shelving, and, if you plan to have customers come by your home, attractive office furniture. You can spend more if you decide to operate a cart or kiosk.

Monthly operating costs will likely run from $800 to $2,500, including supplies, phone/utilities, marketing, and travel/transportation. You may find your expenses increasing rapidly as your books become known in your community, or peaking during seasonal periods and then going through slow periods.

Daily operations will include networking and marketing; book production; shopping for supplies for your business; billing; and bookkeeping.

19. REFERRAL SERVICE

Market research is essential for a referral service. You will need to research who wants and needs to know where your referral products/

services are, and whether there are companies willing to sign up and pay to be on your network. Test the waters with a carefully worded pitch letter to local businesses, explaining the concept and highlighting the personal touch your business would provide. Mention that the operation will be up and running in 60 days and that you're accepting reservations for listings.

Your role in this business is to serve as the go-between for consumers and client companies. Consumers reach you free of charge through your 800 number, and companies pay a fee to be included on your referral database.

Your database, in fact, is the heart of your business, so be organized in collecting client information: name of company, address, phone number, types of services, types of products, hours, and so on. If you decide on professional services, you'll need to get license numbers, certification (if held), type of insurance and bonding (for certain professions), and similar data. To protect yourself from liability, tell your callers that although the information you provide is accurate, they should ask for references from the professional they choose, to ensure that they will be happy.

Once your line is operational, a carefully structured news release sent to local newspapers and cable television stations will help you get your story out to the public. This business is new enough that—especially if your selected product or service is unique—you should attract some attention. Start your release with something like: "Have you ever wondered where you can find a good chili dog at four in the morning, or where you could buy a recording of Spike Jones playing Bach? Don't rely on the Yellow Pages any more, because you know they won't know. But we will. . . ."

Start-up costs will range from a minimum of $5,000 to $10,000–$15,000 on average, depending on how many callers you estimate will respond, based on market research for your referral subject. The number of phone lines and of staff needed to accommodate callers is your main variable. Start-up expenses include your computing system, letterhead stationery, business cards, a business telephone, a fax machine, and office furniture.

Monthly operating costs will run from $1,000 to $5,000, depending on volume and personnel, and will include phone/utilities, advertising/marketing, travel/transportation, and supplies. Remember that phone lines used for your referral service should not have call forwarding, call waiting, or other features that might interrupt the line.

Daily operations will involve list maintenance and updating; adding new subscribers; bookkeeping and marketing; and regular and ongoing market research.

20. SALES/MARKETING SERVICE

Because you will be a salesperson for salespeople, this business requires copywriting and marketing skills (direct mail, telemarketing, brochures, and personal contact) and a penchant for sales. Your principal markets are small businesses and independent sales representatives in need of between 100 and 1,000 sales letters or professional client proposals. For letters, your pricing structure should be based on lots of 100, 250, 500, and 1,000 letters, with prices matching the competition and what the market will bear. Overhead, which, as mentioned later in this chapter, is part of your pricing structure, should be percentaged according to the amount of business generated per client. If, for example, you produce 4,000 letters monthly and a single client generates 35% of your business, 35% of your overhead should be included in your monthly bill. Proposal writing services should be negotiated, in most cases, on a per-project basis. Take a look at the specifications for the proposal, the number of chapters, the questions and answers, and how the client will provide you with the needed information; then make an estimate of the number of hours that will be required. Don't undersell your skills—a good proposal can run a client $3,000 to $5,000, or more.

In addition to your hardware and software (including a high-quality laser printer), start-up costs include phone, stationery, office furniture, brochure printing, and direct-mail costs, and will run between $4,500 to $9,000. Monthly operating costs will run approximately $800 to $2,000.

Daily operations will include meeting with new clients; direct project work; scheduling jobs and client work-review appointments or time frames; billing; bookkeeping; and marketing.

21. SIGN MAKING

Offer more than simple signs to get your business launched. By showing potential clients new, creative ideas—catchy slogans, 3-D effects, original graphics, and so on—you can make yourself and your business known communitywide. By serving as a local, quick source for publicity materials that are often needed on short notice, you can broaden your reach by offering quick turnaround of high-quality products. You should also try to anticipate client needs: upcoming sales, special events, new wings (in stores, hospitals, libraries), community sponsorship, and similar opportunities.

Your first decision will be the types of signs you will offer: those produced solely on computer with color printers, those made with cut vinyl images, or those produced with a four-color print vinyl electrostatic machine set up in your garage or home office addition. (For the latter setup, you will probably need at least 600 square feet for production.) Technological advances are the driving force behind the success of sign-making shops. Years ago, signs were used primarily for storefronts. Today, signs are on the sides of vehicles, in front of homes (placed there by construction, landscaping, and security companies), and in front of booths at fairs or community flea markets. On a smaller scale, you can offer "Grand Opening" and "Sale" banners, or decorative and creative inside banners and signs for retailers, schools, libraries, and restaurants. You might specialize in elegant or fun signs for special occasions, marketed through wedding organizers, party planners, and caterers, for example.

Like personalized children's books, instant sign companies are relatively easy to operate because available systems are user-friendly. Basically, three pieces of equipment are needed to make vinyl signs: (1) a computer screen, (2) a computer keyboard designed for setting type and fonts, and a plotter (a cutting device that is controlled by the computerized keyboard). In addition, a scanner and an art-manipulation program will be necessary if you want to recreate specific images such as company logos. In many cases, your clients will actually have the finished design and artwork they desire for their signs. Still, creative input on your part can help to ensure satisfied customers.

Start-up costs will range from $30,000 to $50,000 minimum, because of the great amount of hardware, software, and accessories you will need to produce high-quality signs. Depending on the types of signs you offer, monthly operating costs will run from $3,500 to $35,000, including supplies, phone/utilities, marketing/advertising, travel/transportation, and personnel. Generally, this is an operation that is difficult to keep going as a one-person shop, unless you stick to small-scale signs and banners that do not involve extensive production work. Consider this carefully when planning on a home-based operation. (It is also important to note that large-scale instant sign stores operated outside the home can incur start-up costs well above $100,000, for rent, equipment, and materials.)

Daily operations will involve scheduling; talking with new clients about their business and needs; sign production; purchasing materials and supplies; and daily bookkeeping and marketing. You may find you need immediate "front-office" help or a full-time production assistant, if you generate a large clientele from the beginning.

22. SOFTWARE DESIGN/CUSTOM SOFTWARE

As mentioned in Chapter 1, the best avenue to success in software publishing is to focus on a narrow, or vertical, market. For example, the
trucking industry seems ripe for computerization. Not only do truck
owners need help with maintenance records, federal and state form-
filing, and per-vehicle data, but truck brokers and agents also need systems to help with their accounting, paperwork, and other management
tasks. We suggest you stay away from obvious vertical markets such as
insurance, law, real estate, medicine, and car-dealership software.

An absolutely essential key to success in developing software for
vertical markets is a complete understanding of the potential users'
needs. Bruce Holmes, creator of software for the mail-order business,
developed his package after running his own mail-order company. "We
needed to computerize, but when I first started out there wasn't anything in the field, so I wrote my own," says Holmes. "I started writing
the program about 12 years ago." Since then, he has made continual improvements and enhancements to the software and offers optimal
technical support to thousands of current clients.

To ensure your success, you must do the same. If you have a software program idea that you're sure will sell, but do not have the requi-
site background, consult with business owners (or other targeted
users) to determine what they want and don't want, the price they'd be
willing to pay for the system, what their ideal program would do for
them, and other particulars. Hire someone, either as an employee or on
a consultant basis, to offer you knowledgeable insight into the potential users' needs.

In addition to the more traditional methods of marketing outlined in Chapter 1, there are software authors' (programmers') agents
today representing entrepreneurs like yourself. The agents usually
work on a monthly retainer and often want a percentage of sales.
Though these agents are not necessary for success, if you find one you
like and have the money to spend, an agent might be worth a try. Have
an experienced lawyer prepare or review any agent contract before you
sign.

There are also software distributors and companies—intermedi-
aries who purchase software from you at a discount, for resale to dealers. Usually, they'll inventory some of your product, making it possible
for dealers to get what they need quickly. Good distributors call on
hundreds of dealers; they act like a sales force, getting your product to
many more dealers than you could on your own. The larger distributors can be pretty demanding. Because of their size and capabilities,
they are cautious about adding new products to their lines. Expect to

spend a fair amount of time "selling" your product to a distributor's acquisition group. Some want to know how much advertising *you* intend to do, and what in-house support *you* will provide (how willing you are to answer users' questions over the phone). Moreover, they'll probably be interested in things like your company's financial strength, track record, and the like. For these reasons, you may find it easier to get started with one or more smaller distributors. How do you find distributors? Through trade shows, the Yellow Pages, word of mouth, directories of software distributors, and computer magazines.

Start-up costs will range from a minimum of $20,000 to $23,000, because of the great amount of hardware, software, and accessories you will need to create and test your software program, and to provide adequate phone service to callers who need technical support following a software purchase (an 800 number is recommended). Besides computer equipment, you will need letterhead stationery, business cards, a business telephone, basic office furniture, and a letter-quality printer. Optional items include a fax machine and a high-quality laser printer.

Monthly operating costs will vary, depending on how you decide to market your product. For example, if you sell your program to a software publisher, the firm will likely buy the rights and thus handle technical support for the program. If you market the software yourself, or through a distributor, you will need at least three phone lines (in the beginning) to offer technical support and customer service to your customers. Plan to spend anywhere from $2,000 to $5,000 per month and up, after making the decision about how you will market. Your costs include business phone/utilities, advertising/marketing, personnel, and regular updates to your computer library for testing and compatibility configurations.

Daily operations will involve networking and marketing; direct project work; shopping for supplies for your business; and regular and ongoing market research of your targeted users. You may also need to handle staffing issues, customer service, inventory tracking and maintenance, shipping, and sales tracking if you plan to set up shop as a software designer, supplier, and full-service operation.

23. UTILITY BILL AUDITING

This is a lucrative business for anyone willing to do the necessary research and keep on top of any changes to telephone and utility company tariffs. The business premise is simple: large corporations such as telephone and utility firms make mistakes, and these mistakes can spell huge savings for businesses that incur substantial bills each month.

As a utility bill auditor, you can work in a home office, examining gas, sewer, electric, water, and telephone bills for inaccuracies in rate classification, billing, meter usage, and taxes. For example, has a company charged tax to a tax-exempt business such as a nonprofit agency? Have the utilities charged rates that exceed their government-approved profit percentages? Have there been meter-reading mistakes? Does the client's normal billing history indicate an excessive month or two that could be worth several hundred dollars?

Start-up costs for this business will range from $8,000 to $17,000 on average, including computer, fax, modem, laser printer, and basic business supplies: letterhead stationery, business cards, telephone, and furniture. You may also want to invest in a notebook computer and a dedicated phone line just for faxing and modem connections. (Setting up with fax and modem capabilities allows you to offer your services over a larger geographic range, an important move once your reputation is established.)

Once clients have agreed to try your service, you will go to their offices for both sales and meetings. Until you have some success stories under your belt, you should charge only a percentage of savings as your fee. Once established, you can charge a setup fee of $100 to $300 (depending on the size of the company and the scope of the bills being reviewed) as well as a percentage of recovered payments. Generally, it is only cost-effective to market your services to medium-size and large businesses that have high-energy usage operations and multiline telephone systems. Though smaller businesses and residential consumers can be charged incorrectly as well, the savings generated are not normally enough to cover the cost of your services.

Monthly operating costs will run from $1,000 to $2,000, including supplies, phone/utilities, marketing, and travel/transportation. Daily operations will involve talking with new clients about their business; research and direct project work; scheduling; and networking. Though new clients will come largely from referrals and networking, cold calling is still a good idea. Especially in metropolitan areas, the number of likely business clients may be large enough to justify newspaper or trade journal advertising as well.

24. WORD PROCESSING

Word processing is the name given to plain old typing as performed on a computer. It has been a boon to businesspeople, writers, students, and others: manuscript mechanics are a breeze and multiple copies and large-scale revisions are run-of-the-mill. A computer allows instant revision, movement and alteration of copy, and essentially error-free pages.

The size and range of such a business is up to you. You can start small, perhaps on a part-time basis, and work up to whatever workload you want to handle. You can offer any range of services, from straight typing, charged by the page or hour, to complete newsletters; weekly or monthly bulletins from businesses, churches, and clubs; product catalogs; resumes; handbooks; pamphlets—whatever your customers need.

If you have specialized knowledge—for instance, if you've worked in a law firm or a dentist's office—seek your first customers among people who will appreciate the fact that you're already familiar with both the forms and jargon they use. If they're pleased with your work, ask them to tell colleagues about your services. Any time you have a satisfied customer, give him or her a few of your business cards to hand out.

However, before you decide what fees to charge and begin soliciting business, you'll want to consider the following:

- How will you bill—by the hour, page, or document?
- How many copies will you provide?
- Can you handle forms?
- What will you charge for revisions of finished work?
- Can you index?
- How long will you store/file client documents for revision?
- Will you offer editing to projects, or simply spelling checks?
- Will you arrange for printing, shipping, or other services? Or will you provide camera-ready masters only?
- Will you offer a wide array of papers, envelopes, and designs, or will the client need you to provide anything more than standard white bond for the finished products?
- How will you protect the clients' material against fire or theft?

Once you know the answer to these and similar questions about the nature of your business, you can set a fee schedule to cover your time and overhead and then advertise your services. The kind of work you do will have a bearing on what your fees will be. One question you may face regarding straight manuscript typing is whether to charge the typical $2.00 to $3.50 per-page fee for a finished manuscript page. On one hand, the ease and speed with which a computer printer can produce fair copy suggest that you could charge less per page. But this has to be balanced against whether your volume justifies the lower fee, the higher cost of the basic equipment package, and the level and type of competition in a given area. You have to know your best potential area market: students will not pay as much as businesspeople; job-hunters will pay more for full-service than for straight typing of their resume, and so on.

One successful entrepreneur got all the work she could handle in the following way: "For a modest fee," she said, "I was able to get 11 lines of advertising displayed on cable television for a week. The local newspaper offered a $4 ad, which I took advantage of. Then I prepared two sets of business letters—one for lawyers and courts, one for businesspeople—and hand-delivered samples in the community."

Another beginner found that advertising her services in a large city newspaper prompted only a few customers to call. But when she put a notice in the local suburban shoppers' weekly, she had to turn away business. People responded to the idea of local service. She currently gets most of her business from doctors, lawyers, and other professionals—people for whom accuracy and quality are paramount. She provides both, and charges accordingly, with no complaints from clients.

Straight text and legal forms make up the bulk of this entrepreneur's work, suggesting that specialization makes sense and that demand for such service is growing. If you can meet it with a high-quality product, you can be your own boss.

Start-up costs for your business will range from $10,000 to $25,000, depending on the extent of services you will offer and whether you will inventory paper and other materials for client jobs. Equipment costs will include a quality computer setup with ample typesetting fonts, a high-quality laser printer, a fax, and a modem—especially if you deal with business clients. Other start-up expenses include letterhead stationery, business cards, telephone, files (many), and office furniture. You may also consider shelving and stationery, binders, and shipping materials.

Monthly operating costs will vary, based on the extent of the services you provide and on whether you choose to run your business as a one-person shop or expand as consumer need dictates. Plan on spending approximately $800 to $2,000 per month, or more if you bring on additional personnel.

Daily operations will include meeting with new clients; direct project work; scheduling jobs and client work-review appointments or time frames; billing; bookkeeping; and marketing. You may also need to dedicate time to tracking your inventory, shopping for new items, and meeting with printers or others, depending on the scope of services offered.

4

SETTING UP
YOUR OFFICE

Location is likely to play a big role in selecting your business. Today's advanced computer technology has changed the way the world conducts business, and entrepreneurs can be competitive from their homes. Modems, fax machines, and overnight mail services allow successful entrepreneurs to be located several thousand miles from their clients.

A HOME-BASED OFFICE: PROS AND CONS

Even when your business is run from your home, you still have locational issues to consider. Are you willing to relocate? If not, then the type of business you choose may be restricted. For example, a sign-making business will be more successful near a large business and shopping area than in a remote residential area.

In addition, some cities are actually more favorable to home-based entrepreneurs than others. Cities with permissible zoning regulations, affordable housing, favorable business programs, active chambers of commerce, good schools, and easy access to major metropolitan areas are the best. Take a look at the community where you live. What are taxes like for businesses? How much do licenses, permits, and renewal fees run in your area? Are there association or neighbor-hood rules that would prohibit operating a home-based business, even if the city permits it?

You may need to consider accessibility and parking. Can clients and vendors easily reach your location? Will neighbors cause prob-lems for you if there is a constant stream of visitors? If you are a renter, keep a close relationship with your building or complex man-ager and stay informed of any impending changes or sales. You may be best off signing a lease that will guarantee your residence for at least one year during start-up. On the other hand, if you anticipate you will be moving soon, you will want to start your business outside of a leasing situation.

Finally, your business neighbors may influence the volume of business you do—even from your home. Their presence can work for you as well as against you, particularly if you locate near businesses in the same affinity class. Studies of the natural clusterings of businesses show that certain businesses do well when located close to one other. For a home-based computer maintenance and repair business, for ex-ample, ideal neighbors may include other office-service businesses such as office cleaning services, office supply stores, and temporary agencies.

Even if you believe that the bulk of your clients will be located far from your home-based operation and this will not cause problems, it is important to know your area. After all, many businesses and con-sumers will support a local operation over one located far from their community.

Important considerations are:

1. Is the population base large enough to support your business?
2. Does the community have a stable economic base that will pro-mote a healthy environment for your business?
3. Are demographic characteristics compatible with the market you wish to serve?

Economic Base

A community's economic base determines your opportunities and po-tential for success. The wealth produced in or near the community greatly affects local employment, income, and population growth. To evaluate a community's economic base, find the following information:

1. The percentage of people employed full-time and the trend in employment.

2. The average family income.
3. Per-capita total annual sales for your products or services.

You can obtain this information by studying census data and other business statistics. You can also learn a great deal about your prospective community by looking and listening. Some danger signals include the following:

1. The necessity for high school and college graduates to leave town to find suitable employment.
2. The inability of other residents to find local jobs.
3. A high number of families and businesses moving out of the area.
4. Declining retail sales and industrial production.
5. An apathetic attitude on the part of local business owners, educational administrators, and other residents.

Favorable signs are:

1. The opening of chain- or department-store branches.
2. Branch plants of large industrial firms locating in or near the community.
3. A progressive chamber of commerce and other civic organizations.
4. Good schools and public services.
5. Well-maintained business and residential premises.
6. Good transportation facilities to other parts of the country.
7. Construction activity accompanied by a minimal number of vacant buildings and unoccupied houses for sale.

Demographic Characteristics

You must know the demographic profile of your potential customers to properly evaluate a community as a potential business location. To evaluate the demographic characteristics of a community you are considering, look at the following:

1. Purchasing power (degree of disposable income).
2. Residences (rented or owned; houses, condos, or apartments).
3. Places and kinds of work.
4. Means of transportation.

5. Age ranges.
6. Family status.
7. Leisure activities.

Detailed demographic information should be available from established businesses within your industry or from a trade association. In addition, the Bureau of Labor Statistics publishes the Consumer Expenditure Survey (CES), which annually samples 5,000 households to learn how families and individuals spend their money. Unlike other surveys that might ask only how much people are spending on household or home appliances, the CES questions participants about nearly every expense category, from alcoholic beverages and take-out food to pensions and life insurance. Bureau of Labor Statistics analysts then sort the information and identify consumers groups by income, household size, race, and other factors.

Once you're established in a location, you must remain aware of the community's demographic characteristics. As neighborhoods and the people within them change, businessowners must either change their locations or redefine the markets they wish to serve. The alternative is reduced revenue or even business collapse.

Tax Requirements and Financial Issues

The most obvious advantage of starting a computer-based business from home is the small initial outlay of required capital. Starting from home will free up money that would otherwise be spent on leasing an office. Ideally, converting a spare bedroom or den into an office provides the best home-based operation; however, if you don't have one available, a corner of the garage, basement, or even the kitchen will be sufficient.

You should be aware, however, that to take full advantage of the available tax breaks, you must choose a room—not just the corner of a room—and it must be used solely as an office. If it also contains a TV and stereo and is used as a den, your home-office deduction won't likely hold up under the scrutiny of an audit. By law, you deduct from your income taxes a percentage of expenses equivalent to the percentage of space your home office occupies. If one room in an eight-room house is used solely as your office, you can deduct as business expenses one-eighth of your rent (or deed/mortgage payment) plus one-eighth of your utility bills, and so on. According to recent federal tax legislation, however, no part of the base rate of the first telephone line into your residence can be deducted, even if you use the telephone for business.

Additionally, in January 1993, the Supreme Court ruled that you need to conduct the majority of your business in your home office space to qualify for a deduction. Under the ruling, unless business owners spend most of their work time within the home, and use it for visits from clients, customers, or patients, the IRS will not allow the deduction.

To qualify for deductions, the home office has to:

1. Be your principal place of business.
2. Be used as a place where clients, customers, or patients visit on a regular basis.
3. Be in connection with your trade if it is a separate place, i.e., the garage.
4. Be used exclusively for business and on a regular basis.

Zoning Restrictions

Before you begin your business in a home office, take the time to review your local zoning codes. As mentioned in detail in Chapter 1 of this book, zoning ordinances that prohibit businesses in residential areas are the most serious legal barriers facing home-based entrepreneurs; some residential zones do not permit home-based businesses at all.

In almost every city and town areas are strictly designated for either commercial, industrial or residential development. Within these broad classifications are further zoning restrictions. A commercial zone may permit one type of business to operate but not another, while a residential zone may or may not permit home-based businesses at all. If the business you choose will have clients visiting your home, this will be an important consideration.

Get to know your city; some cities are actually more favorable to home-based entrepreneurs than others. Become involved in your community and the local chamber of commerce. Also, be sure to find out whether any association or neighborhood rules would prohibit operating a home-based business in your neighborhood even when city rules permit it. (These considerations are especially important if clients or vendors will be visiting your home-based business. Will neighbors cause problems for you if there is a constant flux of visitors?)

Federal restrictions, under the Fair Labor Standards Act, and state laws in 16 states effectively ban employed home work in certain designated industries; in New York and Pennsylvania, employed home work is banned in all industries. (These restrictions do not affect businesses without employees.)

In addition, you should also contact an insurance broker to find out whether your home is adequately insured to protect you against the added liability risks of operating a business from your home.

ORGANIZING YOUR HOME OFFICE SPACE

Naturally, you'll want to keep overhead as low as possible when starting out, because of the time necessary to break even. Don't invest too much in fancy office fixtures and decor in the beginning, but do plan for expansion later on—if needed—as business volume, staffing, or image requirements warrant.

In addition to your home office, you might consider renting a post office box. You can rent one monthly from either the local post office or a private mailbox rental facility. Renting from a private mailbox rental facility allows you to affix a suite number to your post office box, and give the impression that you are operating from a commercial office location. By doing this, you'll present a professional image to the companies with whom you do business and the people buying your product. It will also aid you in attaining a merchant's account from a bank. Some banks will not allow you to open a business account if they know you work from your home (though your business license address may suffice for them).

Your home-based business should be:

- Functional.
- Efficient.
- Free from distractions.
- Well organized.
- Able to accommodate client visitors when necessary.
- Designed to showplace your work (if that is part of your business).

These are important considerations. Most of the home-based entrepreneurs we've interviewed indicated they began working from home to:

- Save money.
- Be with their family.
- Save on child care.
- Break free of commuting (live anywhere they chose).

- Take advantage of the fact that they didn't need a large office, because their business required travel/working at clients' locations.

Don't let the benefits of having a home-based business blind you to the needs of setting up your business office to be an effective workplace. Spending more time with your family and saving on child care dollars are enormous benefits for the home-based entrepreneur, especially since you will need to put in such long hours; but if you are continually distracted, you will not be able to produce effectively. Saving money is also a great home-based benefit; but don't turn around and pour that same money into expensive furniture, paintings, and "extras" until your business earnings justify such expenditures.

In planning your office space, allocate enough production workspace for a computer terminal, a typewriter (if needed for envelopes, forms, or other items), and a conventional desk or worktable. One of your main concerns is to arrange your central processing unit (CPU), monitor, keyboard, and printer so you can enter and print out with minimal effort. Remember, too, that disks must be stored in nonmagnetic surroundings. Plan for special shelving or drawers for data processing materials. Computer documentation should be kept in a drawer or on a shelf of its own.

File and storage space is important, regardless of the type of business you begin. Accurate recordkeeping is crucial to any business, particularly because you'll need to track receivables in a timely manner. Paper, stationery, labels, invoices, resource materials, and so on all need to be kept handy for efficient use.

One entrepreneur we spoke with purchased a portable "office" on wheels that holds her CPU, monitor, keyboard, and printer on a 4' high × 2' wide × 2' long desk/caddie. Paper, stationery, and other supplies are kept on desktop files in a back bedroom. An artist's caddie (with four drawers; also on wheels) houses her pens, markers, paper clips, stapler, tape, floppy disks, and paperwork currently in use. Research and other resource materials are on bookshelves in her bedroom. This setup works well for an entrepreneur who does not have a single room to dedicate to an office and wants the flexibility to work on the living room couch one day, in the dining room the next, or in the bedroom the next—depending, for example, on whether the kids are home or with their grandparents for the day, or whether she is up working late when others are using various rooms in the house.

The square footage required by a home-based business depends on what will take place there on a daily basis. Business owners who currently work from home usually utilize a floor area of 250 square feet to 500 square feet. Available space is usually subdivided into work space and storage space. Depending on the original floor plan and individual design, storage space can take up about 25% of the total.

The less storage space you have, the more room you have to conduct your business. However, storage space is an important part of the floor plan for a home-based business, especially if you are product-oriented. You must allow for shipping and receiving and related chores, take care of paperwork, and store extra supplies and inventory.

If clients will ever need to come by your home for business conferences or deliveries, be sure you have thought this possibility through in designing your office setup. Generally, if there is not easy, direct access to your "office," meet with your clients in the living room, and keep the meeting professional but comfortable. Remove items from your coffee table so there is work space, if needed. Most important, have everything you need for the meeting ready ahead of time in the room where you will work with the client.

If you have converted a spare bedroom or den into your office—and do not need to escort your clients down two hallways and past the kids' bedrooms to get there—this location can work well for client meetings. Again, pay attention to design. If you have several tall, metal filing cabinets, for example, you may want to put them in the closet of the room, so that your office does not look small or cluttered. Be sure there are chairs for your visitors, and a table of some sort on which to work with them. Even if you have severe space limitations, you can plan ahead to maximize the space you have. For example, buying a desk with a left- or right-hand return that is kept clear, and setting the desk at an angle that allows a visitor chair (or chairs) alongside this space, can provide all the "table" you need when meeting with clients.

Furniture

There is only one rule when it comes to choosing furniture for a home office: *If it works, use it.* This is similar to the reasoning that you don't have to fix or replace something that isn't broken. Why spend a lot of money on a "high-tech European-designed ergonomic modular computer station" when a simple pine desk and chair will suffice?

Most entrepreneurs already have the furniture needed to set up an office: a desk (possibly with return or credenza), a chair, one or more filing cabinets, some bookshelves, and perhaps some kind of additional table or countertop. Great buys on these basics can be found at furniture and office warehouses, flea markets, auctions, estate sales, and second-hand stores, if you invest some time looking for what you need. Think about the kind of business you want to start:

- Will clients be visiting you? If so, you will have to design your office appropriately, providing a comfortable place (perhaps a sofa and coffee table) where you can meet to talk business.
- Will you spend most of your time at the desk? Your business relies on computers, so chances are that you will. Put most of your effort into making your desk area functional and organized.
- Do you plan to use your garage to conduct business?
- How much money can you afford to spend on office furnishings?
- Will you be accommodating employees or assistants as well?
- Are you going to house a lot of supplies or inventory?

Conserve your start-up capital and buy only what you absolutely need; when your business volume tells you expansion is necessary, by all means purchase the required furniture instead of trying to operate with what you have. Don't try to avoid purchases if your business volume will suffer because of it.

Lighting

The necessary lighting for a home office depends on the amount of square footage you will use, the way you design your work area, the age of your home, the amount of available natural light, and the brightness you desire. Among the types of lighting available to you are fluorescent, incandescent, and neon. Each has its own distinct qualities, and each is more effective than the other two for certain types of activities. You will do a lot of paperwork and sit in front of a computer most of the time. Incandescent light is probably your best choice because it puts less strain on your eyes. Most industrial plants, large offices, garages, and other work facilities use fluorescent light because it is more cost-efficient, energy-efficient, and practical than incandescent light, which is not to say it is better for the people working under it.

As with every other facet of the home working environment, the best lighting matches maximum usefulness and minimum cost. Your layout will determine what kind of lamps you should use. For heavy office work—the kind that will keep you at your desk for hours on end—small desk lamps can add that perfect degree of extra light without taking much space. Adjustable clamp-on lights have the same space-saving advantages, and allow the addition of light exactly where it is needed. Track lighting, which you install along the ceiling or the walls of your work area, can also be used to improve light conditions.

Proper lighting, especially for heavy computer use, is a must in order to reduce eyestrain and allow you to work productively. This concern may seem trite, but it is one of the most overlooked aspects of the home-based workplace. Spending hours at a desk reading or doing computer work in a poorly lit office is like skiing on a bright clear day without sunglasses—it's something you definitely want to avoid. For a nominal investment, you can give yourself the lighting you need for your kind of work.

Needless to say, there are probably as many ways to design home offices as there are home-based businesses to occupy them.

MOVING INTO OFFICE SPACE

This book focuses on the home-based entrepreneur, but some basic information on selecting office space and understanding leasing arrangements is in order, should your business require you to move from home.

The main reasons why a home-based entrepreneur might move his or her business from home include:

- More space is needed for equipment (expansion).
- The present number of employees can no longer work comfortably in the home-based operation.
- The separation is needed to continue to grow the business.

The last consideration is important. If you find that you cannot dedicate yourself to your business as you should at home, you may need to move to an office just to discipline yourself to put in enough hours and remove yourself from nonbusiness distractions. Know yourself and your work habits well, and don't kid yourself about your ability to commit to your company while at home. Any money that could be saved on an office will be lost from unproductive work habits that develop when you are not able to keep home distractions at bay.

Business Parks and Office Buildings

Individual situations vary, but, in most cases, a move to a commercial office needn't be overly cost-intensive. Unless the number of your employees has grown significantly, your commercial office won't likely need to be larger than 300 to 600 square feet. Rents will range from 90 cents to $1.50 per square foot for the type of secondary commercial or industrial-park location we suggest. If you plan on locating in a high-rent commercial district, plan on paying twice these figures. Also remember that costs for office space vary significantly by city and state.

Office space is commonly leased out on a triple-net basis with the tenants sharing in the maintenance costs of the building. Many times, this maintenance cost will include service to your own office as well as security.

Leasing Property

With office-oriented or unproven businesses, it is safer to arrange for a month-to-month rental at the beginning—though these are often hard to find. Because you began from home, you should already have a good idea of the profits and overhead expenses that your business will generate. However, month-to-month arrangements may still be a positive choice—when you can find them—because if your company once again outgrows its current space, you won't be faced with the problem of subletting your leased office when you move to larger quarters. For more information about leasing, consult *The Entrepreneur Magazine Small Business Advisor* (John Wiley & Sons, 1995).

INSURANCE: MANAGING RISK

Knowing what kind of insurance to carry, and how much, is an important aspect of good risk management. Be sure to ask your homeowner's or renter's insurance agent what specifically is covered in your current policy: Are you covered item-by-item, or simply up to a certain amount of money? Is there a special rate for home-based businesses? Many standard homeowner's insurance policies don't cover personal computers used for business purposes, so it is important to check on your specific coverage. If you do not currently carry insurance, you need to start *now*.

When deciding on insurance coverage, consider:

1. The size of the potential loss.
2. The probability of the loss.
3. The resources available to meet the loss if it should occur.

No business can possibly eliminate or transfer all of the risks of loss; you must assume some of them. How do you decide whether to assume a particular risk or transfer it to an insurance company? Figure the maximum potential loss that might result. If the loss would force your company into bankruptcy or cause serious financial damage, don't assume the risk.

Contrary to popular opinion, a high probability of loss doesn't mean the risk should be insured. In fact, the greater the probability of loss, the less appropriate is the purchase of insurance to cover the risk.

In the first place, losses that occur with relative frequency are predictable and, typically, small. They can be assumed by the business without too much financial difficulty. Often, they are budgeted as part of the normal costs of doing business and figured into the prices charged to customers. A common example is bad-debt loss. Where probability of loss is high, a more effective method of controlling the loss is to adopt appropriate precautionary measures.

The key to purchasing insurance (and all risk management) is: Do not risk more than you can afford to lose.

Insurance Planning

Begin with a consideration of the insurable risks faced by your home-based business. In general, the following risks can be covered by insurance:

- Loss or damage of property, including merchandise, supplies, fixtures, and building.
- Loss of income resulting from an interruption of business caused by damage to the firm's operating assets.
- Personal injury to employees and/or the general public.
- Loss to the business caused by the death or disability of key employees or the owner.

A standard fire insurance policy pays the policyholder only for losses directly due to fire. Other indirect losses, known as consequential losses, may be even more important to your company's welfare. You can protect yourself against these losses by obtaining business interruption insurance. Consequential losses include:

- Loss of use of a facility.
- Continuing expenses after a fire—salaries, inventory items paid in advance, interest obligations, and so on.
- Extra expenses of obtaining temporary quarters.

- If you are a landlord (i.e., a duplex or other rental complex owner), loss of rental income on buildings damaged or destroyed by fire.

The basic business package, many experts agree, consists of four fundamental coverages: (1) general liability, (2) workers' compensation, (3) auto, and (4) property/casualty, plus an added layer of protection over those, often called an umbrella policy.

Under common law, as well as workers' compensation laws, you as an employer are liable for injury to employees at work, if the injury is caused by your failure to: provide safe equipment and working conditions, hire competent fellow employees, or warn employees of an existing danger. In every state, an employer must carry insurance against potential workers' compensation claims. However, employee coverage and the extent of the employer's liability vary from state to state.

Overall, commercial general liability coverage insures a business against accidents and injury that might happen on its premises, as well as exposures related to its products. In some cases, this liability may even extend to trespassers. As a business owner, you may also be liable for bodily injuries to customers, pedestrians, delivery people, and other outsiders—even in cases where you have exercised "reasonable care."

The real trick with general liability is determining how much coverage you need. There are two extremes a business may consider. The first is to buy little or no insurance, to avoid being a target of lawsuits. The sounder approach, however, is to figure out how much you can be sued for and buy the appropriate coverage.

Most businesses own one or more cars and trucks, which are a serious source of liability. Even if no vehicles are owned, under the "doctrine of agency," a business can be liable for injuries and property damage caused by employees operating their own or someone else's vehicle while on company business. This can be especially important if you offer pickup and/or delivery services with your business.

The company may have some coverage under the employee's own liability policy, but the limits might be grossly inadequate. Where it is customary or convenient for employees to operate their own vehicles while on company business, you should acquire nonownership liability insurance.

The best form of liability insurance for the small business consists of a comprehensive general liability policy combined with a comprehensive auto liability policy and a standard workers' compensation policy—especially after you begin using outside employees.

Types of Coverage

You can purchase insurance to cover almost any risk. Following are the types of insurance most commonly used by business owners, and the risk(s) that each protects against:

- Fire and general property insurance: fire losses, vandalism, hail, and wind damage.
- Plate-glass insurance: window breakage.
- Consequential loss insurance: loss of earnings or extra expenses when business is suspended because of fire or other catastrophe.
- Burglary insurance: forced entry and theft of merchandise and/or cash.
- Fidelity bonding: theft by an employee.
- Fraud insurance: counterfeit money, bad checks, and larceny.
- Public liability insurance: injury to the public, such as when a customer or pedestrian falls on the property.
- Product liability insurance: injury to customers arising from the use of goods purchased from or through the company.
- Workers' compensation insurance: injury to employees at work.
- Life insurance: the life of the owner(s) or key employee(s).
- Business interruption insurance: periods when no work or production is possible.
- Malpractice insurance: clients' claims that they have suffered damages as a result of services you perform.
- Errors and omissions insurance: customers' claims that they have suffered injury or loss because of errors you made, or things you should have done but failed to do.

Insurance for Home Computer Owners

The surge in personal computer ownership has sparked a number of spin-off business opportunities. The insurance industry, or at least one company within it, has found just such an opportunity. As mentioned earlier, many standard homeowner's insurance policies don't cover personal computers used for business purposes. Owners of such systems are leaving expensive equipment unprotected from damage caused by fire, theft, vandalism, or natural disaster, not to mention auto accidents during transport or power surges that wipe out memory. Safeware, The Insurance Agency has filled this gap with its comprehensive Safeware policy.

The policy, which protects against these mishaps, is relatively low-priced and simple to set up. Annual premiums range from $39 to $149, depending on the computer's replacement cost (at the high end are systems valued at over $17,000). Because the policy covers the total dollar value of the entire system, instead of the item-by-item valuation common to most floaters, policyholders can change hardware and software without changing their insurance coverage, unless the new gear is worth more or less than the old. A $50 deductible is standard on all policies.

For more information, contact Safeware, The Insurance Agency at the address listed in the Appendix.

PERSONNEL ISSUES

As your business grows, personnel will likely be your most expensive—and necessary—investment. Knowing when to get help, and what type of help you need at different stages, is crucial to keeping your costs in line while growing your company.

Your start as a one-person operation will likely translate into a full-time, seven-day-a-week endeavor—this is the way most entrepreneurs begin. When you're not marketing your business, you're serving clients; and when you're not working for clients, you must be marketing. If you know now that marketing your business will be difficult for you, then your time to hire will come sooner than for others who can get out there and sell their services firsthand.

Unless you started your business to *allow* you to work alone forever (as a freelance writer, graphic designer, or some other solo occupation), you will eventually need to hire others in order to expand your services and accommodate growing client needs. Always a challenge for entrepreneurs, bringing in other people is especially hard when a business is home-based. You worry about the infringement on your personal living space; you worry that employees will not take your business seriously; you worry that qualified workers will prefer a corporate setting to a desk in your home.

The key to hiring in any situation is to be professional, offer a professional workplace, and have a clear idea of what you want your employees to accomplish. If you wish to learn more about hiring personnel and personnel management, consult *The Entrepreneur Magazine Small Business Advisor.*

Part-Timers and Temporary Help

When you first need to hire additional help, consider using temporary help services on a day-to-day basis. Many temporary agencies handle specialized professions—accounting, graphic design, editing, or programming. With this approach, you can take on an especially large job or number of jobs during a busy period, and still find qualified help immediately. Some temporary help agencies, however, will send workers only to commercial locations, not to home offices. Call around for referrals.

You can usually find temporary agencies under the Yellow Pages headings of "Employment—Temporary," or "Employment—Contractors." Temporary employees from these agencies are generally quoted at an hourly charge that is higher than the amount you pay a salaried employee, because included in the charge by the service are payroll taxes, Social Security, workers' compensation, and the profit margin of the temporary help firm. Expect to pay a minimum of about $8 per hour, and as much as $17 or more per hour, for a typical computer-literate worker. If you need highly specialized skills, the rate may be even more, depending on your area.

To get what you need without paying for what you don't need, be *very* specific about the skills you require from a temporary employee. Make sure the agency knows what the job requirements are, what talents you're looking for, and the length of time required for the job. Provide a detailed description of the job(s), so that the agency can get the most qualified person at the lowest possible cost. Don't ask for someone with higher qualifications than those you actually need; you will only be wasting money. By the same token, if you want a highly skilled graphic designer who will also answer the phone and schedule new job orders, say so. This helps the agency look for a graphic designer with previous office experience or other well-rounded skills. If, on the other hand, you ask for a receptionist with basic typing skills, don't expect someone who can use your Macintosh to draft sales letters.

Temporary help is also a good idea if you have a rush order, if your workload increases suddenly but will drop in a few weeks, if an already hired employee is sick or on vacation, or if you need extra help during a seasonal period. Though their hourly cost can be high, "temps" can be more cost-effective than hiring another permanent employee or placing too heavy a workload on your current employees.

Weigh the pros and cons of adding temporary help to current staffing. Can the work get done fast enough with the current staff? Is it financially beneficial to offer overtime pay to present employees? Under the Federal Labor Standards Act, hourly employees must be paid one and one-half times their basic pay for any hours in excess of 40 hours in one week, and, in some cases, overtime pay will be a worse financial drain than hiring temporary help. (Salaried and commissioned employees are not subject to this stipulation, but if you want them to work overtime, there should be some incentive.)

Another good way to begin hiring is with part-time help. You then have a chance to see how much of your work you can transfer without losing equal time to managing and training. Part-time help is also more cost-effective in the beginning than hiring a full-time worker, especially because part-time employees are not entitled to benefits by law.

Local colleges may be a good source for part-time employees, via the college newspaper or college employment service. Many college students are familiar with computers and may be looking for extra money to help with their school expenses. If you need specialized skills, try calling the college department that directly covers your area of need (i.e., marketing, art, computer science) and ask the receptionist if the job can be posted on the department bulletin board. You may even find they have a good internship program.

What the market in your area will bear will affect what you pay. If you insist on quality work and would like to induce employee loyalty, plan on paying at least $5 to $6 per hour in most areas. The fact that the student's classes may come at odd hours is actually a plus for you. You may be able to work out a flexible schedule that's mutually convenient, allowing you to supervise the student's work and give training, and offering the added incentive of your willingness to work around the student's school schedule.

Independent Contractors

As an alternative to temporary help, consider subcontracting some of your work to independent contractors. Independent contractors can be the perfect solution to a common small business dilemma: needing extra help often enough that a steady stream of temporary employees (each needing to be briefed on your business practices, policies, and procedures) becomes disruptive to business, but not so often that you're willing to take on the extra burden (and expense) of hiring and training a full- or part-time employee. Subcontracting projects to independent contractors is beneficial to all involved, in the right situations. You get almost all of the benefits of having an employee, but don't incur the tax-related expenses of employing. Independent contractors reap the fruits of your marketing efforts and obtain work without having to market to various clients on their own.

As you would in hiring a full- or part-time employee, exercise your best business judgment in deciding to whom you will subcontract. Make sure that the contractor will adhere to your high standards of quality and efficiency. Be careful to keep the business relationship one of vendor–client; if an independent contractor can be construed as an employee, *you* will be penalized.

5

LEGAL ISSUES

CHOOSING THE LEGAL FORM FOR YOUR BUSINESS

After deciding to start a business—home-based or otherwise—the first thing you have to consider is the legal form under which it will operate: (1) sole proprietorship; (2) general partnership; (3) limited partnership; or (4) corporation. Though you may be the sole employee of your home-based business, and thus the visible owner/operator, if you have asked others to be involved as "partners" in financing your venture, their investment can change the legal operating form of your company. You may also choose to have your home-based business operate as a corporation.

Sole Proprietorship

"Sole" means only one owner—not even silent partners are allowed. A sole proprietorship provides the easiest method of starting a business. No legal papers are required except a business license and a fictitious-name filing (Doing Business As, or DBA) with the county clerk. No separate income tax returns are necessary (they are with other forms of business). All of your income and expenses are reported on Schedule C of IRS Form 1040. Federal FICA taxes for the owner are less than in other forms of business.

A sole proprietorship has one important disadvantage. Creditors of your business can go after you personally and attach your personal property, bank account, and other resources. You can be harassed for years after you abandon a business, and your personal credit can be ruined.

General Partnership

A partnership of two (or more) people is even more dangerous than a sole proprietorship because each partner is liable for the other's actions. In any legal or creditor action, each partner will be sued personally, and the property, bank accounts, and so on, of each will be attached. If one partner skips town, the other is left holding the bag. Also, when an individual contributes assets to a partnership, he or she retains no claim to those specific properties but merely acquires an equity in all assets of the firm. The partner with the most to lose personally usually gets hit the hardest.

A partnership is like a professional marriage of sorts. Very few partnerships survive without intense conflict, which often causes the business to collapse.

A lawyer's charge for preparing a partnership contract is about the same as for a corporation. Anyone who forms a partnership on a handshake and verbal agreement, without a formal contract, is very unwise. A partnership must secure a Federal Employee Identification number from the IRS, using Form SS-4. It must then file Form 1065 each year as its tax return. Generally, IRS regulations require that a partnership use a calendar year-end.

Each partner reports his or her share of partnership profits or losses on an individual tax return and pays the tax on those profits. The partnership itself does not pay any taxes with its tax return.

Choosing a partner is one of the most important steps you'll take in your venture, so proceed with caution. To ensure a picture-perfect relationship, consider these factors:

- *Divvying up.* Don't assume it's clear who will do what; clearly divide your responsibilities to prevent any misunderstandings.
- *Buyer's remorse.* In case one partner decides to sell out later on, talk about a buy–sell agreement early.
- *Life insurance.* If you or your partner die, a "key person" insurance policy ensures that the surviving partner is able to buy the deceased partner's share from his or her heirs.

- *Consulting outsiders.* Just because you've split responsibilities doesn't mean you've covered all the bases. Make sure to consult an attorney, accountant, or other business expert for matters outside your expertise.

Limited Partnership

In many ways, a limited partnership is like a corporation. The investors become limited partners and are personally liable for the amount of their investment. However, that's all they can lose. The general partner, usually the operator of the business, can be either a sole proprietor or a corporation. There is also the classic "silent partner" situation where one or more partners (limited) put up money and the other partner(s) (general) runs the business. A limited partnership in this case serves to protect the assets of wealthier silent partners and acts as a conduit to pass through current operating profits or losses to them as well as to preserve the special tax character of certain items.

Limited partnerships are commonly used for real-estate syndications. Legal costs of forming a limited partnership can be even higher than for a corporation because in some states the former is governed by securities laws. Another aspect of limited partnerships is that, in some lines of business, the limited partner (also called the passive investor) may be subject to special tax liabilities that can, in certain cases, offset tax-shelter advantages. The IRS tends to look at these facts on a case-by-case basis.

The Tax Reform Act of 1986 limits the amount of losses a limited partner can deduct on his or her personal tax return. If your partnership business is expected to generate tax losses in its early years, you should consult your accountant to determine how and when those losses will benefit you.

Corporation

The most realistic way to start a business is under a corporate structure, because the corporation exists as a separate entity apart from you. It alone is legally responsible for its actions and debts. You are personally protected in most situations, because you will be just an employee of the corporation, even though you may own all or most of the stock. You must operate your corporation in a correct legal and financial manner, or you may lose this protection from its liabilities.

Shareholders forming a corporation can divide ownership into shares, responsibilities can be defined in the corporate minutes, and a shareholder who wants to leave can be accommodated without much legal hassle or dissolution of the business. Stock can be used as collateral; death of one shareholder doesn't stop the business (in a partnership, it sometimes does). And you can enjoy many executive privileges that are difficult to justify in a sole proprietorship or partnership.

Until your corporation has operated successfully for many years, you will most likely still have to sign as being personally liable for any corporate loans made by banks or other financial institutions.

It is advisable to use a shareholders' agreement that provides for the purchase of a deceased shareholder's shares by the supervising shareholders. That agreement will usually provide for a method to determine the price of a selling shareholder's shares, if the remaining shareholders wish to purchase them, or it might grant the other shareholders the right of first refusal.

The only disadvantage is possible double taxation: the corporation must pay taxes on its net income, and you must also pay taxes on any dividends you may receive from the corporation. For fiscal years beginning January 1, 1993, corporate tax rates are as follows:

- 15% on the first $50,000 of income.
- 25% on the next $25,000.
- 34% on all taxable income over $75,000 but less than $10 million.

If a corporation has taxable income over $10 million, it pays a flat 35% tax.

Business owners often increase their own salaries in order to reduce or wipe out corporate profits and thereby lower the possibility of having those profits taxed twice (once to the corporation and again to the shareholders upon receipt of dividends from the corporation).

Subchapter S Corporations

The disadvantage of possible double federal taxation is completely negated by filing a Subchapter S election with the IRS. (Many states do not recognize a Subchapter S election for state tax purposes and will tax the corporation as a regular corporation.) Qualifications for electing Subchapter S were changed when the Subchapter S Revisions Act of 1982 liberalized many of the old rules and gave new flexibility to these corporations, now popular with small and medium-size businesses. Subchapter S allows profits or losses to travel directly through the corporation to you and other shareholders. If you earn other income during the first year and the corporation has a loss, you can deduct against the other income, possibly wiping out your tax liability completely—subject to the limitations of the Tax Reform Act of 1986.

Subchapter S corporations elect not to be taxed as corporations; instead, the shareholders of a Subchapter S corporation include their proportionate shares of the corporate profits and losses in their individual gross incomes. Subchapter S corporations are excellent devices to allow small businesses to avoid double taxation. If your company produces a substantial profit, forming a Subchapter S corporation would be wise: the profits will be added to your personal income and taxed at an individual rate, which may be lower than the regular corporate rate on that income.

To qualify under Subchapter S, the corporation must be a domestic corporation, must not be a member of an affiliated group, and must not have more than 35 shareholders—all of whom are either individuals or estates. You must not have a nonresident alien as a shareholder, you can have only one class of outstanding stock, and, under the new rules, you are allowed an unlimited amount of passive income from rents, royalties, and interest. A passive activity is one in which a taxpayer does not materially participate. Material participation requires involvement in operations on a regular, continuous, and substantial basis.

Under the Tax Reform Act of 1986, losses and credits from a "passive" business activity will be deductible only against passive income. Passive losses and credits will not be usable against nonpassive income, which includes a compensation and portfolio income; however, rental losses and credits can be used against up to $25,000 of nonpassive income.

Therefore, if a shareholder of a Subchapter S corporation does not actively participate in the operation of the business, it is considered a passive activity. That means if the Subchapter S corporation produces a loss during the year, that shareholder's deduction for his or her portion of the loss will be cut back dramatically. However, if income is accrued from the Subchapter S corporation, it can be offset by losses and credits from other passive activities.

For more information on the rules that apply to a Subchapter S corporation, call your local IRS office.

Forming a Corporation

You must incorporate in the state in which you plan to do business. If you locate in any state other than the one in which you incorporate, that state requires you to file corporate papers—as a foreign corporation. The fees are even higher than for a domestic corporation.

Lawyers charge from $350 to $2,000 to file corporate papers; $700 is the average fee. Unless you have more than 10 stockholders or a very complicated partner arrangement, you don't need a lawyer. Incorporation fees are the easiest money an attorney makes. The forms required are no harder to complete than those required for the average credit application.

Limited Liability Corporation (LLC)

A new business form called the limited liability company (LLC) has sprung up in 38 states. The LLC arose from the desire of business owners to adopt a business structure permitting them to operate like a traditional partnership. This distributes the income and income tax to the partners (reported on their individual income tax returns), but also protects them from personal liability for the business's debts, as with the corporate business form. In the case of the entrepreneur, unless a separate corporation is established, the owner and partners (if any) assume complete liability for all debts of the business. Under the LLC concept, on the other hand, an individual is not responsible for the firm's debt.

The LLC offers a number of advantages over S corporations. For example, S corporations can issue only one class of company stock; LLCs can offer several different classes with different rights. In addition, S corporations are limited to a maximum of 35 individual shareholders (who must be U.S. residents); an unlimited number of individuals, corporations, and partnerships may participate in an LLC.

The LLC also carries significant tax advantages over the limited partnership. For instance, unless the partner in a limited partnership assumes an active role, his or her losses are considered "passive" losses and therefore ineligible for use as tax deductions against active income. But if the partner does take an active role in the firm's management, he or she becomes liable for the firm's debt. It's a catch-22 situation. The owners of an LLC, on the other hand, do not assume liability for the business's debt, and any losses can be used as tax deductions against active income.

In exchange for these two considerable benefits, however, the owners of LLCs must meet the "transferability restriction test," which means the ownership interests in the LLC must not be transferable without some restrictions. This feature makes the LLC structure unworkable for major corporations. For corporations to attract large sums of capital, their corporate stock must be easily transferable in the stock exchanges. However, this restriction should not prove to be detrimental to the typical entrepreneurial business in which ownership transfers take place relatively infrequently.

A number of quirks in current state LLC legislation require tricky maneuvering and plenty of advance planning. For example, LLC legislation in Colorado and Wyoming does not allow for continuity of the business. In those states, the business is dissolved upon the death, retirement, resignation, or expulsion of an owner. Although the same is true for both individual proprietorships and partnerships, you must still plan accordingly.

In Florida, the state's 5.5% corporate tax also applies to LLCs. With shortfalls in state tax revenues and strained state budgets, other states may look to LLCs for additional tax revenues, even though similar businesses, such as S corporations, are typically exempt from state and federal income taxes.

Because the LLC is a relatively new legal form for businesses, federal and state governments are still looking at ways to tighten the regulations surrounding it. Most of the impetus to tighten regulations governing LLCs comes from a concern that some investment promoters are using this legal form to evade securities laws. Although most LLCs are legitimate, the Securities and Exchange Commission (SEC) is moving quickly to tighten control of those firms engaged in irregular activity.

If this form of business sounds like it would fit your needs, explore new and pending legislation concerning LLCs in your area.

FICTITIOUS NAME (D.B.A.)

Sole proprietorships and partnerships have the option of choosing distinctive names for their businesses. If you want to operate your business under a name different from your personal name (e.g., Mary Worth doing business as "Information On-Line, Inc."), you may be required by the county, city, or state to register your fictitious name.

In many states, you need only go to the county offices and pay a registration fee to the county clerk. Other states require placing a fictitious-name ad in a local newspaper. Generally, the newspaper that prints the legal notice for your business name will, for a small fee, file the necessary papers with the county.

The cost of filing a fictitious-name notice ranges from $10 to $100. The easiest way to determine the procedure for your area is to call your bank and ask whether it requires a fictitious-name registry or certificate in order to open a business account. If so, inquire where you should go to obtain one.

Fictitious-name filings do not apply to corporations in most states, unless the corporation is doing business under a name other than its own. Documents of incorporation have the same effect for corporate businesses as fictitious-name filings have for sole proprietorships and partnerships.

LICENSES AND PERMITS

Most cities and counties require business operators to obtain various licenses or permits, to show compliance with local regulations. Home-based businesses may require additional considerations, depending on the city or county ordinances. If the business you choose will have clients visiting your home, this may greatly impact the permits needed for your home-based business.

As mentioned in Chapter 1, some cities are actually more favorable to home-based entrepreneurs than others are. However, even if you are lucky enough to be located in a city that is favorable to home-based ventures, you still should be aware of all potential licensing and permit requirements of your area. Many home-based entrepreneurs do not plan to grow, expand, and/or modify their business—but grow they do. Becoming knowledgeable about potential requirements prepares you for the business growth you may end up relishing.

Business License

City business-license departments are operated as tax-collecting bureaus and do not perform any public service. You simply pay a fee to operate your business in that city. In addition to the license fee, some cities receive a percentage of your gross sales.

Your application for a license will probably be processed through the planning or zoning department, which will check to make sure that the zone covering your property allows the proposed use and that there are enough parking places to meet the code, if clients will be visiting your establishment. Home-based businesses may have to meet special requirements, which will be explained to you at the time of filing.

You may not be allowed to operate your home-based business in an area zoned solely as residential, unless you first have a variance or conditional-use permit (explained in "Zoning Ordinances" below).

County Permits

For all commercial enterprises located outside city limits, county governments generally require the same types of permits and licenses that cities require. Educate yourself about county ordinances if your home is located in an unincorporated area outside a city's or town's jurisdiction. In most cases, this should not pose any problems to your home-based business; county regulations often are less strict than those of adjoining cities.

State Licenses

Many states require a license or occupational permit for persons engaged in certain occupations. Often, these persons must pass state examinations before they can conduct business. Your state government can provide a complete list of occupations that require licensing in your state; check this list to see if your intended business appears on it.

Federal Licenses

A few businesses and businesspeople require federal licensing, including common carriers, radio and television stations, and investment advisory services. The Federal Trade Commission can tell you if your business will require a federal license.

Zoning Ordinances

If you want to run your computer-based business from home—and do it legitimately—you will have to find out what the zoning ordinances are for your area. The first rule is: Don't go to the zoning officer for advice. Go to the town/city clerk's office and ask for a copy of any ordinances concerning home-based business. Then find out, if you don't already know, exactly how your residence is zoned.

Once you find out your zoning status, you can get a good idea of whether your planned business is permitted or prohibited. Whatever your conclusion, consult an attorney, who will be better able than you to interpret the fine points of the ordinance. There is often a substantial difference between what an ordinance says and the way it is enforced.

If zoning regulations do not allow operation of the type of business you wish to open, you may file for a zoning variance, a conditional-use permit, or a zone change. A variance or conditional-use permit grants you the privilege (conditionally) of operating a business on land not zoned for that purpose. The filing fee may be as high as $1,200, and it may take 90 days or more before you get a decision. A zone change, on the other hand, amounts to a permanent change in the way a particular area is zoned, and therefore in the way it will be used long into the future. It involves a lengthy procedure—six months or more, in many cases—of filing a petition with the city planning commission, issuing notice, presenting your case at public hearings, and finally getting the city council or other governing body to make a decision.

If your request for a zoning variance or change is approved, many restrictions still apply. In addition to meeting local building codes, you will probably be required to observe minimum setbacks at the front, side, and rear of your home; maximum floor space in relation to land area; maximum heights; minimum provisions for parking; and other factors. We cannot expand on this subject, because each government entity has its own specific policies, but be aware that zoning is a subject to pursue thoroughly.

Essentially, zoning is a way of ensuring that the community's land uses are properly located in relation to each other, that adequate space is available for each type of development, that the density of development in each area is in proper proportion to the development of such facilities as streets, schools, recreational areas, parking, and utility systems, and that the development is sufficiently open to permit light, air, and privacy for persons living and working within the area.

Other Regulations

In addition to licenses and permits, other regulations may apply to your business. Federal and state laws designed to encourage competition prohibit: practices such as contracts, combinations, and conspiracies in restraint of trade; discrimination in price between different purchasers of commodities similar in grade and quality, with the intent of injuring competition; "unfair methods of competition" and "unfair or deceptive practices."

Deceptive practices refers to false advertising, misrepresentation, simulation of competitive products, and bad-mouthing of competitors. Even on violations by a manufacturer or distributor, a retailer may be considered equally guilty if he or she knowingly accepts an illegal concession offered by the vendor.

Any firm conducting business across state lines is subject to federal regulations—usually enforced by the Federal Trade Commission (FTC). Any business that advertises in more than one state is subject to FTC regulations. Even the smallest mail-order business comes under FTC jurisdiction.

A fairly common statute forbids the sale of any article at less than the seller's cost if the intent is to injure competitors. Other laws deal with "bait-and-switch" selling, withholding appropriate refunds on deposits made by customers, misrepresenting warranties and guarantees, and quality requirements for certain products.

The Fair Labor Standards Act is the key federal legislation regarding employees; individual states may have differing or additional legislation. Because of the complexities of these regulations and the penalties imposed for violations, it is essential that you consult a lawyer if your business may be subject to them.

COPYRIGHT

Freelance writers and graphic designers, pay close attention here. If your idea is an original work of authorship, especially in written form, you may be able to obtain protection from a U.S. copyright. You can copyright cartoon characters, sculptures, paintings, plays, maps, songs, scripts, photos, books, and poems, to name a few properties. As long as the material has been fixed in some kind of tangible form, even if it's just a handwritten or typed manuscript, you can obtain this kind of protection.

All you need to do is include a copyright notice on the material. Three elements make up the copyright notice: (1) the word "copyright", the copyright symbol ©, or the abbreviation "copr."; (2) the name of the owner of the copyright; and (3) the year of first publication. Here is an example of a typical copyright:

Copyright by John Doe, 1994.

There are five classes of copyrights:

1. *Class TX: Nondramatic Literary Work.* This broad category includes all types of published and unpublished works written in words or other verbal or numeric symbols. Some of the types of works included in this class are: fiction, nonfiction, poetry, advertising copy, periodicals, textbooks, and reference works.
2. *Class PA: Works of the Performing Arts.* This covers published and unpublished works created for the purpose of being "performed" before an audience, whether this performance is live or "by means of any device or process." Included in this category are dramatic works, musical works, choreographic works, motion pictures, and audiovisual works.

3. *Class SR: Sound Recordings.* This category can apply in two instances: (1) where the claimant seeks to copyright a sound recording alone and (2) where the claimant seeks to copyright a sound recording in addition to the musical, dramatic, or literary work embodied in the sound recording. This does not apply to the audio portion of a motion picture or other audiovisual work.

4. *Class VA: Works of the Visual Arts.* Pictorial, graphic, and sculptural works are protected under this category. Two-dimensional and three-dimensional works such as models, globes, and works of fine art are included, in addition to photography, technical drawings, maps, and advertisements.

5. *Class RE: Renewal Registration.* This category covers renewal of registration for works originally copyrighted before January 1, 1978, extending the copyright protection for an additional 47 years. All classes of copyrights are eligible for renewal under this class.

Should an article you submit for publication be purchased by a magazine, newspaper, or other publication, be sure to inquire as to what rights they are buying to your work. Some publishers buy all rights, others buy first-time rights or first North American serial rights (so they have the first right to publish your work in the United States, Canada, and Mexico). There are publications that will buy only one-time rights or simultaneous publication rights. Generally, you will be paid more for your work when more rights are purchased.

A copyright is good for your lifetime plus 50 years, so that your family or heirs may benefit from your work. It is advisable to register your copyright even though a work is automatically copyrighted upon creation. In cases of infringement, it is always good to have a public record of your copyright and the date it went into effect. In fact, in order for an infringement suit to go to court, it is generally necessary to have your copyright registered with the Copyright Office.

The typical procedure for filing is to send a copy of the work, with a completed official form, to the Copyright Office, Library of Congress, Washington, DC 20559. To request forms, call the 24-hour forms hotline at (202) 707-9100. There is a $20 fee for each application. You may be put on hold for a long time, but the operators are courteous and helpful. You can also call Copyright Information Specialists at (202) 707-5959; the best times to call are Tuesday through Thursday from 9 A.M. to 12 noon Eastern time.

Remember, the copyright protects only the uniqueness of the form in which your idea is expressed, not the idea itself.

Disclosure Document Program

An idea, such as a new software program, can be protected during the development stage through the disclosure document program. This protection is valid for only a two-year period; if you haven't filed for a patent by then, your file is destroyed. However, if you do file for a patent within two years, the Patent Office will maintain your disclosure document in its files for the duration of the patent. This can be helpful in the event of a dispute or infringement suit.

To file, send the Patent Office the following five items: (1) a transmittal letter requesting that the enclosed disclosure be accepted under the Disclosure Document Program; (2) one photocopy of that letter; (3) a check to cover the filing fee; (4) a copy of your invention disclosure; and (5) a self-addressed, stamped envelope.

Your invention disclosure should be a signed document describing your invention's use, function, and structure, in addition to how it differs from similar ideas. Your document must be either a written explanation of your invention or a drawing. Photographs, submitted in duplicate and signed and dated by the inventor, may be used to complete your file.

Some important details: number your pages and use paper that folds to dimensions that do not exceed 8″ × 13″. You must sign and date two copies of the document and have each copy witnessed by two people. Send both copies to: Disclosure Statement, Commissioner of Patents and Trademarks, Patent and Trademark Office, Washington, DC 20231. One copy will be returned to you.

TRADEMARK REGISTRATION

A trademark is any name, word, or symbol with which a business identifies its products, services, or organization. Legal protection for trademarks depends on how distinctive the law considers the trademark in question. Marks that describe a product's function or characteristics usually aren't granted protection because these names resemble everyday words and the government guarantees everybody's right to use them. Generally, names that are not in common usage—arbitrary, fanciful, or coined terms—receive protection.

Because a mark cannot be registered with the Trademark and Patent Office before it is used in conjunction with some product or service, you must protect your mark during the development stage by means of a trade secret. Any information, design, process, formula, technique, device, or composition that is kept secret and gives a company a competitive edge in the market constitutes a trade secret.

Make sure your mark is not descriptive and that it is not already in use, or you will not be able to have it trademarked. Before you register your mark, be sure to use the trademark symbol properly on your product. You must insert the superscript ™ or "(T)" in order for the trademark to be valid.

Once you have used your trademark, you should register it with the Patent and Trademark Office. Afterward, you must indicate this protection by placing the symbol ® or placing "Reg. U.S. Patent & TM Off" on your product.

Four elements make up the trademark application:

1. A written application, including your name, citizenship, address, proof of prior use of the mark, the product the mark is used on, and the class of merchandising. If you don't know what class your product falls into, you can contact the Patent and Trademark Office.
2. A drawing of the mark. If you are seeking protection for a word, number, or combination thereof, a drawing is not necessary. You can simply type the word in capital letters on paper.
3. Five facsimiles or specimens of your trademark. The five specimens you submit must be duplicates of the actual trademark, but not exceeding 8″ × 13″. Specimens must be flat, not bulky or three-dimensional. If your trademark isn't flat, you can submit five photographs in place of the specimens.
4. The filing fee.

For precise information about trademarks, write to the Patent and Trademark Office, Washington, DC 20231, and request the following booklets: *General Information Concerning Trademarks; Trademarks; Trademarks Laws; Trademark Section, U.S. Patent Gazette* (a weekly publication). The Patent Office does not give legal advice on trademarks.

6

GETTING MONEY
AND MAINTAINING
FINANCIAL CONTROL

Raising start-up capital and financing ongoing operations is clearly a wide-ranging subject. It sometimes seems impossible to separate the myriad of details you need to be aware of in order to put your business on a firm financial footing. Because you are starting from home, you have given yourself an advantage in saving on start-up capital. In fact, if you have equity in your home, borrowing against the equity in a good real estate and interest market can be one of the easiest ways to finance your business venture.

How does the "little guy," the home-based entrepreneur who has never raised capital before, go about raising money? Simply stated, you will likely need to raise it through your own resources. However, keep in mind the following: If you seek all of your capital from one large investor, you will end up with a much smaller piece of your company; if you attempt to raise the money yourself from among your own acquaintances, you can normally arrange a much better deal for yourself.

If there is any single item of advice most appropriate for the new entrepreneur in need of money, it is to really think out finance matters thoroughly: make a careful assessment of the proposed value of the new business, determine how much capital you're going to need, in what increments, and over what time period. Then, decide about the source—a Small Business Investment Company (SBIC), a single investor, a private placement of securities with friends and relatives, a private placement through a securities firm, and so on.

In any of these approaches, you're going to need a business plan. Once you've chosen a course of action, follow it without deviation and abandon it for another course only when your first choice has clearly proven unfeasible. *Tenancity is everything.* If your business has merit, a formula for getting start-up capital can usually be found.

CREATING A BUSINESS PLAN

The process of creating a business plan forces you to take a realistic, objective, unemotional, and more or less detached look at your proposed business in its entirety. Why is it so important to see your venture as a whole? Most people who have business ideas deal with them haphazardly. Putting a business plan together and writing down specifics allows you to step outside as the creator and take a realistic look at implementing your creation.

A finished business plan becomes an operating tool that will help you manage your business and work toward its success. The final, completed plan is the chief instrument for communicating your ideas to others—businesspeople, bankers, partners, and others. If you seek financing for your business, the plan will become the basis for your loan proposal.

A strong business plan holds few surprises for its target. It conforms to generally accepted guidelines of form and content. Aside from introductory material, a business plan typically has as many as 13 sections. Each section should include specific elements that will clarify your business goals. The overall structure and sequence are as follows:

  a. Cover.
  b. Title page.
  1. Statement of purpose and summary.
  c. Table of contents.
  2. Description of business.
  3. Market analysis.
  4. Market strategy.
  5. Design and development plans.

   6. Operations plan.
   7. Management structure.
   8. Timetables and schedules.
   9. Potential pitfalls.
   10. Community benefits.
   11. Financial data.
   12. Supporting information.
   13. SBA materials (if applicable).

An important fact to keep in mind when preparing your plan is that you will not be *creating* it in the same order that it is *presented*. Following are some tips on how to prepare each section of your business plan.

Cover

A business plan should have a wraparound cover. It doesn't have to be leather-bound, but it needs to be neat and of adequate size to hold your material. A lender is actually more likely to think well of you if you remain conservative in expenditures on your plan, so don't spend money on unnecessary show. Subtle factors like this reflect your business judgment.

Title Page

Start your business plan with a title page. On this page, put the name of the business, the name(s) of the principals who own it, the complete business address, and the telephone and fax numbers. If you have a professional, businesslike logo, it can be used to dress up your title page.

Statement of Purpose and Summary

Next comes a statement of purpose and summary. Use that wording as its title. The summary should tell the reader what you want: money, time, commitment, and so on. This is very important. All too often, what the business owner desires is buried in the middle of the plan. Make clear what you are asking for in this section. The statement of purpose cannot be completed with numbers until you've calculated your capital needs. Write a draft sentence and leave the numbers blank, to be filled in later. The summary should cite the nature of the business, the legal form of operation (sole proprietorship, partnership, corporation, or limited partnership), the amount and purpose of the loan being requested, a proposed repayment schedule, the equity share of the borrower, and the equity–debt ratio after the loan, security, or collateral is offered. List the market value, estimates, or quotes on the cost of any equipment to be purchased with the loan proceeds.

Suppose you are already operating your business and want to expand. This is how your statement of purpose might read:

> Computer Consulting, Inc., a closely held company incorporated under the laws of the State of Ohio, is seeking a loan of $50,000 to purchase equipment and inventory as well as expanding office space at 520 Olive Street, Springfield, Ohio. The money will be used to perform necessary renovations and improvements, to maintain sufficient cash reserves, and provide adequate working capital to successfully expand this existing computer consulting firm.
>
> The sum, together with the $20,000 equity investment of the principals, will be sufficient to finance the transition through the expansion phase so that this recently started business can operate as an ongoing, profitable enterprise.

Make it easy for the loan analysts to know your wants and capabilities. They can then say yes or no immediately and not waste your time or theirs.

Whether the plan is to be used for financial or operational purposes, its statement of purpose should be kept short and businesslike, probably no more than half a page. It could be longer, depending on how complicated the use of requested funds may be, but the summary of a business plan, like the summary of a loan application, is generally no more than one page.

In financially oriented business plans, the page following might have a table that shows how the loan proceeds will be distributed, and the sources and uses of funds. You can amplify this with a small list showing what is going to be used as collateral and the conditions of the loan you propose.

Table of Contents

Following the statement of purpose comes a table of contents. You will naturally prepare this last, but be aware that you do need to include one. When you or others look over your plan, you should be able to quickly find certain information, financial data, market projections, and the like.

Description of Business

The section describing the business provides the reader with a general idea of the venture. Include any variables that provide insight into the business, the industry, and its markets.

Market Analysis

In this section, your main objective is to provide research defining potential customers, size of the market, competition, and how much of the market share you can reasonably hope to attain. This is perhaps the most important section you'll be dealing with. You'll be developing expected sales figures that define factors to be discussed later in the plan. It may be to your advantage to complete this section before attempting any others.

Market Strategy

Once you have defined your potential market and expected sales figures, you have to detail how you will reach those projections. Based on your marketing analysis, you should describe exactly what your marketing strategy will be.

Design and Development Plans

The section on design and development plans is geared toward detailing the status of the proposed product or service before it is ready to hit the market. If your product or service is already completely developed, you can forgo this section.

If you have developed the idea but not the product (i.e., software), or have plans to improve an existing product, or own an existing company with plans to introduce a new product, this section is extremely important to your business plan. The investor will want to know the development progress of any product or service concept, the costs associated with making it a marketable item, and the estimated period of time.

Operations Plan

In the operations section, you'll want to describe your facility requirements, plus any production or inventory purchasing plans. It is essential to present any costs the business will acquire in the production and inventory cycle.

Management Structure

Investors will be interested in the management structure of the organization. Who will run the business? What type of support personnel will there be? They will also want to know what kind of compensation any management personnel will receive, as well as any equity positions that may be given in order to attract key individuals.

Timetables and Schedules

After the management section, coordinate all the proceeding information into a timetable that will chart the development of the company from start-up to a projected break-even date and beyond. This is an integral step to raising money. Your main task in this section is to interrelate all the major events involved in your company's growth to projected deadlines for the completion of those items.

Potential Pitfalls

The pitfall section is included to show that you have thought of all the potential difficulties you might encounter when starting your business. This type of information lends credibility to your ability to manage and conceptualize the various risks involved in business.

Community Benefits

Aside from the pitfalls, you also want to show potential investors the community benefits that will be derived from your business: the economic impact of your business upon the community in the form of jobs, increased money circulated through the local area, living standards, and so on. In addition, describe how your business will affect the human element as well as the community in general. If you're providing a product or service that is unavailable in that community, this is a definite plus. If your business will increase community pride, that is another benefit.

Financial Data

Your business plan will need to include detailed financial information, such as a projected income statement, cash flow statement, and balance sheet.

Supporting Information

Supporting documents follow the financial data. Some people prefer to put a half-page summary of personal information right after the summary of the business and before the table of contents. This is a matter of discretion; many advisers believe that it makes sense because lenders are investing in the individual as much as or more than they are investing in a business. Frequently, individual tenacity, dedication, and character are the deciding factors of success in small businesses. In any case, it's important for lenders to know that they have a person who can make a business go. Your personal summary should communicate that you are this type of person.

Personal data might show your educational and work history in a functional way, and the things you've done that support your ability to run a business. Credit references and a summarized financial statement can be included as well; any financial statement should be no more than 60 days old. Keep this in mind if you're presenting a plan to different prospects for a longer period, and update your financial statement as required.

SBA Materials

The last section is included only if the purpose of developing your business plan is to obtain SBA financing. Documents required by the SBA may be useful to you in setting up your business.

This is just a brief overview of what is needed in a business plan. For more information that will guide you through the preparation of a business plan, consult the "Business Plan" chapter of *The Entrepreneur Magazine Small Business Advisor*.

OBTAINING START-UP MONEY

Tap Yourself First

The best source of financing for anybody wishing to start a business is, of course, his or her very own money. It is the easiest and quickest form of capital to acquire, there is no interest to be paid back, and you don't have to surrender any equity in your business. But getting any venture off the ground can be a very costly proposition—one that may be beyond your immediate cash reserves. If this is the case, there are several avenues you can turn to in order to obtain the necessary capital.

Friends and Relatives

It may come as a surprise, but after your own resources, those of your friends and relatives are the next best choices. Any money raised this way, however, should be treated as a real loan. Have a lawyer draw up loan papers for each friend or relative who contributes money to your venture. This approach to loans from friends and relatives serves two purposes: (1) it protects their loan, and (2) it prevents them from gaining equity in your business, unless you default on the loan.

Borrowing from Banks

Banks are probably the most visible source of ready financing, and you should already have contact with a few banks through your personal and business accounts. Though banks are logical places to go in order to raise capital, they are many times not the best, because they are notoriously conservative.

Most banks will require some sort of collateral as security for the loan. They will also want to know what the loan is for, so be prepared to show them your business plan. Your personal background information will have a direct bearing on how your loan applications are treated.

Depending on the size of the loan you request, there are several bank loan and collateral possibilities. If you have a *savings account* at a bank, you can use this money as collateral for a short-term loan. This is actually a very good way to get financing, because it lowers your interest rate. For instance, if you take out a loan at 9% and your savings account is earning 3%, the actual interest rate you'll be paying is 6%.

It may be possible to use your *life insurance* policy as collateral if it has any cash value. Usually, loans can be made for up to 95% of a policy's cash value. By borrowing against your life insurance policy, you don't have to actually repay the loan; all you really need to do is pay the interest charges along with your premium. However, if you don't eventually repay the amount borrowed, your policy will decrease that much in value.

Signature or *personal* loans are a possibility if your credit is good. You can usually take out a loan of this type for several thousand dollars, or even more if you have a good relationship with the bank. Timing is everything here: these loans are usually short-term and subject to the current interest rates. Ask your bank about various lines of credit that are available.

Another short-term loan is a *commercial* loan, which is usually issued for a six-month period and can be paid in installments during that time or in one lump sum. Stocks and bonds, your life insurance policy, or your personal guarantee can be used as collateral. If the loan is exceptionally large compared to your assets, the bank may require that you post with them a cash reserve that is equal to 20% of the loan amount.

You can also use as collateral any *real estate* you own. Loans of this nature can be secured for up to 75% of the real estate's value and can be set up for a term of 20 years if necessary.

Should you need expansion money once your business is underway, other loan possibilities include *inventory, equipment,* or *accounts receivable* financing. These types of loans use the value of your inventory, equipment, or accounts receivable as security for a loan. When you use your inventory as collateral, a bank will usually loan up to 50% of its value. Equipment loans will cover 80% of the equipment's value. With accounts receivable, most banks will loan up to 80% of the receivables' value.

SBA Loans

Although it is difficult to get a loan through the Small Business Administration (SBA), it is not impossible. By law, the SBA may not make or guarantee a loan if a business can obtain funds on reasonable terms from some other source. Borrowers must first seek private financing before applying to the SBA. The SBA considers itself to be a lender of last resort.

The SBA recently began offering "micro loans" up to $25,000 for new, small business entrepreneurs. The paperwork involved in applying for these lower-level loans is much simpler than in the past, and, if you are eligible, can be the perfect source for funding. For more information on these loans, call 1-800-8-ASK-SBA.

To qualify for an SBA loan, your loan application must be for financing of an independently owned and operated business. Loans cannot be made to speculative businesses, newspapers, or businesses engaged in gambling; nor can loans be made to pay off a creditor who is adequately secured and in a position to sustain loss, provide funds for distribution to the principals of the applicant, or replenish funds previously used for such purposes.

Be fully prepared to prove to the SBA that your proposed company has the ability to compete and be successful in its particular field. Whether you're seeking a loan for an untried concept or an established one, don't underestimate the importance of the category into which the SBA groups it. The success or failure of your application may rest on the classification the SBA assigns it. Determine which field or area your business can best compete in, state this in your application, and be prepared to back it up.

To help you prepare for this question, you should be aware of how the SBA formulates its guidelines. A key publication it relies on is the *Standard Industrial Classification (SIC) Manual,* published by the Federal Bureau of the Budget. The SBA also uses published information concerning the nature of similar companies, as well as your description of your proposed business. The SBA will not intentionally work against you; therefore, it is up to you to steer the agency in the direction most beneficial to you.

The maximum amount you can borrow under an SBA-guaranteed loan is $833,333. This is based on the SBA's present limit of guaranteeing up to 90% or $750,000—whichever is less—of a bank loan to a small firm. Interest on the loan will be set according to a statutory formula based on the cost of money to the government.

Although loans are available for just 1 or 2 years and for as long as 25 years (for construction and real estate purposes), the vast majority run for 5- to 8-year terms, with 10 years being the limit (except for working-capital loans, which are limited to 7 years).

As collateral for an SBA loan, you can use certain assets as security:

- Land and/or buildings (property).
- Machinery and/or equipment.
- Real estate and/or chattel mortgages.
- Warehouse receipts for marketable merchandise.
- Personal endorsement of a guarantor (a friend who is able and willing to pay off the loan if you fail).

Finance Companies

Geared mostly toward active investors, finance companies will allow for a greater amount of risk in a loan than will banks, but they also charge a higher interest rate. Generally, finance companies will be more interested in your collateral, your past track record, and the potential of your new business, rather than the strength of your credit.

Using Suppliers as Loan Sources

You won't be able to finance your complete start-up through suppliers, but you may be able to offset the cost of the merchandise during your start-up period by obtaining a lengthy payment period, or *trade credit*. When you're first starting your business, suppliers usually will not extend trade credit. They're going to want to make only C.O.D. deals. Try immediately, at the very beginning of your venture, to get on a credit basis with your suppliers. One of the things you can do to make that happen is to have a properly prepared financial plan and negotiate with the owner or the chief financial officer of the supplier.

If you're successful, you may defer payment for supplies from the time of delivery to 30, 60, or even 90 days, interest-free. This is not specifically a loan, but you don't have to pay for the goods right away, and the money needed for those supplies is kept in your pocket during the crucial start-up period.

Using Your Credit Cards

One of the most overlooked avenues of obtaining start-up capital is your credit cards. Most charge extremely high interest rates, but, again, timing is everything: in a competitive market, you can save quite a bit on interest by shopping around for a lower-interest card with ample credit line. This is a way to get several thousand dollars quickly, without the hassle of dealing with paperwork.

We know of one person who had three credit cards with a credit line of $3,000 on each card. He wanted to start an auto-detailing shop and needed approximately $8,000. Using his credit cards, he cashed each in for the full amount and started his shop. Within six months, he had built up a very good business and approached his bank for a loan of $10,000. He received the loan for a 3-year term at 12%. With the $10,000, he paid off his credit card balances, which were incurring (at the time) a 20% annual rate. After another 6 months, he paid off the bank loan of $10,000.

Selling Equity

Sometimes, raising start-up capital requires giving up a portion of your business to private investors. Such money is called *equity capital.* Equity financing means dividing your business ownership among investors who contribute capital but may or may not participate in the operation of the business itself. No loans are associated with equity capital, and no legal obligation is placed on you to pay back the amount invested. All the investor gets in exchange for the money is a percentage of the business and of the losses or profits associated with it.

Equity capital may, at first glance, seem like a good route to take to raise start-up capital (since there is no pressure to pay back a loan monthly), but many drawbacks are associated with this method. First of all, you give up a portion of your business and, with it, some control. That means you have to share your profits with your new partners, and, depending on how you set up the company (partnership, limited partnership, or corporation), you could become responsible for the actions of your partner(s). If your partner(s) goes into debt, you and your company may also.

Second, with some types of equity financing you might relinquish control of your company. Have your lawyer draw up documents for equity investors to sign, stating the amount and value of the equity being offered. Usually, the individual with the idea will retain 50% of the equity in the company, and the other 50% will be sold to investors. The 50–50 rule is fairly common, but everything is negotiable in a deal such as this.

Venture Capital

Obtaining start-up money from venture capitalists is a very difficult and potentially detrimental avenue to take. Luckily, unless you plan to move quickly from a home base and expand your business so much that you will need $100,000 or more before your net sales have begun to approach this mark, venture capital won't be an issue for you.

Although professional venture capitalists invest over $3 billion annually in new and growing businesses, it is in only about 3% of the deals they see each year. Venture capitalists like to invest in relatively new businesses that are risky but have a successful track record and a potential for relatively high profit and growth.

Who are the venture capitalists? There are approximately 400 venture capital firms throughout the United States, about half of which are private partnerships that have been funded by corporate and institutional investors. They are a diverse group of investors with different investment interests, skills, and objectives. Venture capitalists differ in the industries they will finance and the stages of development of the companies they will fund. Some prefer to provide seed money for start-ups, some only do later rounds of financing or leveraged buyouts; some may specialize in a particular geographic area. They have differing parameters on the minimum amount of money they will invest. Some may invest in $50,000 to $100,000 minimums; others will not invest less than $200,000 to $500,000.

Venture capitalists expect two things from the companies they finance: (1) high returns and (2) a method of exit. Because venture capitalists hit the jackpot with only a small percentage of the companies they back, they must go into each deal with the possibility of a return of 5 to 10 times their investment in 3 to 5 years if the company is successful. This may mean that they will own anywhere from 20% to 70% or more of your company. Each situation is different, and the amount of equity the venture capitalist will hold depends on the stage of the company's development at the time of the investment, the risk perceived, the amount of capital required, as well as the background of the entrepreneur.

The key to attracting venture capital is the potential growth prospect for the company. If your company does not have the potential to be a $30 million to $50 million company in 5 to 7 years, you are going to have a difficult time raising money from most venture capitalists. They do not invest in small businesses; they invest in large businesses that are just getting started. There are some venture firms that may have an interest in financing your new computer-based business even if your growth prospects are not that high, but they are difficult to find.

However, if your idea is big and you are willing to give venture capitalists a piece of the action—accepting them as partners in your business—you might be a candidate for venture financing.

Resources

The best place to begin your search for funds is to obtain a comprehensive list of potential investors. Contact the following resources:

- The National Association of Small Business Investment Companies (NASBIC), 1199 North Fairfax Street, Suite 200, Alexandria, VA 22314; (703) 683-1601. Their membership directory, available for $10, lists by state all Small Business Investment Companies that belong to the Association, and provides information about the contract person, investment policies, industry preferences, and preferred investment or loan limits of each individual investment company. To order the NASBIC directory, send a check or money order to: NASBIC Directory, P.O. Box 2039, Merrifield, VA 22116.

- The National Venture Capital Association (NVCA), 1655 N. Fort Myer Drive, Suite 700, Arlington, VA 22209; (703) 351-5269. The directory costs $25 and includes the names and addresses of all NVCA members and the appropriate contact persons at each company. To order the NVCA directory, send a check or money order to the address given above.

MANAGING YOUR ASSETS

How well you manage your financial assets will often determine the extent to which your business is successful. Because of the risks incurred in going into business for yourself, the capital you invest should yield a higher rate of return than could be obtained from an investment in government or corporate securities earning a guaranteed rate of interest.

Generally, financial management centers on five primary factors:

1. Managing old and new assets so they contribute, to the greatest possible extent, to the profitable operation of your business.
2. Managing current assets to ensure the maximum return possible on all money invested in your business.
3. Generating additional capital to acquire additional assets.
4. Evaluating requirements for acquiring new assets in the future.
5. Servicing the debt from current operating capital.

This section is geared toward the efficient management of your money so that you can (1) avoid an excessive investment in fixed assets, (2) understand banking relationships better, (3) maintain receivables and net working capital in proper proportion to sales, and (4) plan your taxes effectively so that they become an asset instead of a necessary evil. The financial difficulty of any firm, regardless of size, can be traced to violation of one or more of these principles of financial management. In this chapter, we will discuss the major tools used in financial planning: the components of working capital and analysis methods.

WORKING CAPITAL

There are primarily six components that fall within the realm of working capital:

1. Cash and liquid assets.
2. Accounts receivable.
3. Inventories.
4. Trade credit.
5. Debt management.
6. Operating expenses and taxes.

Each is outlined individually below.

Cash and Liquid Assets

This is the capital most readily available to your company. It includes all incoming cash from sales or other sources, all marketable securities, and short-term certificates of deposit. Maintaining an accurate and well-planned cash budgeting system is vital to the financial security of your company because it will let you know your cash-on-hand compared to your current expenses. If for any reason the cash-on-hand is not enough to meet expenses that are due and payable, you will run a negative cash flow. You may be able to sustain these losses for a short period of time, but if you begin to run large negatives for successive months, you will eventually file for bankruptcy. Pinpoint your cash peaks and valleys so that you can plan to meet your financial requirements by borrowing the necessary capital ahead of time and/or arranging for adequate credit lines.

Accounts Receivable

Accounts receivable is one of the primary ongoing records needed to track payments and age accounts that are slow in meeting their commitments. We cannot stress enough the importance of proper management of your accounts receivable.

Accounts receivable can be positive as well as negative for a business. These sales are logged into credit accounts that are due and payable based on prespecified terms. However, if you have made a lot of sales on credit accounts but nobody is paying, your business is rich on paper but poor otherwise. You have to watch your accounts receivable very closely and evaluate methods to speed up payment from slow-paying customers and collect from those that have not paid at all.

One way of speeding up slow-paying accounts is to put a due date and percentage penalty amount on each invoice sent. For example,

"This bill is now due and payable. Any amount owed after the 25th of this month will be subject to a 1.5% late service fee." Large companies, especially, try to manage their money by paying bills with penalties—or quick-pay incentives, such as a 1.5% discount for accounts paid within 10 days of billing—before paying bills that have no penalties or discount incentives. They have nothing to lose financially by putting such bills at the bottom of their stack.

Inventories

Some of your capital investment may be in inventory. If this is true of your business (mail order, personalized children's books, computer repair and maintenance), it is very important for you to keep track of your inventory and avoid losing money through overages or shortages.

Trade Credit

It is possible to obtain a large amount of credit from your suppliers, with very agreeable terms, but you must not mismanage or abuse this valuable asset to your company. Never let accounts payable lapse beyond the prespecified terms. It will have a negative effect on both your relationship with your suppliers and your credit rating.

Debt Management

All businesses require some initial capital to get started. Unless existing personal savings are adequate, some type of credit financing will be needed. To determine what type of financing is viable for your business, you have to evaluate your financial situation and the capacity for your business to manage debt. This means knowing when repayment of debts will fall payable and judging whether there will be funds to meet those expenses.

Operating Expenses and Taxes

Items such as utilities, payroll, marketing, insurance, professional fees, and so on, represent month-to-month operating costs. Federal, state, and local taxes are another type of regular and expected expense. Both of these payment types require that the proper funds be available by the due date or your business operations can be drastically affected. If you don't pay your employees, they will not show up for work. If you don't pay your taxes, the government can close you down until you do.

To ensure the current and future financial health of your business, you should constantly monitor these items to note any changes for better or worse. By maintaining complete and accurate records of your working capital, you'll be able to react more quickly to any financial change your business experiences. This monitoring is important so that increased profits can be invested to increase future assets; or, if your business experiences a change for the worse, you can take steps to rectify the situation.

FINANCIAL ANALYSIS METHODS

Over the years, a great many analytical techniques have been developed to enhance financial management skills. These include ratio analyses, return-on-investment guides, and break-even analysis.

Ratio Analyses

Ratio analyses are used primarily to enable small business owners to gauge the financial weaknesses and strengths in their company and take appropriate actions. They also offer a view into the competitive performance of a company compared to that of similar businesses in the same industry. Ratio analyses provide a great deal of illumination, but they have these limitations:

- Ratios are developed for specific periods. If you operate a seasonal business, they may not provide an accurate measure of financial performance.
- Ratios are based on industry averages that are extrapolated from a survey of financial statements, and businesspeople prepare financial statements differently. Some financial ratios may not present an accurate accounting of the average business in your industry.
- Ratio analyses are based on past performance; they don't offer any indications of present or future results.

There are four types of ratio analyses: (1) measure of liquidity, (2) current ratio, (3) acid-test or quick ratio, and (4) inventory turnover.

Measure of Liquidity

This ratio analyzes the amount of available liquid assets your business has at any given time to meet accounts or notes payable. The measure of liquidity tells you how much cash-on-hand you have, the amount of assets that can readily be turned into cash, and, generally, how quickly you can do so. A good rule-of-thumb to determine your financial health is: the more liquid you are, the better.

Current Ratio

Another ratio analysis—perhaps the best known—is the current ratio. This is the difference between your current assets and current liabilities, allowing a safety margin for miscellaneous losses like uncollectible accounts receivable. The current ratio is calculated by dividing your current assets by the current liabilities listed on your balance sheet. For instance, suppose your current assets are $300,000 and your current liabilities are $100,000. The current ratio would be:

$$\$300,000 \div \$100,000 = 3$$

Generally, a current ratio of assets to liabilities that is at least 2:1 is good. You can compare your current ratio with that of similar companies within your industry by referring to surveys conducted by various trade associations and marketing companies.

Acid-Test or Quick Ratio

Like the measure of liquidity, the acid-test ratio measures the liquidity of your business. To find this ratio, total all your liquid assets such as cash-on-hand plus any government securities and receivables, then divide these assets by your current liabilities. For example, suppose your current liquidable assets are $30,000 cash, $50,000 in receivables, and another $20,000 in securities, for a total of $100,000, and your current liabilities are $50,000. You would set up your equation as:

$$\$100,000 \div \$50,000 = 2.0$$

For most businesses, a quick ratio of 2.0 or better is more than sufficient. If, however, there are factors that will slow up payment of receivables or the due dates on your receivables exceed the time stipulation of your payables, then you may need a higher ratio.

Inventory Turnover

This is another aid for determining the correct amount of liquidity when your business operates with an inventory. It provides you with a measure of the amount of capital invested in inventory in order to meet your operation requirements, and indicates how quickly your inventory is being extinguished.

Return on Investment

The performance of a business based on its profitability is measured by its return on investment (ROI). There are several ways to determine ROI, but the simplest and most popular is to divide the net profit by the total assets. For example, suppose net profit is $100,000 and total assets are $300,000. Your ROI would be .33 or 33%.

You can use ROI in several different ways, measuring the profitability of your business via the performance of pricing policies, inventory investment, capital equipment investment, and so on. Some other ways to use ROI within your company are:

- Dividing net income, interest, and taxes by total liabilities to measure *rate of earnings of total capital employed.*
- Dividing net income and income taxes by proprietary equity and fixed liabilities to produce a *rate of earnings on invested capital.*
- Dividing net income by total capital plus reserves to calculate the *rate of earnings on proprietary equity and stock equity.*

Break-Even Analysis

A break-even analysis is important when you are in the planning stages of your business, before actual start-up. The analysis is an essential piece of information for your business plan because it tells you how much money you need to make—daily, weekly, monthly, or per job—in order to make your business profitable.

To put together a break-even analysis, you first have to separate the costs of your business into fixed and variable expenses. Remember that the total overhead of any company will equal the sum of the fixed and variable expenses.

Once you've determined what your fixed and variable expenses are, you are ready to take the next step in your break-even calculation: price of service. The price of service is determined by calculating your labor, materials, and overhead expenses, then applying a profit factor to the sum of those items. For instance, if you want to make a net profit of 20% on the total of labor, materials, and overhead, you would need to apply a profit factor of 25%.

To achieve a detailed break-even analysis, you must first determine what your fixed and variable costs will be on a month-to-month basis. Figure 6–1 shows how.

Figure 6–1   Break-Even Analysis

Break-Even Costs

Fixed Costs

Utilities	$ 75
Owner/Manager Salary	1,500
Accounting/Legal	75
Depreciation	80
Interest	30
Repairs/Maintenance	60
Insurance	125
Rent	0
Total	**$1,945**

Variable Costs

Phone	$ 100
Advertising/Promotion	200
Office Supplies	50
Travel	95
Total	**$ 480**

After you have calculated the fixed and variable expenses, you apply overhead, profit, and other factors to the cost of doing business. For illustration purposes, take an example given in Chapter 2, in which a one-person home-based computer information service contracts with 20 clients per month. The owner starts with the average hourly rate that would be received if freelancing on-site at various businesses; the local market rate, for example purposes, is $20 an hour. To this we factor in a supplies cost of 6% ($1.20), for a total labor-and-materials cost of $21.20. We then add an overhead figure of 19% ($4), for a subtotal of $25.22. Finally, we add to the $25.22 a profit factor of 25% ($6.30) for a total per-job hourly rate of $31.52, rounded off to $32.

The next step in computing break-even is to take the various components in Figure 6–1 and determine at what point, in terms of project hours worked, the service begins to make a profit. To do this, we have to use the break-even equation:

$$\text{Break-even} = F + V \div S$$

where

F = fixed expenses
V = variable expenses
S = selling price

Now let's input our data from Figure 6–1:

Break-even = $1,945 + $925 ÷ $32 = 89.6 hours

According to this break-even analysis, if we don't change price or reduce expenses, we will need to have a total of 90 hours worked (rounded off from 89.6) before we start making a profit.

PROFITABILITY MEASURES

Making money is what being in business is all about. Besides return on investment (ROI), there are several measures that help determine just how profitable your business is: asset earning power, return on owner's equity, net profit on sales, and investment turnover.

Asset earning power is a ratio that is calculated by taking your earnings before taxes and interest and dividing that number by your total assets. This measure is designed to illustrate the earning power of your total assets, not just your liquid assets. For instance, if you had total earnings before taxes and interest of $100,000 and total assets of $300,000, you would have an asset earning power of .33 or 33%. Your total assets are earning you 33% of their present marketable value.

The *return on owner's equity* determines what return your business is producing on the amount you've invested in it. Equity in a company, usually based on capital investment, includes both initial and ongoing capitalization. You can also include any intangible assets—such as patents or trade secrets—that have been contributed to the business in exchange for equity. If you are the only investor in your company, you control the total equity.

To compute the return on owner's equity, you first have to calculate what your average equity investment in the business has been over a 12-month period. You can usually find this number on your balance sheet. Divide your net profit by the average equity and you will have computed your return on owner's equity. For example, if you have an average equity in the business of $75,000 and your net profit is $50,000, your return on owner's equity would be .66 or 66%.

Net profit on sales measures the difference between your net sales and the amount you spend to operate your business. To determine your net profit on sales, you have to divide the net profit by the net sales. If we use the net profit of $50,000 from the above example and have net sales of $300,000, your net profit on sales would be .16 or 16%.

Like inventory turnover, *investment turnover* expresses the number of times, each year, that your total investment or assets revolve. To calculate your investment turnover, divide your total annual net sales by your total assets. If your net sales are $500,000 and your total assets are $300,000, your investment turnover would be 1.6.

FINANCIAL STATEMENTS

Financial statements are the tools used in business to keep score. There are two important statements that you should be familiar with in order to determine your financial condition: (1) the *balance sheet* and (2) the *profit and loss* or *income statement*. These statements are integral for planning and attracting start-up or expansion capital and will be important in forming your business plan—as well as for outlining day-to-day business operations.

The Balance Sheet

A balance sheet is a table of the assets and liabilities (i.e., a summary of credits and debits) as well as the capital, or owner's equity, of a business at a given point in time. A balance sheet is typically generated when books are closed after a specific period—monthly, quarterly, or annually.

The top portion of the balance sheet lists your company's assets, classified as either current or long-term/fixed assets. Current assets are assets that will be converted to cash or will be used by the business in a year or less. They include:

- Cash.
- Accounts receivable.
- Inventory.
- Supplies.

Other assets that appear in the balance sheet are called long-term or fixed assets. These assets are durable and will last more than one year. They include:

- Buildings.
- Fixtures.
- Furniture.
- Equipment.

The bottom half of the balance sheet lists the liabilities of your business and the amount of equity or capital you have accumulated.

Like assets, liabilities may be classified as current or long-term. If the debts are due in one year or less, they are classified as current liabilities. If they are due in more than one year, they are long-term liabilities. Examples of current liabilities are:

- Accounts payable.
- Salaries.
- Utilities.
- Taxes.

Long-term liabilities include:

- Bonds payable.
- Mortgage payable.
- Notes payable.

Finally, capital comprises the claim that the business owner has on the assets of the business. This is also referred to as owner's equity. Capital is not money in an accounting sense. Capital is equal to net assets, or the total value of assets minus the liabilities. Figure 6–2 is a sample balance sheet.

Income Statement

Whether the primary purpose of a projected operating statement is to obtain a bank loan, estimate cash requirements, or provide information for management planning, you should create such a statement *before* you start your business. Later, as operating data become available, update and refine your projections regularly.

The steps for estimating monthly sales and profits are as follows:

1. Estimate how many people in your market area you can reasonably hope to attract as customers or clients.
2. Estimate the average revenue to be generated by each customer or client.
3. Calculate the total annual sales volume: Dollars per client × Number of clients = Total sales.
4. Estimate the seasonal sales patterns for the business, attributing varying percentages of the total volume to each month of the year.
5. Allocate the total annual sales calculated in Step 3 to months: Annual sales × Monthly percentage = Monthly sales.

Figure 6–2   Sample Balance Sheet

Monthly Balance Sheet

The following balance sheet is based on a home-based computer information service two years after start-up. The business is earning $48,000 at the low end and $120,000 at the high end. Aside from monthly gross sales (listed below as accounts receivable), the business's assets include equipment, furniture, and inventory. Liabilities include payroll costs, phone/utility expenses, and accounts payable (cost of sales)—consisting of accounting/legal and insurance costs. The business has no long-term liabilities such as bonds payable or mortgage payments.

ASSETS

CURRENT ASSETS	LOW	HIGH
Cash	$10,000	$30,000
Accounts Receivable	4,000	10,000
Inventory	500	1,100
Supplies	50	120
Total Current Assets	**$14,550**	**$41,220**
FIXED ASSETS		
Office Furniture	$250	$500
Equipment	3,200	9,540
Total Fixed Assets	$3,450	$10,040
Total Assets	**$18,000**	**$51,260**

LIABILITIES & EQUITY

CURRENT LIABILITIES		
Accounts Payable	$480	$1,370
Utilities	175	400
Taxes	60	160
Total Current Liabilities	$715	$1,930
EQUITY/CAPITAL		
Owner's Equity	$17,285	$49,330
Total Equity	18,000	51,260
Total Liabilities & Equity	**$18,715**	**$53,190**

Figure 6–3   Sample Income Statement

Monthly Income Statement

The following income statement is based on two computer information services earning $48,000 at the low end and $120,000 at the high end. The low end represents a one-person home-based business servicing 20 clients that pay an average of $200 per month. The high end represents an office-based business occupying 300 square feet, with 50 clients paying an average of $200 per month. Cost of service includes subcontracted labor when needed, cost of materials, and database access fees.

INCOME	LOW	HIGH
Gross Sales	$4,000	$10,000
(Cost of Sales)	(480)	(1,370)
Gross Profit	$3,520	$8,630
EXPENSES		
Rent	$0	$450
Utilities/Phone	175	400
Manager's Salary	1,500	2,000
Sales & Marketing	200	500
Professional Services	75	150
Supplies	50	120
Depreciation	80	170
Interest	30	75
Repairs/Maintenance	60	140
Licenses/Taxes	75	190
Travel	95	270
Insurance	125	220
Total Expenses	$2,565	$4,985
Net Profit Before Taxes	$955	$3,645
Net Profit as a Percentage	23.88%	36.45%

6. Adjust these normal monthly sales totals to reflect the start-up period; this is strictly a value judgment.
7. Deduct from the monthly sales totals all your labor, materials, and overhead expenses. What's left is your net profit before taxes.

Figure 6–3 is a sample income statement.

By using the tools described above, you can take control of your finances. You must know exactly how profitable you are at all times. If you discover that you aren't making as much money as you need to survive, take corrective measures immediately.

7

RECORDKEEPING AND TAXES

There are three main reasons to keep accurate records of a business operation: (1) records are required by law, (2) they are useful to you as a manager, and (3) they are necessary for documenting allowable tax deductions. From a managerial aspect, maintaining accurate records is vital to the day-to-day operation of your business. Information about your business's financial condition will help you identify and correct any income/expense problems before they become major catastrophes. From a tax perspective, accurate recordkeeping can be like money in the bank for you and your business when it comes time to itemize deductions.

Records are also kept to determine the tax liabilities of your business. Regardless of the type of bookkeeping system employed, these records must be permanent, accurate, and complete, and must clearly establish income, deductions, credits, employee information, and anything else specified by federal, state, and local regulations. The law does not require any particular kind of records, only that they be complete and separate for each business.

When you start in business, establish the type and arrangement of books and records most suitable for your particular operation, keeping in mind the taxes for which the business is liable and when they fall due. If you are not competent in this area, call in outside professional help. A system for good recordkeeping need only be set up once; doing it efficiently makes things easier later on.

ACCOUNTING METHODS

Two systems of accounting are used for recordkeeping purposes: (1) cash basis and (2) accrual basis. Which one will be best for your computer operation depends greatly on your sales volume, how you legally choose to form your business, and whether you extend credit.

Cash Basis

In cash basis accounting, you do business and pay taxes according to your real-time cash flow. Cash income begins as soon as you ring it up on the register or receive it in the form of a check. Expenses are paid as they occur. Both income and expenses are put on the books and charged to the period in which they are paid or received.

If you're on the cash basis system, you can defer income to the following year as long as it isn't actually or constructively received by you in the present year. A check received by you in the present year but not cashed until the following year is still income to you for the present year. Therefore, if you want to shift income to the following year, you will have to either delay billing until the following year or bill so late in the present year that payment before year-end is unlikely.

If you want to accelerate expenses to the present year, you should pay any bills received and log them as the present year's expenses. An expense charged to your credit card will count as an expense in the year it was charged, not when you pay the card company. But be careful of paying next year's expenses in advance. Generally, expenses prepaid in excess of one month have to be prorated over the specified payment period. However, dues and subscriptions can be currently deducted if prepaid for the forthcoming year.

Accrual Basis

With accrual basis accounting, income and expenses are charged to the period to which they (should) apply, regardless of whether the money has been actually received or spent. For instance, suppose you are a contractor using accrual basis accounting, and you have done work for which you haven't been paid. You would recognize all expenses incurred in connection with that contract during the period in which it was supposed to have been completely paid and expensed, regardless of whether you have been paid for them yet. If an employee works for you this month, but you haven't paid him or her, you still take the deduction for that expense because that person has earned the money.

The accrual method is mandatory for purchases and sales when and where inventories are used in a business. Under the Tax Reform Act of 1986, if your gross sales receipts exceed $5 million per year and your business is a corporation, partnership, or trust, the IRS will not permit you to use the cash method of accounting; you must use the accrual accounting method. There are several exceptions that permit some businesses to use the cash method of accounting no matter how large their gross receipts. These exceptions apply to the farming business, partnerships without corporate partners, sole proprietorships, "qualified" personal-service corporations, and those performing services in the fields of health, law, accounting, actuarial science, performing, or consulting. In addition, 95% of the stock of the corporation must be owned by shareholders who are performing services for the corporation.

In accrual basis accounting, it doesn't matter when you receive or make actual payment. Income is reported when you bill. Expenses are deductible when you are billed, not when you pay. This accounting method has more tax benefits for a company with few receivables and large amounts of current liabilities. Advance payments to an accrual basis taxpayer are held to be taxable income in the year received.

Unlike payments for services rendered, advance payments for merchandise are reported by an accrual basis taxpayer when properly accruable under this method of accounting. If you choose this accounting procedure, you must use it for all reports and credit purposes. If you run two or more businesses at the same time, you may use different accounting methods for each business. Therefore, you can run one business on the cash basis and the other on the accrual basis.

RECORDKEEPING

When developing a recordkeeping system, your goal should be to keep it as simple as possible. Your time is valuable, and if your records are too complex, you will spend too much time maintaining them. Also, to maintain complicated records, you may have to hire an accountant or bookkeeper. Develop a comprehensive recordkeeping system—but one that is also easily understandable.

Keep in mind, as you enter data into your records, that the information should have a direct bearing on the financial condition of your computer-based business. Don't maintain records that are irrelevant and time-consuming. The records that you want to maintain should be kept up-to-date with current and pertinent information entered in a uniform manner throughout the entire system.

Bookkeeping Systems

Double-entry bookkeeping, which makes use of journals (Figure 7–1) and ledgers, is usually the preferred method of keeping business records. Transactions are entered first in a journal, then monthly totals of the transactions are posted to the appropriate ledger accounts. The ledger accounts include five categories: (1) income; (2) expense; (3) assets; (4) liability; and (5) net worth. Income and expense accounts are closed each year; asset, liability, and net worth accounts are maintained on a permanent and continuing basis.

Single-entry bookkeeping, although not as complete as the double-entry method, may be used effectively in a small business, especially during its early years. The single-entry system can be relatively simple. The flow of income and expense is recorded through a daily summary of cash receipts, a monthly summary of receipts, and a monthly disbursements journal (such as a checkbook). This system is entirely adequate for the tax purposes of many small businesses.

Records to Keep

Your business will generate four basic records that have to be accounted for through your recordkeeping system. They are:

1. Sales records.
2. Cash receipts.
3. Cash disbursements.
4. Accounts receivable.

Sales records include all income derived from the sales of products or the performance of a service. They can be grouped into one large category called *gross sales* or into several subcategories depicting different product or service lines so that you know which segments are doing well and which ones aren't.

Cash receipts account for all moneys generated through cash sales and the collection of accounts receivable. This is actual income collected; it does not include earnings from your sales records unless you choose to operate a cash-and-carry business—for example, a computer repair and maintenance business, or a personalized children's book service. In a cash-and-carry business, your cash receipts should theoretically match your sales records.

Figure 7-1 Sample General Journal Page

GENERAL JOURNAL

MONTH OF _____

DATE	ACCOUNT DEBITED	ACCOUNT NUMBER	AMOUNT	ACCOUNT CREDITED	ACCOUNT NUMBER	AMOUNT

Cash disbursements are sometimes referred to as operating expense records or accounts payable. All disbursements should be made by check if possible, so that business expenses can be well-documented for tax purposes. If a cash payment is necessary, a receipt for the payment, or at least an explanation of it, should be included in the business records. All canceled checks, paid bills, and other documents that substantiate the entries in the business records should be filed in an orderly manner and stored in a safe place. Breaking the cash disbursement headings into different categories—supplies, postage, maintenance, advertising, and so on—may be easier to deal with than just one large category.

A petty cash fund should be established for expenses that are immediate and small enough to warrant payment by cash. The Small Business Administration (SBA) suggests cashing a check for the purpose of petty cash and placing the money in a safe or lockbox. Record items purchased from the petty cash fund on a form that lists date of purchase, amount, and purpose. When the petty cash fund is almost exhausted, total the cost of all the items and write a check for the specified amount in order to replenish the account.

Accounts receivable (Figure 7–2) account for sales stemming from the extension of credit. Maintain these records on a monthly basis so you can age your receivables and determine just how long your credit customers are taking to pay their bills. If an account ages beyond a 60-day period, start investigating the reasons why the customer is taking so long to pay.

OTHER RECORDS YOU SHOULD RETAIN

Records supporting entries on a federal tax return should be kept until the statute of limitations (ordinarily, three years after the return is due) expires. Copies of federal income tax returns should be kept forever; they may even be helpful to the executor of your estate.

In addition to the four basic records and your tax documents, you should maintain records for three other important items: (1) capital equipment, (2) insurance, and (3) payroll.

Capital Equipment

Equipment records should be kept only for major purchases, so that you can determine what your depreciation expenses will be for tax purposes. Don't keep records on small items like staplers, tape recorders, answering machines, and similar items, and don't list leased equipment

Figure 7–2 Sample Accounts Receivable Aging Form

AGING OF
ACCOUNTS RECEIVABLE

REPORTING PERIOD

FROM: _____   **TO:** _____

DATE	INVOICE NUMBER	ACCOUNT	ACCOUNT NUMBER	DESCRIPTION	AMOUNT			
					30 DAYS	60 DAYS	90+ DAYS	TOTAL

in this section. Leased equipment should be maintained under cash disbursements because you do not own it; it is a liability that is payable each month.

Maintain records only on capital equipment you have purchased, whether outright, on a contract basis, or through a chattel mortgage. Major equipment you have purchased is considered an asset, even though you may have financed it. As you pay off your loan obligation, you build equity in the equipment that can be entered onto your balance sheet as an asset.

Information you should keep in your equipment records includes: the vendor's name, the date when each piece of equipment was purchased, a brief description of the item, how it was paid for (and the check number, if appropriate), and the full amount of the purchase.

Insurance

Keep all records pertaining to your company's insurance policies—auto, life, health, fire, and so on—and any special coverages you may obtain to decrease the risk of liability in a specific area. List the carriers for the policies and the underwriting agents that issue the coverages. Maintain records on any claims made against your policies, in order to resolve any misunderstandings that may arise.

When updating your records, enter all information about the payment of premiums: the date the check was written, the amount, and which policy it was written for. This will help you in payment disputes and for tax purposes.

Payroll

Payroll records present another set of challenges. An employer, regardless of the number of employees, must maintain all records pertaining to payroll taxes (income tax withholding, Social Security, and federal unemployment tax) for at least four years after the tax becomes due or is paid, whichever is later.

There are 20 different kinds of employment records that must be maintained just to satisfy federal requirements. These records are summarized below.

Income Tax Withholding Records

1. Name, address and Social Security number of each employee.
2. Amount and date of each payment of compensation.

3. Amount of wages subject to withholding in each payment.
4. Amount of withholding tax collected from each payment.
5. Reason that the taxable amount is less than the total payment.
6. Statements relating to employees' nonresident alien status.
7. Market value and date of noncash compensation.
8. Information about payments made under sick-pay plans.
9. Withholding exemption certificates.
10. Agreements regarding the voluntary withholding of extra cash.
11. Dates and payments to employees for nonbusiness services.
12. Statements of tips received by employees.
13. Requests for different computation of withholding taxes.

Social Security (FICA) Tax Records

1. Amount of each payment subject to FICA tax.
2. Amount and date of FICA tax collected from each payment.
3. Explanation for the difference, if any.

Federal Unemployment Tax (FUTA) Records

1. Total amount paid during calendar year.
2. Amount subject to unemployment tax.
3. Amount of contributions paid into the state unemployment fund.
4. Any other information requested on the unemployment tax return.

Payroll for a small firm is a simple task with a good pegboard or "write-it-once" system. Any office supply store can show you samples of different one-write systems. A good accounting clerk can be taught how to use one in about 15 minutes. Most accountants recommend these systems because they reduce errors and save time in making payroll entries.

Business Papers

Carefully preserve all underlying business papers. All purchase invoices, receiving reports, copies of sales slips, invoices sent to business firm customers, canceled checks, receipts for cash paid out, and cash register tapes must be meticulously retained. They are not only essential to maintaining good records but may be important if legal or tax questions are ever raised.

How Long Should I Keep These Records?

Price Waterhouse, a leading accounting firm, offers the following guidelines:

- Income tax, revenue agents' reports, protests, court briefs: Retain indefinitely.
- Annual financial statements: Retain indefinitely.
- Monthly financial statements used for internal purposes: Retain for three years.
- *Books of account.* General ledger and general journal: Retain indefinitely. Cash books: Retain indefinitely, unless posted regularly to the general ledger. Subsidiary ledgers: Retain for three years. ("Ledgers" refer to the actual books or the magnetic tapes, disks, or other media on which the ledgers and journals are stored.)
- Canceled, payroll, and dividend checks: Retain for six years.
- Income tax payment checks: Retain indefinitely.
- Bank reconciliations, voided checks, check stubs, and check register tapes: Retain for six years.
- Sales records such as invoices, monthly statements, remittance advisories, shipping papers, bills of lading, and customers' purchase orders: Retain for six years.
- Purchase records, including purchase orders, payment vouchers authorizing payment to vendors, and vendor invoices: Retain for six years.
- Travel and entertainment records, including account books, diaries, and expense statements: Retain for six years.
- Documents substantiating fixed asset additions, such as the amounts and dates of additions or improvements, details related to retirements, depreciation policies, and salvage values assigned to assets: Retain indefinitely.
- Personnel and payroll records, such as payments and reports to taxing authorities, including federal income tax withholding, FICA contributions, unemployment taxes, and workers' compensation insurance: Retain for four years.
- Corporate documents, including certificate of incorporation, corporate charter, constitution and by-laws, deeds and easements, stock, stock transfer and stockholder records, minutes of board of directors' meetings, retirement and pension records, labor contracts, and licenses, patents, trademarks, and registration applications: Retain indefinitely.

RECORDING TRANSACTIONS

A manual or one-write system of recording company financial transactions is a system where each check that you write is recorded automatically in the cash disbursements journal. This is popular with
many small businesses because it saves time. If you are writing a low
number of checks per month, it makes sense to use a manual or one-
write system. Maintaining your general ledger (Figure 7–3) on a normal basis should give you all the financial information you need to
make good business decisions. This type of system works well with
personal service businesses. An accountant is an example of someone
in a personal service business. He or she pays the rent, some miscellaneous bills, and perhaps writes only 20 checks on the business account per month. Though CPAs use a computer for many clients, they
often do their own books manually because their practice requires
very few checks.

If you write a large number of checks per month, consider
changing to batch processing of your general ledger postings. Data
processing services will handle this for you if the volume is large, or
you can invest a small amount of money and purchase a small business finance program, such as *Quicken*, that lets you write business
checks straight off of your computer, and automatically places each
expenditure into the proper recordkeeping category. You develop the
expense codes for the types of checks you write. You can then get a
computer printout of your general ledger, with all of your checks
listed according to their expense codes.

If you are spending a lot of money in cash rather than by check in
your business, you should list these expenditures on an expense report
form. Such forms are readily available at stationery or office supply
stores. Expenses are designated by category: travel, entertainment, office supplies, and so on. Attach the receipts to the form on which an expenditure is entered. Then add the expense codes and write a check to
yourself for reimbursement of the expenses. In this way, all cash disbursements are handled by company check—even out-of-pocket expenses. Accordingly, if you spend $200 out of pocket, fill out an
expense report and pay yourself back for the amount you spent. This
method ensures that those expenses are entered into your bookkeeping system.

We cannot stress enough that you should try to pay as much as
you can by check, to give you a record of all debits to your company.
Additionally, most bookkeeping veterans agree that it is best to work
out of one checkbook for the business, if at all possible. Nothing
drives an accountant crazier than having interaccount transfers—the
source of many businesses' financial problems. You might run the

Figure 7–3   Sample General Ledger Record Form

GENERAL LEDGER

ACCOUNT _____   **MONTH OF** _____

ACCOUNT NUMBER _____

DATE	ITEM	TRANSACTION		BALANCE	
		DEBIT	CREDIT	DEBIT	CREDIT

risk of recording an investment in the business as income, or making a similar error.

In some lines of business, legal restrictions prevent running the business out of one checkbook. Lawyers and collection agents are usually required by law to maintain trust accounts on behalf of their clients. These accounts represent money held in trust on the client's behalf until it is disbursed in the form of client receipts (e.g., court-awarded damages or collection moneys) or, ultimately, service fees.

WORKING WITH AN ACCOUNTANT

A good accountant will be your most important outside adviser. The services of a lawyer may be vital during specific periods in the development of your business or in times of trouble, but your accountant will have the greatest impact on the ultimate success or failure of your business.

Once you are in operation, you will have to decide whether your volume warrants a full-time bookkeeper, an outside accounting service, or merely a year-end accounting and tax preparation service. Even the smallest unincorporated businesses employ an outside public accountant to prepare their financial statements.

When you borrow money, your bank manager will want to see your balance sheet and your operating statement. If these have been prepared by a reputable public accountant, they will have more credibility than if you have prepared them yourself. (If you are borrowing less than $500,000, most banks will accept unaudited financial statements prepared by a public accountant.)

Public accountants must meet certain proficiency levels in order to be licensed by the state in which they practice. This does not ensure that an independent business accountant will automatically do a good job for you, but it does narrow your chances of running into an unqualified accountant.

If you are organizing a corporation, your accountant should counsel you in the start-up phase in order to determine the best approaches for your tax situation. If you are starting as a sole proprietor or in a partnership, you'll want the accountant to set up a bookkeeping system you can operate internally.

Experienced independent accountants will usually be familiar with accounting problems peculiar to your business and will be able to advise and direct you wisely. Before the calendar year ends, always ask your accountant to organize your records for the tax year coming to a close.

Ideally, an accountant should help organize the statistical data concerning your business, assist in charting future actions based on past performance, and advise you on your overall financial strategy with regard to purchasing, capital investment, and other matters related to your business goals. Today, however, much of an accountant's time is spent keeping the business owner in substantial compliance with the shifting interpretations of the laws and regulations.

Accountants specialize in legal requirements that affect you. You need their services if you expect to succeed as a small-business operator. If you spend your time finding answers to perplexing questions that accountants can answer more efficiently, you will not have the time to manage your business properly. Spend your time doing what you do best, not trying to do your own accounting.

Where do you find a good accountant? Ask other small business owners, your banker, or your lawyer for recommendations. How much does a good accountant charge? Accountants' fees, like those of lawyers, doctors, and other professionals, vary widely. A small-town accountant in business as an independent may charge $60 and up per hour; some of the large, nationally known firms might charge $150 to $300 per hour, or more, for their personnel.

WHAT YOU NEED TO KNOW ABOUT TAXES

As a business owner and employer, you will be responsible for collecting various state and federal taxes and remitting these to the proper agencies. In addition, you will be required to pay certain taxes yourself.

When reading the following sections, remember that, at the time this book went to press, all tax information reflected current law. But Congress has been passing tax legislation at the rate of one major act every two years. Therefore, it is important that you check for any major tax changes before making a decision that will affect the tax structure of your business.

Employer Tax Identification Number

If you employ one or more persons, you are required to withhold income tax and Social Security tax from each employee's paycheck and remit these amounts to the proper tax-collecting agency.

You will need to obtain an employer tax number from the federal government, using IRS Form SS-4. If your state has an income tax, you need a number from the state as well. Call the local numbers of the federal and state agencies listed in the white pages under "United States" and your state name. The federal agency will send you your number as well as charts to determine payroll tax deductions, quarterly and annual forms, W-4 forms, tax-deposit forms, and an instruction manual (you guessed it) on filling out forms. No advance fees or deposits are required.

Child Care Deduction

If you employ someone to watch your children for you while you run your business, you are still entitled to the current child care deduction on your personal taxes. Working from home is legitimate work, and your home-based business will likely require your undivided attention, making child care a necessity even when you are at home.

Social Security (FICA) Tax

The Federal Insurance Contributions Act (FICA) requires employers to withhold two different taxes: (1) Social Security and (2) Medicare. You need to know the difference between them because their tax rates are different.

As of 1994, the FICA tax (for both employers and employees) was 6.2% for old-age, survivors', and disability insurance (OASDI), commonly known as Social Security, for wages through $60,600; and it was 1.45% for Medicare on all earnings (there is no limit). For self-employed individuals, the 1994 OASDI tax rate was 12.4% on wages through $60,600 and 2.9% for Medicare on earnings (no limit).

As an employer, you have two responsibilities in regard to FICA: (1) you must withhold 7.65% from your employees' wages as FICA; (2) you must pay another 7.65%—the same amount of Social Security tax as the employee does.

Both the federal withholding and the full 15.3% FICA tax are reported on Form 941, Federal Payroll Tax Return. Form 941 is filed quarterly, and as long as total taxes due per quarter are less than $500, you can pay the entire amount when you file the return. The returns are due the last day of the month following the end of the quarter.

As a new employer, if you don't fall under the less-than-$500 quarterly exemption, you qualify with the IRS as a monthly depositor. You must deposit FICA and federal withholding for every calendar month by the 15th day of the following month. January taxes, for example, must be deposited by February 15. Monthly deposits must be made with Form 8109, Federal Tax Deposit (FTD) Coupon. For new employers, the IRS will send you an FTD coupon book five to six weeks after you receive your EIN.

Charts and instructions for Social Security deductions come with the IRS payroll forms. Be aware that Congress has accelerated the requirements for depositing FICA and withholding taxes. Failure to comply subjects a business to substantial penalties.

You must file four different reports with the IRS district director in connection with the payroll taxes (both FICA and income taxes) withheld from your employees' wages:

1. Quarterly return of taxes withheld on wages (Form 941).
2. Annual statement of taxes withheld on wages (Form W-2).
3. Reconciliation of quarterly returns of taxes withheld, along with annual statement of taxes withheld (Form W-3).
4. Annual Federal Unemployment Tax return (Form 940).

Federal Unemployment Tax

In addition to the FICA taxes, the Federal Unemployment Tax Act (FUTA) requires payment under certain conditions. If you paid total wages of $1,500 or more in any quarter during the calendar year, or if you had any employee who worked at least one day during 20 different weeks, you must pay FUTA tax on behalf of your employees.

The FUTA rate is 6.2% of the first $7,000 of wages. Any state unemployment tax rate you pay is subtracted from your federal rate, up to 5.4%. If you qualify for the full 5.4% credit, your FUTA rate could be reduced to 0.8%. You pay your employees' FUTA tax when you file Form 940, Employer's Annual Federal Unemployment Tax Return (or Form 940EZ with restrictions). Form 940 is due on or before January 31 of the following year.

W-2 and W-3 Forms

Form W-2 provides the employee and the government with a record of the employee's earnings and withholding for federal income tax, state income tax, and FICA taxes. The form must also contain the employee's full name, address, and Social Security number.

Form W-2, Wage and Tax Statement, is a five-part form that must be mailed or delivered to each employee by January 31 of the year following the end of the tax year. The employee gets three copies; the fourth copy is for your records; the fifth you mail to the Social Security Administration (SSA).

The SSA copies of Form W-2 must be summarized on Form W-3, Transmittal of Income and Tax Statements, and mailed to the SSA by February 28.

State Payroll Taxes

Almost all states have payroll taxes of some kind. You must collect them and remit them to the appropriate agency. Most states have an unemployment tax that is paid entirely by employers. The tax is figured as a percentage of total payroll and remitted at the end of each year. The actual percentage varies with the state and the employer.

Some states impose an income tax that must be deducted from each employee's paycheck. As an employer, you have the responsibility of collecting this tax and remitting it to the state. A few states have a disability insurance tax that must be deducted from employees' pay; in some states, this tax may be split between employee and employer.

Most states have patterned their tax-collecting systems after the federal government's. They issue employer numbers and similar forms and instruction booklets. As discussed above, you may apply for your employer number and various forms and booklets by calling the local office of the appropriate state agency.

Independent Contractors

Hiring individuals as independent contractors requires filing an annual information return (Form 1099) to report payments totaling $600 (or more) that were made to any individual in the course of trade or business during the calendar year. If this form is not filed, you will be subject to penalties. Be sure your records list the name, address, and Social Security number of every independent contractor you hired, along with pertinent dates and the amounts paid each person. Each payment should be supported by an invoice submitted by the contractor.

Other than licensed real estate agents, very few people who perform services on your business premises qualify as independent contractors. If the IRS feels an individual should have been treated as an employee, you will be liable for payroll taxes that should have been withheld and paid, plus penalties and interest.

Some factors that are reviewed by the IRS to determine whether an individual is really an "independent contractor" include:

- Does the independent contractor have its own business license?
- Does it have cards, stationery, and a business address?
- Does it have a business bank account?
- Does it regularly sell its services to various customers?

Personal Income Tax

Operating as a sole proprietor or partner, you will not be paid a salary like an employee; therefore, no income tax is withheld from money you take out of your business for personal use. Instead, you must estimate your tax liability each year and pay it in quarterly installments on Form 1040 ES. Your local IRS office will supply the forms and instructions for filing estimated tax returns. When applying for the forms, also request the *Tax Guide for Small Business* (Publication 334).

At the end of the year, you must file an income tax return as an individual and compute your tax liability on the profits earned in your business for that year.

Corporate Income Tax

If your business is organized as a corporation, you will be paid a salary like other employees. Any profit the business makes will accrue to the corporation, not to you personally. At the end of the year, you must file a corporate income tax return.

Corporate tax returns may be prepared on a calendar- or fiscal-year basis. If the tax liability of the business is calculated on a calendar year, the tax return must be filed with the IRS no later than March 15 each year.

Reporting income on a fiscal-year cycle is convenient for most businesses because they can end their tax year in any month they choose. Pursuant to the Tax Reform Act of 1986, a corporation whose income is primarily derived from the personal services of its shareholders must use a calendar year-end for tax purposes. In addition, most Subchapter S corporations are required to use calendar year-end statements.

Sales Taxes

Sales taxes are levied by many cities and states at varying rates. Most provide specific exemptions—certain classes of merchandise, or particular groups of customers. Service businesses are often exempt altogether. Contact your state and/or local revenue offices for information on the law for your area, so that you can adapt your bookkeeping to the requirements.

Levying taxes on all sales would present no major difficulties, but because this is not the case, your business will have to separate tax-exempt sales from taxable sales. You can then deduct tax-exempt sales from total sales when filing your sales tax returns each month. Remember, if you fail to collect taxes that should have been collected, you can be held liable for the full amount of uncollected tax.

Advance Deposits

Many states require an advance deposit against future taxes to be collected. For example, in California, if you project $10,000 in taxable sales for the first 3 months of operation, you must deposit 6.5% ($650) with the state tax bureau when applying for your sales tax permit number.

In lieu of the $650, the bureau will accept a surety bond for that amount from your insurance company. If you have a fair credit record, the bond is usually simple to obtain through your insurance agent. The cost varies according to the amount and the risk; 5% is a rule of thumb, but 10% is not unusual for small dollar amounts.

If your state requires a deposit or bond, you can keep the amount down by estimating sales on the low side. This is a wise tactic; most new business owners tend to overestimate early sales.

The Seller's Permit

In many states, wholesalers or manufacturers will not sell to you at wholesale prices unless you can show them your sales tax permit or number, also called a seller's permit. You will usually have to sign a tax card for their files.

Where and how do you get such a permit? Agencies issuing permits vary with each state, but generally they are: the Equalization Board, the State Sales Tax Commission, or the Franchise Tax Board. Contact the entity responsible for governing taxes in your state, and apply for your resale tax or wholesale permit. You will have to provide documentation to prove you are a retailer. Usually, your business permit is acceptable.

Your resale permit allows you to avoid putting out money for sales tax at the time you purchase merchandise from suppliers. This does not mean you won't be remitting taxes on the merchandise; it means you'll be deferring them until you sell the merchandise to your customers. The sales taxes will then be added (where applicable) to their purchases. You must remit the taxes to the appropriate agency, using the forms designed for that purpose.

When conducting business across state lines, you are required to collect taxes only for the states in which you maintain offices or stores.

TAX REPORTING SUMMARY

Every government entity, bureau, or agency that has any legal jurisdiction whatsoever over your business requires that you submit a written report, usually accompanied by a payment, on a monthly, quarterly, or annual basis.

These taxes don't apply in every state or city. We have covered the important ones in the foregoing pages. Any other taxes you must pay in your area will come to you automatically. In other words, the agencies doing the collecting will find you.

STANDARD BUSINESS DEDUCTIONS

General and Administrative Expenses

There are deductible general and administrative expenses in your business. These include all office expenses such as telephone, utilities, salaries, legal and accounting expenses, professional services, dues, and subscriptions to business publications.

Many people working out of their homes want to claim a home-office expense. That deduction was severely limited by the Tax Reform Act of 1986, which said that one could claim a home office only if it was the sole and primary place of doing business. If you have another office somewhere, you will not be able to deduct the cost of a home office as well. You might still deduct some business-related telephone charges made from your home, as well as business equipment and supplies, but you will not be able to deduct any part of your rent or depreciate any part of the property as a business expense.

A deduction is allowable to the extent that a portion of your home is used "exclusively" and "regularly" as your principal place of business for any business that you operate. Normally, that portion of your residence must be used to meet clients, store inventory, and perform your work. If you perform the majority of your work somewhere else, such as at your clients' offices, your home office may not be deductible.

Home office expenses that are eligible for deduction would include all normal office expenses plus interest, taxes, insurance, and depreciation on the portion of your home used exclusively as your office. The total amount of deduction is limited by the gross income derived from that business activity, reduced by all of your other business expenses other than those connected with the home office. Therefore, a home office cannot be used to produce tax losses for an otherwise profitable business. Any disallowed losses can be carried over and used in a year when the limitation is not exceeded.

Allocation of home office expenses is generally made on the basis of the ratio of square footage used exclusively for business to total square footage of the residence.

When it comes to your home office business computer, the Deficit Reduction Act of 1984 severely limits the conditions under which computers in the home can be used as a means of limiting tax liability. Actually, the test is simple: a home computer used for business over 50% of the time can qualify for appropriate business deductions or credits. As of 1985, business owners using home computers have to document, in writing, their business and personal use of the machine.

Section 179

The biggest tax break for start-up entrepreneurs is the newly revised rule on depreciation for equipment purchased in 1993 and after. The government allows you to take a depreciation deduction based on the usable life of equipment purchased for your business. One such depreciation deduction is called Section 179, which allows you to deduct up to $17,500 for equipment used in the course of doing business. This deduction had previously been $10,000.

Therefore, for each piece of equipment purchased on or after January 1, 1993, you could deduct up to $17,500 provided that (1) you do not exceed $200,000 and (2) the amount is less than or equal to your taxable income. If the amount exceeds your taxable income, the excess would then be carried forward to the next tax year.

Automobile Expenses

Almost everybody doing business in the United States has to drive an automobile to conduct that business. At this writing, business-related automobile mileage is deductible at 28¢ a mile. Once your vehicle is fully depreciated, you can deduct only 11.5¢ for each mile driven. Keep abreast of any changes the IRS may make.

Calculating your straight mileage deductions is very simple. Suppose you drive a car 20,000 miles a year. Of those, 12,000 are for business purposes. Your deduction is 28¢ × 12,000 miles, or $3,360.

The distance you drive from your home to your place of business is not deductible, but mileage you accumulate when driving from your place of business to any other location for business purposes is. Business miles accumulate when you drive for the purpose of either *doing* business or *seeking* business; going to talk to a potential client or doing something related to the promotional aspects of your business is considered business mileage. Keep in mind that you are required to maintain a log of your business miles for tax purposes. Enter your mileage on your appointment calendar at the end of each day.

There is another method of deducting the cost of driving, using actual operating expenses. The normal deductions in this area are gasoline, maintenance, insurance, and depreciation. As an example, assume that you are going to take a depreciation deduction of $3,120. Add to this the following expenses for operating your car: insurance, $400; maintenance, $500; gasoline, $1,600. You have $5,620 in deductions. Take this number and multiply it by the fraction of business miles (numerator) over total miles driven (denominator): 12,000 business miles divided by 20,000 total miles, or 60% business mileage. Sixty percent of $5,620 is $3,372. If you elect the second method, you get a deduction of $3,372 for the same mileage versus the $3,360 for straight mileage calculation.

If you use this second method, you must stay with it for the life of the vehicle. If you sell the car for a profit, you have to take the depreciation off its cost to determine its tax basis. If you sell it for more than its base, you'll have a gain that will result in a tax at your regular income tax rate.

Generally, straight mileage is best if you are driving an older car for many miles. If you are driving a fairly new car with a fairly high cost (over $10,000), the operating expenses/depreciation method might offer you more deductions.

Entertainment and Travel

If in your business you entertain clients for promotion, you have to maintain a log to deduct for entertainment, travel, and related expenses. Use a standard appointment calendar and write down whom you were entertaining, the nature of the business, where you were, and how much you spent. Contrary to popular belief, you do not need receipts for expenditures on entertainment under $25—but you must maintain your log. In certain instances, you can even claim business-related home entertainment; have clients or prospects sign a guest log. If you prepare a meal or serve drinks, your expenses are deductible as part of the expense of doing business.

Beginning in 1994, the limit on business meals and entertainment was reduced from 80% to 50%. For entertainment expenses, which are 50% deductible, all of these elements must be proved:

- The amount of expenditure.
- The date of expenditure.
- The name, address, and type of entertainment.
- The reason for entertainment and the nature of the business discussion that took place. General "good will" is not acceptable by the IRS.
- The occupation of the person being entertained.

Since the 1986 law, a deduction has no longer been permitted for travel, food, and lodging expenses incurred in connection with attending a conference, convention, or seminar related to investment activities such as real estate investment, stock investments, and so on. However, the cost of the actual seminar is still deductible.

Business travel deductions would include the cost of air, bus, or auto fares; hotels, meals, and incidentals, including dry cleaning; or little expenditures such as tips and taxis. However, the rule is that you must stay overnight in order to claim travel incidentals deductions.

The things you do to expand your awareness of and your expertise in your field of business are tax-deductible. Accordingly, deductions are allowed for convention expenses. *Note:* Rules limiting the amount that can be deducted for attending conventions in foreign countries have been toughened. Also, there are limits to the deductibility of conventions held on cruise ships. The cost of getting to and from the convention and the cost of your stay there are deductible. If you stay three days after the convention ends, these expenses would not be deductible. Deductions for your spouse are not allowed unless he or she is active in the business.

TAX ADJUSTMENTS

If the IRS wants to look at one of your tax returns, the examination must be done within three years of the time you filed it. In a case of alleged fraud—deductions claimed with the intent to defraud the government out of tax revenues—or unreported income, the government may look at tax returns that have been filed at any time. Assuming, however, that you are doing a proper job of tracking your tax credits and liability, the IRS has three years to look at your records.

The statute of limitations for assessment of taxes starts from the date you file your tax return. If you fail to file your tax return, the statute does not start to run. If you omit from gross income an amount in excess of 25% of the gross income reported on your return, the statute of limitations for an audit and assessment is six years.

Conversely, this means you have three years to straighten out tax matters as they arise. If you discover something that results in a change in your taxable income in any of three previous years, you may file a one-page amended return, known as a Form 1040X, and indicate the changes that are on the amended return. You may be paying more taxes. On the other hand, if you've had business deductions you didn't take, you can file an amended return and claim a refund—plus interest.

TAX PLANNING

Good tax planning minimizes your taxes and provides more money for your business or investments. As an entrepreneur, you should view tax savings as a potential source of working capital.

From a working capital perspective, there are two important rules to follow in your tax planning. First, don't incur an additional expense solely for the sake of getting an extra deduction. For instance, suppose your accountant tells you that you are in the 33% tax bracket and need more deductions. To get an extra $1,000 interest-expense deduction, you incur $1,000 in finance charges from credit card purchases. These finance charges are incurred not because of a cash flow problem or for business reasons, but solely for the benefit of writing off $1,000. If you think you are money ahead because you saved $330 in taxes, think again. You actually lost money. In effect, you avoided paying one party $330 by giving another party $1,000. You just spent $770 out of your pocket.

The second rule to remember is that immediately deferring taxes allows you to use your money interest-free before paying it to the government. Interest rates may justify deferring taxes for even a year, though this may cost you more taxes in a later year.

Estimated Tax Underpayments

If you have not paid sufficient amounts of estimated income tax, you may be able to avoid or reduce penalties for underpayment by arranging to increase the amounts withheld from the paychecks remaining in the present year. All withheld income tax is treated as if spread equally over the calendar year, even when a disproportionately large amount is withheld in December. Individuals required to make estimated tax payments should pay special attention to other techniques that may be beneficial, especially if their income is irregular or seasonal.

Careful planning and analysis of required tax payments are warranted in all categories of small business because of the high non-deductible penalty rates in effect.

Equipment Purchases

Primarily because of tax incentives, the year-end is the time to consider buying business equipment. The tax incentive is the $10,000 expensing deduction which, under Section 179 of the Internal Revenue Code, is not prorated for the period of the year that you hold and use the equipment. Consequently, you will get the same deduction whether you buy the equipment and put it into service at the beginning or the end of the year.

You can only take this deduction for tangible personal property used in your business. It is not available for real estate or automobiles.

You can expense up to $10,000 in costs of equipment purchased for a trade or business. The expensing deduction may be deducted in full, even though the property is acquired and used in the last days of the year. But if you purchase the equipment in the present year and don't use it until the following year, the expensing deduction won't be allowed for the present year. To the extent you take the expensing deduction, you must reduce the cost basis for the equipment in computing its depreciation, using the methods previously discussed.

Inventory Valuation

You don't automatically get a deduction for purchasing inventory items for your business. You must reduce the amount paid for inventory purchases by the value of the inventory at the end of the year. For example, if you paid $10,000 for merchandise in one year, and your inventory at the end of the year is $7,000, you can deduct only $3,000 for purchases in the year, even though you paid $10,000.

A change in how your inventory is valued can save a substantial amount of taxes. Given the trend toward rising costs, a switch to last-in, first-out (LIFO) in a typical year will give your company a one-shot loss deduction for the increase in prices of the items in your inventory. The switch to LIFO is made by filing Form 970 with your tax return. Once you adopt the LIFO method, IRS approval is required to return to first-in, first-out (FIFO).

Postponing Income

If you are employed by someone else when you first begin your home-based business and you expect to receive a year-end bonus or other additional compensation, you may want to defer receipt of the money until the succeeding year—especially if you will be in a lower tax bracket in the following year. This is often the situation for first-time entrepreneurs who quit their job and do not have a steady income during the time needed for their new business to break even. If your employer uses the accrual method of accounting, the bonus should still be deductible in the current year, provided it is fixed by year-end and paid shortly thereafter, and the employer is legally obligated to pay it.

As for compensation expected to be received for future services, you may want to negotiate an agreement with your employer whereby part of your earnings will be deferred and paid in either one or several future years. Because the employer will have the use of the funds during the deferral period, an interest factor may be added. If certain requirements are met, deferred compensation will generally not be taxed to you; similarly, it will not be deductible by your employer until actually paid.

Computations of projected tax liability are needed to evaluate the desirability of postponing compensation. Any potential tax advantage of deferring compensation will be offset, at least in part, by the loss of interest or other income that can be earned if the compensation is received currently, unless the deferred compensation is increased. Credit risk is another important factor to consider.

You should, however, seek consultation prior to entering into deferred-compensation agreements. Deferring compensation may reduce your retirement or other benefits because it may reduce the base-period figure used in calculating the benefits. Also, special rules apply for employees of state or local governments or tax-exempt organizations.

Postponing the reporting of taxable investment income, if possible, is almost always advantageous. It enables you to defer taxes and use funds for an additional period of time. However, tax-rate prospects for future years must be evaluated. Some mechanisms for postponing taxable income include:

Treasury Bills and Bank Certificates

Investors in short-term securities can shift interest income forward into a succeeding year by buying Treasury Bills or certain bank certificates with a term of one year or less, which mature in the next year. This applies to individuals as well as businesses.

Savings Bonds

U.S. Savings Bonds have become a more viable investment for some investors. Bondholders may elect to postpone the tax on the interest until the bonds are cashed in, which may be 30 years or more if the Treasury continues to extend maturities as it has in the past. Alternatively, the income tax may be reduced or avoided by giving the bonds, at the time of purchase, to minor children who are in low tax brackets and having them elect to report the interest currently.

This election, once made, applies to all savings bonds owned now or in the future, and the election cannot be reversed. The election by the children will not be considered an election by the donor. If you have accumulated untaxed savings-bond interest for many years and now require current funds, you can extend the tax postponement if you exchange the bonds for Series HH bonds, which pay interest semiannually.

Deferred Annuities

Taxes can be postponed on earnings from capital put aside for long-range goals by purchasing a deferred annuity. Annuities are arranged by contract with an insurance company. There is no tax deduction for the amount contributed, but all interest earned and compounded will be tax-free until it is withdrawn, which may be as late as age 70 for some plans.

Deferred annuity purchases may be made in installments or with a single payment. Early withdrawals will be deemed taxable to the extent the cash value of the contract exceeds the investment in the contract. Only after any excess has been withdrawn as taxable income will it be possible to receive nontaxable early withdrawals of principal.

8

BOOTING UP
FOR BUSINESS

The first part of this chapter outlines the latest information regarding on-line services. These services are of increasing importance to the operation of nearly any computer-based businesses. Day-to-day management and the pricing of your services—one of the most important aspects of operating a business, and certainly one of the most crucial factors affecting the success of that business—are then addressed.

ON-LINE ACCESS

If you have a modem, communications software, and a telephone, you can access any number of databases around the world by using one of the two major communications networks—SprintNet (formerly Telenet) and BT/MCI Data Services (formerly Tymnet). Known as packet-switching networks, they provide free on-line information to users who know the proper commands (which differ with each network). The on-line information includes local database-network phone numbers.

Packet switching refers to the process networks use to connect you with various database utilities—in effect, they put your commands into "packets" (electronic envelopes) "addressed" to the service you request. (For our purposes, we're defining utilities such as America Online and Dialog as *services* that, in turn, provide access to databases; some services can also be accessed through their own networks.) The network sends your packet to the service through a series of computers, "switching" the packet from one computer to the next en route.

The Internet

The Internet is an evolution of a U.S. Department of Defense communications network. It was designed in 1969 to withstand the fallout of a nuclear war. There is no "Internet company" that owns or manages the Internet; rather, it is a free-existing entity that is accessible through various "gateway" companies to anyone with a computer and a modem. Costs are minimal: about $20 per month plus phone charges. One of its biggest draws is that e-mail can be sent through the Internet to literally anyone in the world who is also connected. About 25,000 educational, research, and corporate computer networks are now on the Internet, and 20 million people are believed to have access.

A drawback on the Internet has been difficulty of use; the language, UNIX, is generally known only by techies and researchers. Luckily, the National Center for Supercomputing Applications (NCSA) in Illinois created "Mosaic"—an application that allows the "Windows generation" to point and click their way through what had been a horrible maze for nontechnical users. At publication, Mosaic is being given free to any noncommercial Internet user who requests it. Its developers and others are hard at work to produce improved commercial versions.

On-Line Services

The on-line services described next offer a wide variety of databases, which are growing at a rate of approximately 35% a year. A handy reference tool is the *Directory of On-Line Databases,* published by Gale Research, Inc., in Detroit (see Appendix F for the address). Actually one book of a two-volume set (the second volume lists manufacturers of portable computer accessories such as CD-ROMs), the *Directory* includes summaries of the services and their databases, company addresses and phone numbers, and indexes by subject, service name, and network (i.e., which network accesses each service). The two-volume set is $315; the *Directory of On-Line Databases* alone runs $135. Each includes an annual update in July. (The directory was formerly published by Cuadra Associates in Los Angeles, manufacturer of

STAR, a proprietary database development and information-retrieval system designed for use on small business computers. Cuadra Associates continues to sell the software, which can be used with laser video disks.)

In addition to being invaluable research aids, on-line services facilitate worldwide distribution of desktop-published documents. Bulletin boards and services like CompuServe and General Electric's GEnie offer access to layout templates, fonts, and images. These can be accessed through CompuServe by typing GO ALDUS (Aldus, Inc.), GO ADOBE (Adobe Systems), and GO GRAPHICS (for graphics utilities). GEnie's forums are subject- rather than company-based. Adobe screen fonts can be downloaded through GEnie's Winchell Typesetting Service Bureau. Utilities and templates are accessed via the National Association of Desktop Publishers by typing WTS or NADTP. (When uploading or downloading, we recommend that customers use a data-compression utility such as Arc 5.13.) For on-line distribution, we recommend that customers use electronic mail services such as MCI Mail (listed in the Appendix).

America Online

America Online (AOL) has recently become a powerhouse in the on-line services arena, offering more than 600,000 subscribers access to 31 magazines, 2 newspapers, and *Compton's Encyclopedia*, as well as Morningstar's mutual funds reports. On-line investment trading is accomplished through Quick & Reilly and E*Trade. One of AOL's biggest draws is its Internet-link offerings: access to news groups, e-mail, and mail lists with an easy-to-use search tool that guides subscribers through the Internet maze. The basic rate at publication is $9.95 per month, with 5 free hours plus $3.50 per each additional hour.

CompuServe

A unit of H&R Block, based in Columbus, Ohio, CompuServe is touted by many as the best of the best, offering subscribers a variety of news and financial information sources, including major wire services, Dow Jones News/Retrieval, the National Weather Service, and Grolier's Academic American Encyclopedia, updated quarterly. In all, over 2,000 databases are available via CompuServe. It offers access to ValueLine and Standard & Poor's databases, in addition to e-mail and bulletin board services. As with America Online, on-line investment trading is accomplished through Quick & Reilly and E*Trade. In addition, CompuServe offers a Travelshopper service enabling users to book airline reservations. Connect fees have recently been lowered, but vary with baud rate (at this time, the basic rate is $8.95 per month, with extended services running $4.80 per hour at 2,400 baud and $9.60 per hour at 9,600 baud). Membership kits like "Information Manager" can be purchased in stores for about $50, and include a $25 on-line credit.

DIALOG

DIALOG, a Knight-Ridder company, provides more than 450 databases containing over 330 million records. Because of the size of the databases and the amount of information available, many sources are summarized, though the "complete text of articles from more than 2,500 journals, magazines, and newsletters" is available. Databases include Bowker's *Books in Print*, a keyword-searchable magazine index, a daily index of over 2,000 news stories from over 1,700 publications, and an index of book reviews from over 380 publications. Additional databases track developments in medical technology, science and engineering, law, government, and education, and include U.S. copyrights, U.S. patents (1971 to the present), and TRADEMARKSCAN®.

The initial sign-up charge for the main DIALOG service is $295, and includes $100 worth of free on-line connect time (to be used within the first 90 days) and a mailbox on DIALOG's DIALMAIL service—an e-mail, conferencing, and bulletin board system. There is no monthly fee. Subscribers are charged only for time spent on-line, and there is no minimum monthly requirement. Connect time varies by database, with a display charge record. There is, however, an annual password fee of $75. An optional (but necessary) manual, the *Guide to DIALOG Searching*, is available at additional cost, as are a series of publications called *Database Chapters* (offering detailed summarizations of databases).

Dow Jones News/Retrieval (DJN/R)

Originally designed to provide on-line abstracts of *The Wall Street Journal*, *Barron's*, and other papers published by parent corporation Dow Jones & Company, DJN/R has since grown into a large and varied financial service offering: databases that can track up to five of their on-line portfolios (providing current quotes and information); a search service culling 350,000 news stories from 1979 to the present; and a full-text *Wall Street Journal* search service. Additional databases offer real-time quotes, SEC information on over 8,700 publicly held companies, same-day Japanese business coverage, corporate earnings forecasts, Standard & Poor's profiles of over 4,600 companies, an on-line dictionary of investment terms, computerized shopping, movie reviews, sports coverage, e-mail services, and foreign currency exchange surveys. The DJN/R membership kit includes a manual, a user's agreement, and a free subscription to the magazine *Dowline*, plus 5 hours of free connect time. Connect rates vary with time and baud rate; frequent users are able to take advantage of special membership plans. Contact Dow Jones News/Retrieval, listed in the Appendix, for further information.

CDP Technologies and ORBIT•Questel

These are similar to DIALOG but not as extensive. Both offer bibliographic abstracts from over 600 news and information publications; over 6.5 million entries from *Chemical Abstracts*; abstracts from some 4,000 biomedical journals worldwide; updated coverage of more than 3,500 engineering and government journals; a database specializing in physics, electrotechnology, and computers; and ERIC, an educational database also available on DIALOG.

CDP Technologies offers a medical database of over 3,000 international publications, and a 200,000-record database of government publications. ORBIT•Questel databases include lists of over 2,000 government and private grants, the *Index to Publications of the United States Congress*, and indexes of the *Congressional Record, Federal Register*, and *Washington Post*.

Costs for CDP Technologies include connect time (which varies according to the type of account you set up); database royalty charges; and telecommunications costs. In addition, CDP Technologies charges an annual password fee. The monthly *CDP Bulletin* is sent to subscribers at no charge. ORBIT•Questel's database costs vary, and there is no initial sign-up fee.

Delphi

This is a smaller service founded by programmer/marketer Wes Kussmaul. The service charges lower communications fees than most others, and there is no monthly minimum. Among other things, Delphi offers mail and messaging services, computer conferencing, and bulletin boards.

GEnie

General Electric's on-line service includes GE Mail, an electronic mail service; a live-wire CB simulator, with user communication via keyboard; a round-table forum called Personal Computing, which includes over 8,000 down-loadable soft fonts; travel services, including American Airlines' EAASY SABRE, an on-line reservations service; TRAVEL DATA database, rating hotels/restaurants worldwide; a travelers' information service (round table); Desktop, a publishers' round table; business, financial, and shopping services; U.S./world news databases; and reference library databases. The sign-up fee includes 2 free hours of non-prime-time usage and a user's manual. At publication, basic rates are $9.00 per month for 4 hours, with each additional hour at $3.00.

LEXIS/NEXIS

A product of Mead Data Services, a subsidiary of Mead Corporation, LEXIS/NEXIS is an easy-to-use full-text service with offerings ranging from the *New York Times* (1980 to the present) and transcripts of the *MacNeil/Lehrer NewsHour* from 1982 to the present, to over 50 magazines including *Time, Newsweek, Fortune, Forbes, U.S. News & World Report,* and *Aviation Week & Space Technology.* Also available are 16 wire services, 4 patent databases, the complete texts of 50 industry newsletters, along with *InfoWorld,* the *Manchester Guardian Weekly,* and the *Los Angeles Times.* A database called the AP Political Service offers information on election campaigns, state propositions, national polls, and local and national political issues. Also included are Information Access Company's databases—Trade and Industry ASAP and Magazine ASAP. The monthly subscription fee and the basic connect rates vary, depending on location. LEXIS/NEXIS adds varying "file charges" to its connect rate for each file change; the service considers a user's first search statement to be his or her search—everything added after that is labeled a modification. The service doesn't charge for the display of retrieved information, but charges a minimal fee per line plus transmission time to download an entire document on disk. LEXIS/NEXIS subscribers receive the 900-page *Guide to LEXIS/NEXIS* and related services, as well as a reference manual explaining the LEXIS/NEXIS search language.

NewsNet

This is a collection of over 300 full-text newsletters on more than 35 subjects, ranging from aerospace and electronics to entertainment, energy, finance, government, and telecommunications. One of its features is a keyword search of all user-specified publications. Over 80% of all newsletters on the system are transmitted directly from publisher's workstations. The subscription fee includes network communications charges.

Prodigy

Prodigy offers subscribers access to about a dozen magazines (including *Consumer Reports*), more than 30 news services, and *Grolier's Encyclopedia,* as well as numerous bulletin boards. On-line investment trading can be accomplished by signing up with PC Financial Network. Basic rate at publication is $14.95 per month, with 2 free hours of "plus" services that otherwise cost $3.60 per each additional hour.

MANAGING A COMPUTER-BASED BUSINESS FROM YOUR HOME

Whatever your business orientation, you'll want to separate personal and business activity in your home to the greatest extent possible. Establish definite business hours so you can plan to have a private as well as professional life. In any home office, time management is a primary concern. One of the advantages to being home-based is that you can work long and odd hours, but doing so without any time off in your own home will not be healthy for you or your company.

Depending on your location and the business you choose, you may be up at 6:30 A.M. to make East Coast phone calls from your West Coast home, or you may be able to postpone starting your day until mid-morning. Your first hour or so should be spent on follow-up calls and on lining up clients for interviews, as well as overseeing scheduling and any outstanding in-house bookkeeping tasks. Personal sales visits should begin around 10 A.M. On the way, you can stop by your post office box to pick up mail.

Try to dedicate at least one hour a day to marketing. If you have no sales calls on a given day, use the hour to call on new advertising possibilities, make phone calls, or plan an upcoming sales promotion.

The morning is a good time to red-flag any problems on jobs you are finishing. By catching these problems early, you can reach your clients well ahead of time and discuss steps to get the job completed as needed.

Time Management

A one-person shop serving many different clients is not going to do very well if time isn't managed effectively. To optimize your workday, schedule all "field work" (pickups and deliveries, personal sales calls, business purchasing, and so on) at pretty much the same time. This allows you to set aside in-house periods of work without disruption.

Many sophisticated time management software programs are on the market now. MeetingMaker™ by On Technology Corporation, for example, allows you to set meetings and activities with persons either connected to a network with you, or simply for your own scheduling purposes. You program your computer to remind you ahead of time of each meeting and/or activity (you select how far in advance you want notice), and a message appears on the screen to remind you. You can also set regular, recurring meetings and meetings far in the future. The program alerts you when a meeting or activity you are about to schedule conflicts with another commitment that is already on the program.

Organization and Scheduling

Organization and effective client scheduling are crucial to your success, whether you do most of your work at home or on the road at your clients' facilities. For most service businesses, you'll want to assign each client a separate floppy disk and (ideally) a backup disk so you can easily keep individual records.

If you decide to hire employees, consider beginning with someone who can handle client phone calls professionally, maintain your schedule, and help with basic job-completion duties. If you're a freelance writer, you can still have someone make initial phone calls to set up interviews for you. If you're a business plan writer, you'll benefit from a fresh pair of eyes proofreading your drafts. Graphic artists can have helpers pick up supplies from the various stores they frequent, and computer training services can assign helpers to have new packets of training material copied, collated, bound, and readied for the next session.

Maintaining strong customer relations should be the chief yardstick against which you measure allocation of staff duties. If your phone is answered quickly and professionally, your schedule maintained effectively, and your office stocked with everything you need to be effective, this could be the best way to ensure optimal client services. On the other hand, if you need to have deliveries made on time, projects typed, proofed, and faxed on deadline, or research completed by noon for a client, then use skilled employees accordingly.

PRICING YOUR SERVICE

How should you price your service? Procedures vary with each business, but the same three elements apply in every situation: (1) labor and materials (or supplies), (2) overhead, and (3) profit.

Labor and Materials

Until you establish records to use as a guide, you must estimate your costs of labor and materials. Labor costs include both your own time and the wages and benefits you pay your employees and/or contractors who perform services for you.

Labor cost is usually expressed as an hourly rate. The going rate for individual employees may range from $5.50 to $12 or more per hour, depending on employees' experience and your local market. But your own labor cost may come in at a rate resembling that of consultants, from $25 to more than $50 per hour. Data-entry clerks work at the low end of the scale; managers and supervisors are at the high end.

Check in your library's reference area for government publications that give national and state salary ranges for different occupations. The editors of trade publications might have such information. Check for current rates in classified newspaper ads and with your chamber of commerce.

Labor can be subcontracted. Under this system, you do not put a worker on your payroll as an employee. This eliminates the time and expense associated with time records, payroll preparation, payroll taxes, and benefits. Frequently, when labor is contracted out, the full cost is agreed on in advance, allowing the owner to accurately figure that part of his or her labor costs into the job estimate.

Carefully estimate the labor time it will take to accomplish each job on which you bid. For example, if you estimate that a large word processing job for a client would take 2 hours of labor during each 24-hour period, 5 days a week, with 2 hours of supervision in each 21-day work-month, you would compute your labor and materials cost for a month as follows:

	Hours/Month	Rate	Cost
Labor	2 hours × 21 workdays	$6.50/hr	$273
Supervision	2 hours	$8.00/hr	16
Total labor cost*			$289
Supplies			
(at 6% of labor cost)			17
Total labor			
and materials			$306

*If you put people on payroll, add 15% to this total to cover payroll taxes, workers' compensation, and paid vacation. If you plan on providing benefits, add 30%.

Overhead

Overhead comprises all the nonlabor, indirect expenses required to operate your business "through thick and thin." (A detailed description of these expenses can be found later in this chapter, under "Costs.") If you have past operating expenses to guide you, figuring an overhead rate is not difficult. Total all your expenses for one year, excluding labor and materials. Divide this number by your total cost of labor and materials to determine your overhead rate. For example, suppose your costs and expenses for a one-year period were as follows:

Overhead expenses	$31,200
Labor and materials cost	$52,000
Overhead rate ($31,200 ÷ $52,000)	60%

If you do not have past expenses to guide you, figure that overhead will cost you from 45% to 65% of your labor and materials cost. You can raise or lower that figure to suit the realities of your operation.

Using an overhead rate of 60% as just computed, and continuing with our example, we now have:

Labor/Materials cost	$306
Overhead (60% of $306)	184
Subtotal of operating expenses	$490

Profit

Most business operators look to make a net profit of 15% to 30% out of their gross revenue. This net profit must be figured into the estimate by applying a percentage profit factor to the combined costs of labor/materials and overhead. This profit factor will be larger than the actual percentage of gross revenue you'll end up with for your net profit. For example, if you plan to net 20% (before taxes) out of your gross revenue, you will need to apply a profit factor of about 25% to your labor and materials plus overhead, to achieve that target. Doing this in our example, we now have:

Subtotal of operating expenses	$490.00
Net profit (25% of $341)	122.50
Price you quote customer	$612.50

Compare the price of $612 above with the cost of labor ($306) already estimated, and you will notice that the quote is double the labor charge. Some contractors use this ratio as a basis for determining price. They estimate their labor costs and then double that figure to arrive at their quote.

Pricing can be tedious and time consuming, especially if you don't have the knack for juggling numbers. Some contractors seem to have a "sixth sense" when it comes to pricing and estimating; they know what they need to ask to make a job profitable to them.

If you're just starting out, you won't have the skill of a pro. If your quote is too low, you will either rob yourself of some profit (or worse, lose money) or be forced to lower the quality of your work to meet the price. If you estimate too high, you may lose the contract altogether, especially if you are in a competitive bidding situation. Make it your business to learn how to estimate labor time accurately and how to calculate your overhead properly. When you quote a price, you can then be competitive and still make the profit you require.

ESTIMATING A JOB

The price you quote a client will be based on your estimate of labor costs. Your ability to make an accurate estimate is largely a matter of experience.

Survey the Job

The first step in preparing an estimate is to identify the variables that will affect the time it takes to complete a particular project. A key variable is the kind of computer-assisted operation you have. If you're performing straight word processing services, the condition of the copy you're given will be a key factor. If you're designing an ad for a client, the specifications ("specs") concerning typeface, point size, and leading will have to be marked by the client, and the number of changes you have to make from the original to the client-approval stage will be a factor in the completion of the job. If your business is an electronic clipping service, how specific the client is about the desired types of clips will be important. If you're compiling a home inventory list, the completeness of the information provided will be important. If there are special problems, areas requiring unusual attention, a high frequency of duties, or extraordinary client specifications, these variables will affect the amount you charge.

Plan the Operation

Once you have a general idea of the type of service your client wants, the next step is to map out tasks, deciding who will complete each one. If you plan to subcontract any of the labor, aim for a time estimate that is realistic—don't pad. This approach will give you a firm basis for offering the job to a subcontractor with minimal negotiation.

Determine, as best you can, the time it will take to do the job to client specifications. Don't ignore the time needed to set up equipment and put it away. Some projects may require you to write and/or run special programs, and you'll need to know exactly how much of this you can absorb. Establish the time when the work can begin and the time when it must be finished. This is especially important if your service may interfere with your client's business operation. In apportioning the work, think in terms of number and type of staff vs. job tasks. If you have not hired employees, you need to be realistic about how much you can accomplish on your own, within the client's specified time frame. If you have staff, you need to decide which workers you will use and how much supervision time they will need. If you plan to act as supervisor, be sure to include supervision time as part of the labor cost in your final estimate.

Calculate Your Costs

Once you estimate the number of hours required for you and your staff (if any) to do the tasks according to the client's specifications, you can calculate labor costs. If you're bidding on a job that calls for a monthly fee, figure the number of hours each worker will work in a month. If the job needs to be done 5 times a week, figure 21 workdays in a month. If it is to be done 3 times a week, figure 13 workdays in a month. Then multiply the wage rate for each worker (or your own time) by the number of hours you schedule for the job.

Next, calculate the cost of materials and supplies. If you don't have actual cost records, estimate your supplies cost as a percentage of labor. Later, as you do business and develop records, you can prepare estimates based on your purchases of materials and services such as computer paper, diskettes, and time on-line doing various research.

Pricing Goods for Resale

A commonly asked question is whether tangible items that you sell along with your services should be marked up—for example, you may sell stationery, envelopes, and report holders as part of your word processing service. In part, whether and how markups should occur will depend on the scope of your business. If, for example, you're arranging to sell a computer-hardware system to a business, you may be able to purchase hardware at dealer cost or slightly above, and mark up the hardware to retail price. More typically, however, a computer consultant who makes a deal with a local retailer to purchase hardware at a trade discount, in turn discounts the hardware to the client. The fact that your client does not pay full retail price makes him or her better appreciate your value as well as the value of the hardware.

But suppose you're a word processor preparing and printing 5,000 brochures for your client. You'll incur costs with your vendor—the printer. The client could take your master of the brochure and have the 5,000 copies printed. Instead, you offer full service by doing the word processing and the printing. In this case, it is customary to mark up the cost of the printing by a small margin to cover the cost of your services.

There are no universal standards for *what* items are marked up or how much the markup should be. We believe that the practice in the ad agency business, a minimum markup of 17.65% (15% margin), makes sense. Adjust the markup upward if the job is extraordinarily complex.

Because this kind of markup is just one element of a pricing system, using different markups for different kinds of work is usually preferable to adopting a single markup for all jobs. The compensation you receive should correspond closely to the nature of the work an individual client requires. Your charges will then be easier to justify.

Theoretically, if your business involves merchandising product lines or selling ancillary items, every item you sell should be priced to cover its wholesale cost, freight charges, a proportionate share of your overhead (fixed and variable operating expenses), and a reasonable profit. In reality, some items will warrant a high gross profit, and others will require a low- or no-gross profit in order to move them quickly. As long as the aggregate gross and net profits are sufficiently high, your business is successful.

COSTS

Overhead

We use "overhead" here to refer to all nonlabor expenses required to operate your business. Expenses can be divided into *fixed*—those that must be paid, usually at the same rate, regardless of the volume of business—and *variable* (or semivariable)—those that change according to the amount of business:

- *Fixed expenses.* No matter what the volume of sales is, these costs must be met every month. A good example is business insurance or basic phone rates for your business line. If your business insurance is $180 per month, irrespective of profits, it is a true fixed expense. Other fixed expenses are: depreciation on fixed assets (such as cars and office equipment); skeleton-staff salaries and associated payroll costs; utilities; membership dues and subscriptions (though these can sometimes be affected by sales volume); and accounting and legal costs. All of these continue at the same rate with little or no relation to your company revenues.

- *Variable expenses.* Most so-called variable expenses are really semivariable. They will fluctuate from month to month in relation to sales and other factors, such as promotional efforts, seasons, and variations in the prices of suppliers' products and services. In this category are: phone calls; office supplies and business forms (the more business, the greater the use of these items); printing; packaging; mailing; and advertising and promotion. In estimating variable expenses, it is common to ignore month-to-month variations (unless they are large and can be accurately predicted in advance) and use an average figure based on an estimate of the yearly total.

Cost of Services

Cost of services, also known as *cost of sales,* refers to your expenses in providing services to your clients. Accountants segregate the cost of providing services on an operating statement because it provides a measure of gross profit margin when compared with total sales—an important yardstick for measuring the firm's profitability.

Normally, the cost of goods or services bears a close relationship to sales. It will vary, however, if there are increases in the prices paid for merchandise (for example, on-line service costs for an information broker) that cannot be offset by increases in sales prices, or if special bargain purchases are made that increase profit margins. These situations seldom make a large percentage change in the relationship between cost of goods/services and sales. Therefore, the cost of goods and services is a semivariable expense.

COMPUTING MARGIN

Gross profit margin, also known as *gross profit* or *gross margin,* is the difference between net sales (total sales minus any discounts and/or returns) and the cost of those sales. For example:

Net sales	$1,000
Cost of sales	−300
Gross profit margin	$ 700

Gross profit (GP) margin can be expressed in dollars or as a percentage. As a percentage, the GP margin is always stated as a percentage of net sales. The equation is: (Total sales − Cost of sales) ÷ Net sales. In the above example, the margin would be 70%: ($1,000 − $300) ÷ $1,000. (We assume total sales and net sales are equal here, with no discounts or returns.)

When all operating expenses (rent, salaries, utilities, insurance, advertising, and so on) and other expenses are deducted from the GP margin, the remainder is the net profit before taxes. If the GP margin is not sufficiently large, there will be little or no net profit.

Some businesses require a higher GP margin than others in order to be profitable, because the costs of operating different kinds of businesses can vary tremendously. If the operating expenses in one line of business are comparatively low, then a lower GP margin will still yield the owner an acceptable profit.

The following comparison illustrates this point. Keep in mind that operating expenses and net profit are shown as the two components of GP margin (i.e., their combined percentages (of net sales) equal the GP margin):

	Business A	Business B
Net sales	100%	100%
Cost of sales	40%	65%
Gross profit margin	60%	35%
Operating expenses	43%	19%
Net profit	17%	16%

In the first example, the cost of sales (40% of net sales) is lower than in the second example (65% of net sales), leaving a higher GP margin (60% vs. 35%). But because operating expenses are also higher in the first business, when they are deducted from GP margin, they leave a net profit that's comparable to that of the second business.

COMPUTING MARKUP

Markup and (gross profit) *margin* are often confused in pricing goods and services. The reason is that, when expressed as percentages, margin is always figured as a percentage of the selling price, and markup is traditionally figured as a percentage of the seller's cost. The equation is: (Total sales − Cost of sales) ÷ Cost of sales.

Using the numbers from the preceding example, if you purchase goods for $300 and price them for sale at $1,000, your markup *in dollars* will be $700. As a percentage, this markup comes to 233%: ($1,000 − $300) ÷ $300. In other words, if your business requires a 70% margin in order to show a profit, your average markup will have to be 233%.

You can now see from our example that, although markup and margin may be the same in dollars ($700), when expressed as percentages (233% vs. 70%), they represent *two different things*. More than a few new businesses have failed to make their expected profits because the owner assumed that if the markup is X%, the margin will also be X%. This is not the case.

AVOIDING BUSINESS PITFALLS

One of the biggest pitfalls of computer-dependent businesses is loss of data on their hard drive. If you accidentally erase a file that you'd like to recover, you have to know the basics of your internal operating system—or hire someone who does. For example, if your computer is an MS-DOS machine, you might be able to use the MS-DOS Recover command. Before you try that, however, you might also look into utilities software that will help protect you from such accidents. As outlined in Chapter 2, the two most popular utility programs for Windows, DOS, and the Mac are The Norton Desktop (PC) and Norton Utilities (Mac) by Symantec, and PC Tools and Mac Tools by Central Point Software.

As with any business service company, another potential problem is allowing your receivables to age too long. You want your clients to be long-term users. To keep good customers who don't get too deeply into debt with you, insist on timely payment of all bills. No-pays are less of a problem in service businesses than slow-pays. The looser you are with credit, the more problems you'll have staying solvent.

A potential pitfall—but one that seldom occurs—is that employees will get delusions of grandeur and decide it's just as easy to start their own businesses as to keep working for you. Typically, such people exhaust their clients and contracts within 6 months and haven't a clue as to how to get more. Unlike you, they don't understand that a successful business, like those outlined above, is 50% marketing and 50% technical knowledge or well-earned expertise. Your commitment to marketing your service and marrying it with your technical and/or special business abilities will keep you well in front of the competition.

FAILURE FACTORS

Most small business surveys show that the primary reasons for business failure lie in the following areas:

1. Inefficient control over costs and quality of product.
2. Bad stock control.

3. Underpricing of services and goods.
4. Bad customer relations.
5. Failure to promote and maintain a favorable public image.
6. Bad relations with suppliers.
7. Inability of management to reach decisions and act on them.
8. Failure to keep pace with a management system.
9. Illness of key personnel.
10. Reluctance to seek professional assistance.
11. Failure to minimize taxation through tax planning.
12. Inadequate insurance.
13. Loss of impetus in sales.
14. Bad personnel relations.
15. Loss of key personnel.
16. Lack of staff training.
17. Lack of knowledge of merchandise.
18. Inability to cope adequately with competition.
19. Disregard of competition due to complacency.
20. Failure to anticipate market trends and act accordingly.
21. Loose control of liquid assets.
22. Insufficient working capital or incorrect use of capital borrowings.
23. Growth without adequate capitalization.
24. Bad budgeting.
25. Ignoring data on the company's financial position.
26. Inadequate financial records.
27. Extending too much credit.
28. Bad credit control.
29. Overborrowing or using too much credit.
30. Bad control over receivables.
31. Loss of control through creditors' demands.

9

MARKETING
YOUR SERVICES

You can offer impeccable service, unequaled efficiency, and praisewor-
thy results, but if no one knows about your business, you will find
yourself with a lack of clients.

Each home-based business targets a different clientele that re-
sponds to different advertising methods, but the key to effective advertising for *all* businesses is twofold: (1) get known, and (2) use your
market research information—who your clients are, where they are,
and what type of services they demand—to tailor your efforts and "get
known" accordingly.

ADVERTISING

Your first step in advertising is to learn as much as possible about your
target market. If you thought market research wasn't critical before, it is
essential to a successful advertising campaign. Consider the following:

- Who are my potential customers?
- How many are there?

- Where are they located?
- Where do they now obtain the services I want to sell them?
- Can I offer them anything they are not currently getting?
- How can I persuade them to do business with me?

Steps to Follow

The advertising process involves four steps:

1. Budgeting, based on what you can afford and where your advertising dollars may be most effectively spent.
2. Determining the best way to reach prospective customers so money is not wasted on nonproductive audiences.
3. Choosing a minimal number of points to be emphasized in your ad message.
4. Evaluating market and advertising information gathered to justify the dollars to be spent.

Creating the Ad Budget

How much is enough for an ad budget? Many businesses peg their ad budgets at 2% to 5% of their projected gross sales. Generally referred to as the *cost method*, this practice theorizes that an advertiser can't afford to spend more money than it has. For instance, if your projected gross sales for the first year are $60,000 based on your business plan, and you are using the cost method to determine your advertising budget (figuring 3%), you would have $1,800, or about $150 a month, to work with.

This may not seem like much, and for some businesses it won't be; they need to spend more on advertising to get their message out to the right people. These companies based their advertising budgets on the amount of money needed to move the product. This is called the *task method* of estimating. There are many different ways to determine the amount of money needed to move a product (or sell a service). The most common way is through experience.

Companies just starting out, however, won't have past records to guide them. Using the task method during start-up to determine an advertising budget, you'll have to refer to your business plan and market survey. You want to find out what media will be appropriate and what the cost will be to effectively advertise using those media.

Purposes of Advertising

Advertising provides a direct line of communication regarding your service to customers and prospective customers. Its purposes are to:

- Convince customers that your company's service, pricing, and quality are the best.
- Enhance the image of your business.
- Point out the need and create a desire for your services.
- Announce new specials and/or programs.
- Reinforce individual sales/marketing messages.
- Draw customers to your business.

Effective advertisements have six characteristics:

1. They are simple and easily understood.
2. They are truthful.
3. They are informative.
4. They are sincere.
5. They are customer-oriented.
6. They tell who, what, when, where, how, and why.

Good advertising creates a desire for your services and an inclination to do business with *your* company. Most importantly, good advertising causes action. It persuades the prospective customer to try your service.

Consumers may not realize their need for certain services until educated by advertising. This is why new ideas require extensive methods of promotion and advertising, and it explains, in part, why advertising expenses are higher during the first few years of a new business. If customers do not want a particular service, however, advertising alone cannot create acceptance.

When you first invest in advertising media, it is important to remember that advertising has a cumulative effect. Response is slow at first but increases with time. Sporadic splurges rarely pay off. It is much better to advertise regularly and continuously on a smaller scale than to place a single large advertisement infrequently.

SELECTING THE RIGHT MEDIA

The advertising media generally used by the homebased entrepreneurs we interviewed included the following:

- Referrals/Networking.
- Cold calling/Telemarketing.
- Direct mail.
- Telephone directories.
- Trade magazines.
- Newspapers.
- Radio.
- Other media (catalogs, samples, handouts, brochures, and so on).

Another relatively inexpensive medium is specialty advertising—distribution of such items as matchbooks, pencils, calendars, gummed labels, telephone pads, shopping bags, and the like, with your company name, logo, and phone number on them.

In appraising prospective advertising media and comparing them in effectiveness, you should consider the following:

- *Cost per contact.* How much will it cost to reach your specific prospective customers?
- *Frequency.* How frequent should these contacts or message deliveries be, and how often can you employ this medium (daily, weekly, monthly, bimonthly)?
- *Impact.* Does the medium in question offer full opportunities for appealing to the appropriate senses, such as sight and hearing, in presenting design, color or sound?
- *Selectivity.* To what degree can the message be restricted to those people who are known to be your most likely prospects?

Frequency

As stated, frequency and repetition are important. It is much better to advertise regularly and frequently in a small space ad than to run a one-time full-page advertisement. We recommend running ads in six-week flights in electronic media or publications that are dailies or weeklies. If you are advertising in a monthly, run the ad for six months straight.

DESIGNING THE AD

No matter what communication vehicle(s) you select, all good advertising follows established rules for form and content. Rules are made to be changed and broken, and innovators are often successful when they do that; however, first learn to imitate and follow the styles and techniques of successful advertisers.

An ad doesn't necessarily have to be logical or even artistic to be effective. It doesn't even have to look or sound good. As long as your ad is memorable, your name will stick in the minds of your consumers.

To put together an effective advertisement, you first have to analyze your company, the specific services to be plugged, and the type of clients you want to contact through the ad. Next, you have to design an appeal—that is, something that will benefit the target audience—and incorporate it into your ad copy. Some guidelines to help you create strong, response-getting ads are:

1. *Create a sense of immediacy.* Because response diminishes over time, advertising relies on getting people to act immediately. Most people like to be led—particularly when in unfamiliar territory; tell your audience what response you want. At different points throughout the ad, and especially at the conclusion, ask for a physical response: "Act quickly," "Limited-time offer," "Call now," and so on.

2. *Repetition sells.* That's why we keep repeating it. Keep weaving and reweaving the same sales pitch throughout the ad, each time adding a slightly new slant to the significant features and benefits of your service. Repetition sells because the more often someone hears or reads something, the more believable it becomes. Repetition is particularly important in advertising (as in speeches), because it normally does not pull in the full attention of the audience. Many people find writing repetitiously difficult because they were taught in school to avoid redundancy at all cost. When writing ad copy, forget this training and repeat, repeat, repeat.

3. *Hit the right "buttons" for your market.* Different people will be turned on by different things about your service: one person may admire quality, another may like easy access or personalized service. Decide what is unique and exciting about your service and then tell your target audience how and why they need what you have to sell.

4. *"Sell the sizzle, not the steak."* This is an old advertising axiom. It means sell the action—or benefits of the service—not merely the service itself. There's nothing wrong with talking about your service features briefly, but unless you spell out how your clients will directly benefit, your ad won't have maximum effectiveness. To excite your audience, describe how much better their life will be by using your service or buying your product.

When writing ads, use plain, simple English and be straightforward. Keep your ad copy at a level understandable by an 11- or 12-year-old; anything higher, and you'll lose much of your audience. Evaluate other ads—collect all kinds and study them. This is a habit of all good ad-makers. Use ideas that are worthwhile; emulate the strengths of others who are successful with their advertising, and add your own imagination and creativity.

For print ads, visual art is key. Your visual element should create human interest, emotion, and realism; your design should reflect professionalism and creativity.

If you can afford photography in print ads, use it. Photographs are generally more believable than illustrations, and they're usually more easily remembered. If not, there are other ways to add visual impact to a print ad. One is to create an ad with a lot of white space. These kinds of ads work well because of the dense columns of type used in some publications. Anything that breaks up the pattern stands out.

This variation is true not only for the design of the print ad, but for its size as well. Ads that are different in size from standard formats will stand out in a publication. For instance, a diagonal ad will break up standard media formats, as will running three ads in rapid succession. Placing an ad that runs across two pages can also be effective, but is likely more expensive.

SUCCESSFUL MARKETING APPROACHES

Referrals

Word of mouth is always important to business growth. Each happy customer can steer dozens of new ones to your business, and most will do so gladly. Home-based businesses that rely heaviest on word of mouth and referrals include architectural services, information brokers, and business consultants. However, *all* businesses can benefit significantly from referrals.

To make referrals easy, make sure that you have business cards and/or flyers and brochures handy for clients to pass on to others. If your clients do not come to your home office, send cards and information with their billing statements—along with a thank-you for using your service and recommending you to others.

Another good referral mechanism is to reciprocate advertising referrals with other businesses in your area that service similar clients. For example, if you offer computer training, business consulting, business plan writing, or the like, try reciprocal advertising referrals with office supply warehouses, computer hardware/software stores, printers, copier services, and courier/messenger companies. Offer to hand out their business cards and literature to your clients in return for let-ting you leave your cards and brochures at their business. Make good on your promise; generally, your clients will appreciate a referral to a business you recommend, if they are happy with your services.

Networking

Successful operators in any business are frequently well known in their communities. This is no accident. Smart business people know the importance of making contacts; they become active in their commu-nities—joining and leading civic organizations, attending charity events, speaking at seminars, getting involved in politics, and attend-ing openings of other businesses and events at local institutions. Proper running of your business comes first, but time spent developing contacts is essential to a home-based venture.

Take networking a step further by becoming a local expert in your business. Offer to write articles for local publications or trade maga-zines (editors appreciate free articles by experts to round out their ed-itorial well without raising costs). Become a local speaker on your business or specific business skills. Apply for awards when they are of-fered in your field, especially those sponsored by organizations you have joined. Your involvement reinforces the image of you as an expert.

Most importantly, reach out to your community. Can you sponsor a scholarship or a local baseball team? Donate your business services to a worthwhile cause? Your return on this type of investment will likely be high, because nearly all home-based businesses rely heavily on word of mouth.

Cold Calling/Telemarketing

Many entrepreneurs dread the three words above, but these are highly effective techniques for selling your service to business clients. Believe it or not, some companies operate exclusively via the telephone. It has been reported, for instance, that some telemarketing firms, selling only office supplies, are grossing $10 million to $15 million annually. Telephone solicitations *can* generate considerable business.

Home-based businesses that rely on cold calling and telemarket-ing include newsletter publishers (who need business advertisers) and inventory control services. In the early stages of market research, how-ever, nearly all entrepreneurs would benefit from telemarketing.

Telemarketing costs vary, depending on several factors, one of which is the cost to purchase calling lists. For this reason, collecting names, addresses, and phone numbers in the marketing research phase of your business is crucial. You can buy lists that include telephone numbers, but these cost considerably more than standard lists. Whether such a list is worth the extra cost is difficult to predict. Consider testing on a limited basis.

Follow-Up: Selling the Client Face to Face

Contact potential clients by phone to set up an appointment, and prepare yourself well for the first meeting. Look and act sharp—this is coat-and-tie or heels-and-dress time, even if you live in a casual area. Be prompt; being late for this appointment is a sure way to hurt your chances.

Bring samples of your work to this meeting—or a list of references, if visual copies of your work are not possible. A portfolio of testimonial letters or of work samples gives the prospect an idea of the quality of your services. The pitch you make in person should include an explanation of how cost-effective your service is for your clients. Remember: benefits, benefits, benefits.

Direct Mail

Direct-mail advertising controls distribution of information to a selected audience, offering you more flexibility in budgeting and greater selectivity in choosing prospects than other kinds of advertising. It also allows you to send a personalized sales message to prospective customers. The U.S. postal regulations provide special rates for direct mail, making this highly effective medium available at a reasonable cost.

Home-based businesses that rely heavily on direct mail include computer consulting, software design, research services, bulletin board services, and data detectives. Mail-order companies and newsletter publishers constantly advertise through direct mail simply by sending out their products.

Your direct-mail advertising should be personal, informal, and selectively directed. Careful study of charge-account and delivery records, as well as your personal knowledge of your customers, will enable you to classify most of your clientele into groups that have common buying interests. If you thoughtfully word your direct-mail pieces, you can create an impression of individualized attention to each recipient.

Today, computer systems linked to your telephone are capable of identifying a new person who is calling your business for the first time. When this happens, the software program automatically prints a mailing label so that you can send the caller further information on your business, and the program stores the information.

You can also rent mailing lists from list brokers. Mailing lists today are ultrasophisticated, and you can get lists in just about any category you want. The one-time rental fee for these names is usually between $35 and $50 per thousand, with a minimum rental of 5,000 names.

How do you pick a list? Use the RFM formula: R stands for recency, F for frequency, and M for money. Because people and businesses move and their economic status changes, recency is vital to the success of a list. Frequency refers to how many times the people on the list purchased your type of service. Money refers to how much they spent.

Because good mailing lists are essential for the success of a direct-marketing campaign, check out the list as thoroughly as possible. Buy only from established services. You can find mailing list brokers in your Yellow Pages under "Advertising—Direct Mail," but if possible ask other business owners for referrals.

One question to ask before paying for a list is: How many times has the list been sold in the previous six months? Get the names and telephone numbers of some of the buyers, and call and ask them what their response rate was with the list, how many pieces were returned because of bad addresses, and whether they thought the list was worth the cost.

Once you've got your own list of clients, consider trading lists with other established businesses to save money and share good leads. A good way to develop your own list is to attend trade shows that attract consumers from your targeted market, and offer a drawing for a prize (i.e., money or free services). Business cards will be thrown into your drawing bucket. You select one lucky winner, and then walk away with the names, addresses, and phone numbers of many new prospective clients. Another good way to generate contacts is to offer to be a columnist or product reviewer (for hardware, software, and other components) for a trade journal or other publication. In your column, invite readers to write you with questions, and respond sincerely. Then use the names and addresses collected to build your contact list.

Telephone Directories

Most local businesses advertise their goods and services in a local telephone directory, usually the Yellow Pages. With the exception of bulletin board services and mail-order companies, there is no reason *not* to place an ad in the Yellow Pages to reach prospective clients. Follow the lead of other word processing services, sign makers, multimedia companies, and computer service businesses that advertise regularly in the Yellow Pages, and consider purchasing a sizable ad.

Yellow Pages advertisements may be illustrated and can vary in size from simple one-line listings to quarter-page, full-page, or multi-page (repeat ads) spreads. The phone company has specific categories in which it classifies businesses. Be careful to choose the most appropriate one(s). Sometimes it may be worthwhile to cross-reference your listing. Be careful about making the Yellow Pages deadlines for sending in your ad(s). Missing them can mean going a whole year without advertising in this important medium.

The "800" Telephone Number

The 800 number exploded in the early 1970s as a national and regional marketing tool. If your customers are scattered across the country and would have to invest in a long-distance call to get in touch with you, consider an 800 number a necessity. (Some businesses, like mail order, automatically install an 800 number for customer orders or service.)

Even with home-based businesses, 800 numbers have become so common that businesses that market and sell throughout a wide territory and don't have one are at a competitive disadvantage. The opposing argument is that an 800 number, if not handled right, encourages a certain number of "shoppers"—a.k.a. *unqualified leads*—on whom your time and money are largely wasted.

You must determine whether the costs outweigh the benefits for the clients you will be serving. The installation, monthly service charges, and usage rates can add up to a substantial sum. (Your phone company will give you the current fees.)

Newspapers and Trade Magazines

Generally, local newspapers will be the best placement if you plan to use newspaper advertising for your services. Most of the home-based entrepreneurs we interviewed did not use this medium; however, there are two good reasons to consider local publications if your budget allows it. First, your ad helps place your business in the minds of editors at small papers. Editors with passing interest on a story about how computers allow small-scale entrepreneurs to conduct large-scale businesses from home may be sold on the idea once they get to know you and your business. (Local editors also are normally some of the best-known people in town—highly desirable contacts for networking.)

Second, you can advertise cost-effectively in many newspapers and magazines by asking about "remainder space" advertising rates. Generally, this means that you provide the publication with a standard ad that it will place automatically—at reduced rates—whenever it has unexpected ad space to fill.

Trade magazines are used regularly by the following home-based entrepreneurs: bulletin board services, business plan writers, computer consultants/programmers, data detectives, information brokers/research services, multimedia services, and software designers. To select the right trade magazines for your business, study your market research information and find out where your competitors are advertising.

BROCHURES

As a medium for explaining the services you offer, a brochure conveys professionalism. A brochure can give the impression of a serious, established, high-quality business—even if you just opened up yesterday.

Your company brochure does not have to be a four-color job. To keep expenses down, go for a light-colored card stock measuring 7 ¼" × 8 ½". With one center fold lengthwise, the brochure fits easily into a No. 10 envelope. This makes it an ideal companion for your direct-mail marketing efforts, as well as an excellent handout. We stress the size because an ordinary-size sheet of paper will tend to blend in with other stacks of paper, and an oversized brochure can be pretentious as opposed to professional.

If you know that you write well and persuasively, then write the brochure yourself. If you have any doubt about your ability to do a top-notch job, trust the writing and the design to professionals. To save on costs, see about trading your services with those of a freelance writer and/or graphic designer in your area.

Be careful about typeface: your message should be easy to read and no smaller than 10 point. It should take not much more than a minute for anyone to scan your brochure; however, those 60-odd seconds should communicate memorable information. Many companies do not use brochures. Give yourself the extra advertising edge and professionalism a brochure provides.

SPECIALTY ITEMS

You can inscribe your company's name and/or logo on matchbooks, calendars, pens, pads of paper, balloons, and other handouts. The list of potential products is practically endless. Inexpensive specialties can be given free to customers who patronize your business. Others can be left with local businesses or given out at seminars, community meetings, and other gatherings, to advertise your business.

Ad specialties help your customers enjoy an identification with your company while providing an inexpensive—and useful—advertising tool.

SOLICITING FEEDBACK AND MEASURING ADVERTISING EFFECTIVENESS

As a business owner, you should never stop surveying and studying your customers. If a client drifts away, try at once to determine why.

It may sound strange, but you should actively solicit complaints from your clients. Even happy clients can provide valuable suggestions on making your service even better, if they are invited and encouraged to give you feedback.

When clients complain, take notes while they are talking. This allows you to place some emotional distance between yourself and the complaint, and ensures that you will have specifics regarding the complaint instead of remembering only the emotion with which it was conveyed. Regardless of the nature of a complaint, validate the client's concerns. Even if you feel the complaint is petty or unfounded at the time, you may be surprised to hear the same complaint again in the future, or to find a different meaning in the complaint when read a day or two later.

Clients' complaints offer truly golden opportunities for you to effectively stop problems that you may not have realized existed. Follow up with clients who have complained or provided suggestions, and thank them for their input. If you have changed operations to reflect improvements based on their input, let them know of your action.

Check the effectiveness of your advertising programs regularly, using tests like the following:

1. Advertise one item or service in one ad only. Have no references to the item or service on the business premises. Then count the calls and requests for the advertised item.
2. Run the same ad in two different publications, and place an identifying mark on each. Ask the reader to turn in the ad to receive a special price or discount. Track how many ads come in from each source.
3. Omit a regular advertising project for intermittent periods and watch any change in sales.
4. Check sales results when you place a new advertisement.

These tests cannot provide precise measurements, but they can give you some idea of how your program is performing. Timing, season, economic conditions, and similar factors can affect any advertising program. If results are not significant, the program may still have served an institutional purpose by telling people your firm is there. Some readers may give you their business in the future.

SALES PROMOTION

You need sales promotion to attract new clients and hold present ones, to counteract competition, and to take advantage of opportunities revealed by your market research.

Plan your sales promotion activities at the beginning of each business year, and revise them as needed during the year. Base your strategies on market opportunities indicated by reliable market research that tells you what to promote, where to promote, and when to promote.

Determine what to promote by considering where the best profit opportunities lie and noting which market areas hold the greatest promise for development.

If your analysis of company sales shows that normal sales efforts are not penetrating certain areas of town, you may have to plan a special promotion to open up those areas.

PROMOTING THE BUSINESS

Do not let your business keep a "low profile" simply because you work from your home. Local newspapers are most interested in local news, and that's what you are as a local business owner. When you start a new business, when you have a contest promotion, when you do something charitable, when something unusual happens to you, your business, or your employees—these are newsworthy events worth letting the local media know about. Why is publicity so important, and what will it do that advertising won't? In general, a news story or magazine article takes more time to read than an ad. The more time a reader spends with your story, the more likely he or she will remember you.

Appreciate the factor of "reach." You can place news and feature stories in more periodicals than you could afford to reach through paid advertising. Besides, an article in a respected newspaper or magazine, or an appearance on radio or cable television occurs only if it meets the standards of the editor or programming director. It therefore gives to your story third-party credibility that cannot be duplicated with paid advertisements.

When you begin any publicity campaign, it's important to make the right media contacts. For newspapers, the most likely contact is the city editor; for radio or cable television, get in touch with the programming director. Just call up the newspaper or broadcast station, ask for the name of the person, and be sure you have the correct spelling/pronunciation of the name and the correct address. This is common courtesy and is extremely important to some media people. Take time to track down the right people; this contact will pay off for you.

Keep alert to anything that can give you publicity. Not everything may be accepted by the media, but whatever is accepted will be a form of free advertising for you. Be sure to reprint all your publicity stories and news releases. Use them as highly credible advertising handouts and mailers.

IMAGE AND IDENTITY

Image—the way your company and its services are viewed by the public—is very important. You establish your image through your advertising, your service, your community networking, and your work product. It is helped or hurt by every dealing you or your employees have with consumers who come into contact with your business.

Identity is different from image. Your business identity is the "Who am I? What service do I offer?" of your company.

Identity can change over time, but, as business changes occur, entrepreneurs must always stay aware of who they are and what they offer. Identity gives companies focus. It affects decision making and directs change. To be successful, remember to have a clear picture of your company's identity and market niche. Know your strengths, know your limits, and be mindful of changes to your business identity that should be affecting your decision making.

Appendix

RESOURCES

ASSOCIATIONS

Computer and Business
   Equipment Manufacturers
   Association
1250 Eye Street, NW, Suite 200
Washington, DC 20005
(202) 737-8888

Computer Dealers and Lessors
   Association
1212 Potomac Street, NW
Washington, DC 20007
(202) 333-0102

Electronics Technicians
   Association International
602 N. Jackson
Greencastle, IN 46135
(317) 653-8262

Independent Computer
   Consultants Association
933 Gardenview Office Parkway
St. Louis, MO 63141
(314) 997-4633

Institute of Electrical and
   Electronics Engineers, Inc.
   (IEEE)
Computer Society
1730 Massachusetts Avenue, NW
Washington, DC 20036-1992
(202) 371-0101

National Electronic Service
   Dealers Association
2708 W. Berry, Suite 8
Ft. Worth, TX 76109
(817) 921-9061

EQUIPMENT MANUFACTURERS

Adobe Systems
411 First Avenue South
Seattle, WA 98104
(206) 622-5500

Apple Computer, Inc.
1 Infinite Loop
Cupertino, CA 95014
(408) 996-1010

Borland International, Inc.
1800 Green Hills Road/100
        Borland Way
Scotts Valley, CA 95067-0001
(408) 431-1000; (800) UPGRADE

CE Software, Inc. (QuickMail)
P.O. Box 65580
West Des Moines, IA 50265
(515) 221-1801

Corel Corporation
1600 Carling Avenue
Ottawa, Ontario,
        Canada K1Z8R7
(613) 728-8200; (800) 772-6735

Delrina Technology
6830 Via Del Oro, Suite 240
San Jose, CA 95119
(408) 363-2345

IBM PC Company
Route 100, Bldg. 1
Mailstop 1197
Somers, NY 10589
(914) 766-1425; (914) 766-1563;
(914) 766-1813

Intel Corporation
5200 NE Eloam Young Pkwy.
Hillsboro, OR 97214
(800) 538-3373

Intuit, Inc.
P.O. Box 3014
Menlo Park, CA 94026
(415) 592-7600

Lotus Development Corporation
55 Cambridge Pkwy.
Cambridge, MA 02142
(617) 253-9150; (800) TRADE-UP

Microsoft Corporation
16011 NE 36th Way
Box 97017
Redmond, WA 98073-9717
(206) 454-2030

On Technology Corp.
        (Meeting Maker)
1 Cambridge Center
Cambridge, MA 02142
(800) 548-8871

Quark, Inc.
1800 Grant Street
Denver, CO 80203
(303) 894-8888;
(800) 676-4575

Quarterdeck Office
        Systems
150 Pico Blvd.
Santa Monica, CA 90045
(310) 392-9701

Software Publishing Corp.
        (Harvard Graphics)
3165 Kifer Road
P.O. Box 54983
Santa Clara, CA 95056-0983
(408) 986-8000

Symantec Corporation
D10201 Torre Avenue
Cupertino, CA 95014-2132
(408) 253-9600;
(800) 441-7234

WordPerfect Corporation
1555 N. Technology Way
Orem, UT 84057-2399
(801) 225-5000 corporate;
(800) 451-5151

MAJOR SOFTWARE MANUFACTURERS' TECHNICAL SUPPORT CONTACTS

Word Processing Software

Lotus AmiPro
(404) 399-5505

Microsoft Word
(206) 462-9673

Microsoft Word-(MAC)
(206) 635-7200

Wordperfect
(800) 228-9907

Spreadsheet Software

Lotus 1-2-3 for Windows
(800) 386-8600

Microsoft Excel
(206) 635-7070

Microsoft Excel (MAC)
(206) 635-7080

Novell Quattro Pro
(800) 861-2773

Accounting Software

Intuit Quicken, Quickbooks
(415) 858-6035

Microsoft Profit
(800) 723-3333

Peachtree
(404) 279-2099

Communications Networks

MCI Data Services
P.O. Box 49019
San Jose, CA 95161-9019
(408) 922-0250

Sprint
1850 M Street, NW, Suite 1100
Washington, DC 20036
(800) 877-2000

Contact Management Software

Cognitech Sharkware
(800) 487-4275

Database Software

Borland Paradox
(408) 461-9155

Lotus Approach
(800) 386-8600

Microsoft Access
(206) 635-7050

Insurance

Safeware, The Insurance Agency
2929 N. High Street
P.O. Box 02211
Columbus, OH 43202-9980
(800) 800-1492

Presentation Software

Lotus Freelance
(800) 386-8600

Microsoft Powerpoint
(206) 635-7145

SPECIALIZED SOFTWARE AND HARDWARE VENDORS

Adobe Systems
1585 Charlston Road
P.O. Box 7900
Mountain View, CA 94039
(800) 833-6687, (415) 961-4400

American Medical Software
7 Glened Professional Park
Edwardsville, IL 62025
(800) 423-8836

American Small Business
    Computers
1 American Way
Pryor, OK 74361
(918) 825-7555

Business Resource Software
2013 Wells Branch Parkway,
    Suite 30500
Austin, TX 78728
(800) 423-1228

Cambridge Educational
90 MacCorkle Avenue, SW
South Charleston, WV 25303
(800) 468-4227

Chronicle Guidance
    Publications
66 Aurora Street
P.O. Box 1190
Moravia, NY 13118-1190
(800) 622-7284

Computer Medica Corporation
860 5th Avenue, Apt. 10-E
New York, NY 10021
(212) 794-2000

Computer Place Inc., The
916 East Baseline Road, Suite 225
Mesa, AZ 85204
(800) 333-4747

Computer Sports World
1005 Elm Street
Boulder City, NV 89005
(800) 321-5562

Context Software
241 S. Frontage Road, Suite 38
Burr Ridge, IL 60521
(800) 783-3378

Corel Systems Corporation
1600 Carling Avenue
Ottawa, Ontario K1Z 8R7
(613) 728-8200

Deneba Software
7400 SW 87th Avenue
Miami, FL 33173
(305) 596-5644

Dydacomp
150 River Road, Suite N-1
Montville, NJ 07045
(800) 858-3666

Dynacomp, Inc.
Dynacomp Office Building
178 Phillips Road
Webster, NY 14580
(800) 828-6772

Dynamic Pathways Company
180 Newport Center Drive
    Suite 100
Newport Beach, CA 92660
(800) 543-7788

Electronic Arts
1450 Fashion Island Boulevard
San Mateo, CA 94404
(800) 245-4525

Elite Software Developers
P.O. Box 1194
Bryan, TX 77806
(800) 648-9523

Engineering Consulting
583 Candlewood Street
Brea, CA 92621
(714) 671-2009

Foresight Resources Corporation
10725 Ambassador Drive
Kansas City, MO 64153-1216
(800) 231-8574

Group 1 Software Inc.
4200 Parliament Place, # 600
Lanham, MD 20706-1844
(800) 368-5806

Hewlett Packard Company
P.O. Box 58059, MS 511L-SJ
Santa Clara, CA 95051-8059
(800) 752-0900, (208) 323-2551

Institute of Business Forecasting
P.O. Box 159
Flushing, NY 11367
(718) 463-3914

Ioline Corporation
12020 113th Avenue, NE
Kirkland, WA 98034
(206) 821-2140

Janac Enterprises
P.O. Box 394
Hebron, IL 60034
(815) 648-2492

Kent-Marsh Ltd.
3260 Sul Ross
Houston, TX 77098
(800) 325-3587, (713) 522-5625

Lifestyle Software Group
63 Orange Street
St. Augustine, FL 32084
(800) 289-1157

Microtek Lab, Inc.
680 Knox Street
Torrance, CA 90502
(800) 654-4160, (213) 321-2121

Now Software
921 SW Washington Street, # 500
Portland, OR 97205
(503) 274-2815, (800) 237-2078

ProHelp Systems
P.O. Box 1284
Lawrenceville, GA 30246
(404) 962-6425

Roland Digital Group
1961 McGaw Avenue
Irvine, CA 92714
(714) 975-0560

RSA Data Security, Inc.
100 Marina Parkway, Suite 500
Redwood City, CA 94065
(415) 595-8782

Soft Run Software
68 Pine Hill Estates
Kenova, WV 25530
(304) 453-6775

Spreadware
P.O. Box 4552
Palm Desert, CA 92261-4552
(619) 360-7881

TE Corporation
P.O. Box 140
Campton, NH 03223
(603) 726-4700

usrEZ
18881 Von Karman, Suite 1200
Irvine, CA 92715
(800) 482-4622, (714) 756-5140

Wellsource, Inc.
P.O. Box 569
Clackamas, OR 97015
(800) 533-9355

Wintergreen Orchard House
P.O. Box 15899
New Orleans, LA 70175
(608) 845-8410

ON-LINE SERVICES

America Online
8619 Westwood Center Drive
Vienna, VA 22182-2285
(800) 827-6364

CDP Technologies, Inc.
333 7th Avenue, 4th Floor
New York, NY 10001
(800) 289-4277

CompuServe Information
    Services
5000 Arlington Centre Boulevard
P.O. Box 20212
Columbus, OH 43220
(800) 848-8199

Delphi Internet Services
1020 Massachusetts Avenue
Cambridge, MA 02138
(800) 544-4005, (617) 491-3342

DIALOG Information Services,
    Inc.
Marketing Dept.
3460 Hillview Avenue
Palo Alto, CA 94304
(415) 858-3785, (800) 334-2564

Dow Jones News/Retrieval
    Service
P.O. Box 300
Princeton, NJ 08543
(609) 452-1511

GEnie
G.E. Information Services
401 N. Washington Street
Rockville, MD 20850
(800) 638-9636

LEXIS/NEXIS
Mead Data Central
9393 Springboro Pike
P.O. Box 933
Dayton, OH 45342
(513) 859-5398, (800) 543-6862

NewsNet
945 Haverford Road
Bryn Mawr, PA 19010
(215) 527-8030, (800) 345-1301

ORBIT•Questel
8000 Westpark Drive
McLean, VA 22102
(800) 456-7248

PUBLICATIONS

Byte Magazine
McGraw-Hill, Inc.
One Phoenix Mill Lane
Peterborough, NH 03458
(603) 924-9281

*Computer Buyer's Guide and
    Handbook*
Bedford Communications, Inc.
150 Fifth Avenue, Suite 714
New York, NY 10011
(212) 807-8220
(features software reviews)

Computer Data
501 Oakdale Road
North York, Ontario, Canada
    M3N1W7
(416) 746-7360

Computer Reseller News
600 Community Drive
Manhasset, NY 11030
(516) 365-4600

Computerworld
375 Cochituate Road
Framingham, MA 01701
(508) 879-6700

Computing Canada
255 Consumers Road, Suite 110
Willowdale, Ontario, Canada
   M2J5B1
(416) 497-9562

Desktop Publishing With Style
And Books
702 S. Michigan
South Bend, IN 46601
(219) 232-3134

Directory of On-Line Databases
Gale Research, Inc.
P.O. Box 33477
Detroit, MI 48232-5477
(800) 877-GALE

Encyclopedia of Information Systems
   and Services
Gale Research, Inc.
835 Penebscot
Detroit, MI 48226
(313) 961-2242

Home Office Computing
Scholastic, Inc.
555 Broadway
New York, NY 10012
(800) 288-7812

Information Times: The Annual
   Directory of the Information
   Industry Association
Information Industry Association
555 New Jersey Avenue, NW,
   Suite 800
Washington, DC 20001
(202) 639-8260

Macintosh Buyers Guide
660 Beachland Boulevard,
   3rd Floor
Vero Beach, FL 32963
(407) 231-6904

MacUser
1 Park Avenue
New York, NY 10016
(800) 289-0429 subscriptions

Mini-Micro Systems
275 Washington Street
Newton, MA 02158
(617) 964-3030

PC Magazine
Ziff-Davis Publishing Co.
1 Park Avenue
New York, NY 10016
(212) 503-5255

PC World & Macworld
PCW Communications, Inc.
501 Second Street, Suite 600
San Francisco, CA 91407
(415) 243-0500

Personal Computing
Penton-VNU Business
   Publications, Inc.
10 Holland Drive
Hasbrouck Heights, NJ 07604
(201) 393-6000

Publish!
PCW Communications, Inc.
501 Second Street, Suite 600
San Francisco, CA 94107
(415) 243-0600

Service News
P.O. Box 995
Yarmouth, ME 04096
(207) 846-0600

Software Digest Magazine
Plymouth Corporate Center
Box 1000
Plymouth Meeting, PA 19462
(215) 878-9300

GLOSSARY

GENERAL BUSINESS*

accounts receivable: A record used to account for the total number of sales made through the extension of credit.

accrual basis: An accounting method used for recordkeeping purposes where all income and expenses are charged to the period to which they apply, regardless of whether money has been received.

acid-test ratio: An analysis method used to measure the liquidity of a business by dividing total liquid assets by current liabilities.

asset earning power: A common profitability measure used to determine the profitability of a business by taking its total earnings before taxes and dividing that amount by its total assets.

Audit Bureau of Circulation (ABC): A third-party organization that verifies the circulation of print media through periodical audits.

balance sheet: A financial statement used to report a business's total assets, liabilities, and equity.

bonding: Generally used by service companies as a guarantee to their clients that they have the necessary ability and financial backing to meet their obligations.

break-even analysis: An analysis method used to determine the number of jobs or products that need to be sold to cover all expenses and begin to earn a profit for a business.

business plan: A plan used to chart a new or ongoing business's strategies, sales projections, and key personnel in order to obtain financing and provide a strategic foundation for growth.

---

*See also the *Dictionary of Business and Management,* by Jerry M. Rosenberg, published by John Wiley & Sons, Inc.

Business Publications Audit (BPA): Similar to the Audit Bureau of Circulation, the BPA is a third-party organization that verifies the circulation of print media through periodical audits.

capitalization: Capital may be in the form of money, common stock, long-term debt, or some combination of all three. With too much capital, a firm is overcapitalized; with too little capital, it is undercapitalized.

cash basis: An accounting method used for recordkeeping where income is logged when received and expenses are charged when they occur.

chattel mortgage contract: A credit contract used for the purchase of equipment where the purchaser receives title to the equipment upon delivery but the creditor holds a mortgage claim against it.

collateral: Assets used as security for the extension of a loan.

commercial loan: A short-term loan, usually issued for a term of six months.

conditional sales contract: A credit contract used for the purchase of equipment where the purchaser doesn't receive title of the equipment until the amount specified in the contract has been paid in full.

cooperative advertising: A joint advertising strategy used by a manufacturer and another firm that distributes its products.

copyright: A form of protection used to safeguard original literary works, performing arts, sound recordings, visual arts, and renewals.

corporation: A legal form of operation that declares the business a separate legal entity guided by a group of officers known as the board of directors.

cost-of-living lease: A lease where yearly increases are tied to the government's cost of living index.

cost per thousand (CPM): Terminology used in buying media. CPM refers to the cost it takes to reach 1,000 people within a target market.

current ratio: A ratio used to determine the difference between total current assets and total current liabilities.

demographic characteristics: The attributes such as income, age, and occupation that best describe a target market.

depreciation: The lessening in value of fixed assets that provides the foundation for a tax deduction based on either the declining-balance or straight-line method.

disability insurance: A payroll tax required in some states that is deducted from employee paychecks to ensure income during periods when an employee is unable to work due to an injury or illness.

disclosure document program: A form of protection that safeguards an idea while it is in its developmental stage.

dollar control system: A system used in inventory management that reveals the cost and gross profit margin on individual inventory items.

Dun & Bradstreet: An agency that furnishes subscribers with market statistics and the financial standings and credit ratings of businesses.

equipment loan: A loan used for the purchase of capital equipment.

equity capital: A form of financing where equity in a business is sold to private investors.

exploratory research: A method used when gathering primary information for a market survey, where targeted consumers are asked very general questions geared toward eliciting a lengthy answer.

Fair Labor Standards Act: A federal law that enforces minimum standards that employers must abide by when hiring.

Federal Insurance Contributions Act (FICA): A law that requires employers to match the amount of Social Security tax deducted from an employee's paycheck.

fictitious name: Often referred to as a DBA (Doing Business As). A fictitious name is frequently used by sole proprietors or partnerships to provide a name, other than those of the owners or partners, under which the business will operate.

first in, first out (FIFO): An accounting system used to value inventory for tax purposes. Under FIFO, inventory is valued at its most recent cost.

fixed expenses: Expenses that must be paid each month and do not fluctuate with the sales volume.

flat lease: A lease where the cost is fixed for a specific period of time.

frequency: The number of times you hope to reach your target audience through your advertising campaign.

401K plan: A retirement plan for employees that allows them to deduct money from their paychecks and place it in a tax-sheltered account.

income statement: A financial statement that charts the sales and operating costs of a business over a specific period of time, usually a month. Also called a profit and loss statement or an operating statement.

inventory loan: A loan that is extended based on the value of a business's inventory.

inventory turnover: An analysis method used to determine the amount of capital invested in inventory and the total number of times per year that investment will revolve.

investment tax credit: A tax credit that allows businesses to write off the first $18,000 of equipment purchased for business use.

investment turnover: A profitability measure used to evaluate the number of times per year that total investment or assets revolve.

Keogh: A pension plan that lets business owners contribute a defined portion of their profits toward a tax-sheltered account. There are several Keoghs to choose from, such as profit-sharing and defined-contribution plans.

last in, first out (LIFO): A method of valuing inventories in which items sold or used are priced at the cost of the most recent acquisitions and those remaining are valued at the cost of earliest acquisitions.

leasehold improvements: The repairs and improvements made to a facility before occupation by the lessee.

liability: A term used when analyzing insurance risks; describes possible areas of exposure. While a business may be liable for numerous comprehensive and special coverages that blanket almost every known exposure, there are three forms of liability coverage that insurers usually will underwrite: (1) *general liability,* which covers any kind of bodily injury to nonemployees except that caused by automobiles and professional malpractice; (2) *product liability,* which covers injury to customers arising as a direct result of goods purchased from a business; and (3) *public liability,* which covers injury to the public or visitors when they are on your premises.

market survey: A research method used to define the market parameters of a business.

markup: The amount added to the cost of goods in order to produce the desired profit.

measure of liquidity: An analysis method used to measure the amount of available liquid assets to meet accounts payable.

Modified Accelerated Cost Recovery System (MACRS): Used in accounting to define the rate and method by which a fixed asset will be depreciated for tax purposes.

net leases: Typically, there are three net leases: (1) a net lease, (2) a double-net lease, and (3) a triple-net lease. A net lease is a base rent plus an additional charge for taxes. A double-net lease is a base rent plus an additional charge for taxes and insurance. A triple-net lease is base rent plus an additional charge for taxes, insurance, and common area expenses.

net profit on sales: A profitability measure that determines the difference between net profit and operating costs.

open to buy: The dollar amount budgeted by a business for inventory purchases for a specific time period.

overhead: All nonlabor expenses needed to operate a business.

partnership: A legal form of business operation between two or more individuals. The federal government recognizes several types of partnerships. The two most common are general and limited partnerships.

patent: A form of protection that provides a person or legal entity with exclusive rights to exclude others from making, using, or selling a concept or invention for the duration of the patent. Design, plant, and utility patents are available.

percentage lease: A type of lease where the landlord charges a base rent plus an additional percentage of any profits produced by the business tenant.

personal loans: Short-term loans that are extended based on the personal integrity of the borrower.

point-of-sale (POS) systems: A computerized network that is operated by a miniframe computer and linked to several checkout terminals.

profit: There are generally two kinds of profit: (1) gross profit, the difference between gross sales and cost of sales, and (2) net profit, the difference between gross profit and all costs associated with operating a business.

reach: The total number of people in a target market to be contacted through an advertising campaign.

return on investment (ROI): A profitability measure that evaluates the performance of a business by dividing net profit by total assets.

return on owner's equity: A profitability measure used to gauge the earning power of the owner's total equity in a business by dividing the average equity investment of the owner by the net profit.

signature loans: See *personal loans.*

sole proprietor: A legal form of operation where only one owner can exist.

specific research: A method used when gathering primary information for a market survey. Targeted customers are asked very specific, in-depth questions geared toward resolving problems found through exploratory research.

Standard Rate and Data Service (SRDS): A company that produces a group of directories that list rates, circulation, contacts, markets serviced, and so on, for different types of media.

step lease: A type of lease that outlines annual increases in the tenant's base rent, based on an approximation of what the landlord thinks maintenance and repair expenses may be.

Subchapter S: Under federal law, small corporations in this category can pay out all income proportionately to their shareholders, who then claim the income on their personal income tax returns.

sublet: The leasing by the original lessee, of space in a rented facility.

unit-control system: An inventory management system that tracks inventory using bin tickets and physical inventory checks.

variable expenses: Business costs that fluctuate in successive payment periods according to the sales volume.

venture capital: A source of financing for either start-up or expansion capital that is based on providing private investors with equity positions within the business.

workers' compensation: A privately managed or state insurance fund that reimburses employees for injuries suffered on the job.

working capital: Net current assets required for a company to carry on with its work; the surplus of a firm's current assets over its current liabilities.

COMPUTER-RELATED TERMS*

bus: The highway along which instructions from the central processing unit (CPU) pass to the other components of the system.

card: A component that attaches to the motherboard to supplement the electronic capabilities of the computer.

CD-ROM: A device that reads data from, but cannot write data to, a compact disk.

clock speed: The speed in which computer instructions are processed, as measured in millionths of a second, or megahertz (MHz).

CPU: The central processing unit of the computer, often called the "chip" because it is made of a small wafer-size chip of silicon. It is the brains of the package, directing everything that happens with the computer.

disk drive: The storage place for computer programs and data.

DOS: One type of special software, called an operating system, that provides basic instructions to the computer for printing, storing and copying files, and other functions.

DPI: Dots per inch.

gigabyte: The expression used for a million bytes, or 1,000 megabytes.

megabyte: A million bytes, with one byte equivalent to a character. Thus, a 200-megabyte hard disk drive has the capacity to hold 200 million characters.

megahertz: Millionths of a second; the speed in which computer instructions are executed.

modem: A device that allows digital computer information, including fax images, to be transferred over analog telephone lines to any location where another modem will receive them.

motherboard: The main electronic component of the computer on which the CPU or memory chips (RAM) reside. It is a flat piece of plastic inserted into the computer case to which all the other components are attached or welded.

network: Two or more computers connected to share files or peripheral devices such as printers.

operating system: The software program that handles all basic instructions—printing, copying files, and so on, so that each of the application programs does not have to build in replicated instructions for these functions.

optical character recognition (OCR) program: A program used to convert the scanned image to actual letters and other characters that can be edited.

PCMCIA (expansion) slots: Outlets on a computer that provide room for adding more memory, disk space, modems, and so on.

---

*See also the *Business Dictionary of Computers,* by Jerry M. Rosenberg, published by John Wiley & Sons, Inc.

portable computer: Also known as a notebook, subnotebook, or laptop computer: the notebook and subnotebook are smaller, lighter, and less powerful. (All battery-operable computers in this text are referred to as portables.)

RAM: Random access memory, or just *memory* for short. The workspace, much like a tabletop, where all the computer's work is done. RAM is directed by the CPU according to instructions given out by the operating system and application software.

scanner: A piece of equipment that captures an image and turns it into a digital representation that can be stored on a disk drive or manipulated with special software.

tape backup: A method of transferring data on a hard disk drive onto a small tape cartridge that is easily stored; a backup if something happens to the data on the disk drive, like a fire, theft, or disk crash (unrecoverable failure).

UPS: Uninterruptible power supply, that is, a battery backup in case of an electrical failure.

video driver: A component that takes some of the load off the CPU by acting as the interpreter of instructions to the monitor, serves to speed up the computer's operation.

Windows: The trademarked name used by Microsoft to refer to its graphical view of DOS, which makes it easier to use.

INDEX

1995 Expo Schedule

CHICAGO
April 8-9, 1995
Rosemont Convention Center

ATLANTA
May 20-21, 1995
Cobb County Galleria

DALLAS
Sept. 30-Oct. 1
Dallas Market Hall

SAN FRANCISCO
October 28-29, 1995
Moscone Center

PHILADELPHIA
November 18-19, 1995
South Jersey Expo Center

MJWE

Get your FREE Small Business Development Catalog today!

Name: _____

Address: _____

City: _____

State/Zip: _____

MJWC

To receive your free catalog, return this coupon to:
ENTREPRENEUR MAGAZINE,
P.O. Box 50370, Boulder, CO 80321-0370.
OR CALL (800) 421-2300, Dept. MJWC
Step-by-step guidance to help you succeed.

Get the book. **FREE!**